84 - 00085

FAMOUS UTOPIAS

of the

RENAISSANCE

Introduction and Notes

by

FREDERIC R. WHITE

HENDRICKS HOUSE, INC.
PUTNEY, VERMONT

Title page illustrations by courtesy of:
The Rare Books and Manuscripts Division
New York Public Library
Astor, Lenox and Tilden Foundations

ISBN: 0-87532-115-1 (paper)

PRINTED IN THE UNITED STATES OF AMERICA

CONTENTS

PUBLISHER'S PREFACE TO THE 1981 EDITION

Interest continues both in utopias and in the thought that prompted them. Therefore, we are happy to be able to reprint Frederic R. White's excellent edition as it stands, merely supplementing his bibliography by adding some more recent books, both on utopias in general and on the specific writers included in this book. The general bibliography is at the end of the introduction, the more specific bibliography on the back of the title page of each relevant section. The cover of the book shows More's Utopia.

H.H.

INTRODUCTION

Man has always sought to embody in literature his visions of a better life. Probably the rude Neanderthaler had his songs about a larger and better cave, just as the American Indian has his poems about the Happy Hunting Ground. Every man, of whatever clime or time, may take as his motto the quatrain of Omar the Tentmaker:

Ah, love, could you and I with Him conspire
To grasp this sorry Scheme of Things entire,
    Would we not shatter it to bits—and then
Re-mould it nearer to the Heart's Desire?

Here, in this human revulsion from the sorry scheme of things, is a vast common ground where primitive man scuttling through the miasmal swamps joins hands with the atomic scientist, where the disconsolate lover agrees with the sour misanthrope, where the reactionary who would turn back from the present concurs with the revolutionary who would press on to the future, and where the practical tinkerer with broken watches and the artist in his ivory tower may meet in a common disdain for current reality and a common desire for something a little nearer the heart's desire.

For man is perennially dissatisfied with what he has and perennially longs for what he lacks. Shelley's lines, "We look before and after, and pine for what is not," are both a melancholy comment on the way most of us spend our lives and a sound interpretation of that *elan vital* that underlies evolution. By his eternal dissatisfaction with things as they are and his eternal desire to make them better, man was led to descend timidly from his tree, to balance himself precariously on two hind legs, to clothe his poor naked body, to fashion fire, tools, houses, and civilizations, and to formulate, finally,

vague generalizations about why he had gone to all this evo-
lutionary bother in the first place. Not Master Gaster, as
Rabelais taught, but man's divine discontent seems to lie at
the root of all progress and most literature. It is this divine
discontent that leads him, even in these mad times, to draw
up schemes for some saner life. It is this inspired disgust with
things as they are that creates the literature of Utopia.

The impulse to create utopias, then, lies close to the fundamental motives of all human activity. Sometimes, to be sure,
they seem to be written in a spirit of mere play. This is the
popular interpretation of such perennial favorites as *Baron
Munchausen, Alice in Wonderland,* or the delightful worlds
of Sir William Gilbert. Yet the mature reader senses, even
here, a clear distinction between the author's revulsion from
reality and his wishful pursuit of the ideal. The playful
fantasy of Aristophanes' *Clouds,* the witty *Voyages to the
Moon* of Lucian and Cyrano de Bergerac, or the grim humor
of Swift's *Gulliver's Travels* originated in discontent and
desire. And the major utopias, those of Plato, Augustine,
More, Cabet, Butler, Bellamy, Morris, and Wells, are, without exception, grounded in their authors' attempts to escape
from contemporary reality into an ideal realm. All take
their origin from those fundamental forces of nature which
Empedocles distinguished as love and hate, which the physi-
cist defines as attraction and repulsion, and which the psy-
chologist studies under the more complicated labels of
compulsive neuroses and aversion psychoses.

No doubt this motivation lies behind all writing, but its
visible manifestations are most easily discernible in the literature of utopia. Utopias, in fact, are distinguished from all
other forms of literature by their patent idealism. They are
ideal in both of the common senses of the word. Negatively,
they are ideal in that they are deliberately non-real; and,
positively, they are ideal in that they portray an exemplary
pattern of culture. These two kinds of idealism are implicit
in the word "utopia" itself, which may refer both to an

ou topos or No-Place and to an *eu topos* or Place-Where-All is-Well. Sir Thomas More, the coiner of the term, seems to have taken it in both senses. He suggests the non-reality of his ideal commonwealth by naming the principal river Anyder ("without water"), its principal city Amaurot ("unknown"), and its king Ademus ("without people"). The positive nature of his ideal realm is suggested by the use of the label Macariens ("happy ones"), by the whole tenor of his arguments, and by the concluding words, "there are many things in the Commonwealth of Utopia that I rather wish, than hope, to see followed in our government." Both senses of utopian idealism have often been illustrated by titles. The non-reality of these states is indicated by Aristophanes' Nephelococcygia or Cloud-Cuckoo-Land, by Augustine's *City of God,* by Carroll's *Wonderland,* or by Butler's *Erewhon,* which is simply Nowhere spelled backwards. The eutopic aspect of idealism is illustrated by the sixteenth century treatise of Stiblimus, *The Commentary on the Republic of Happy Men,* by Rabelais' *Theleme,* where one follows his "wishes," or by von Faramond's *The Happiest Island.*

These two generic characteristics of utopian literature, the outopic revulsion from reality and the eutopic desire for a better world, appear most clearly in periods of abrupt transition. And the Renaissance was, above all, an age of transition. The Renaissance is a somewhat loose but convenient label for that tract of time lying between the fourteenth and the seventeenth centuries. By convention it is limited in space to western Europe, although it had repercussions throughout most of the inhabited globe. Within this small frame of space and time a small number of men gathered together all their strength in a mighty impulse that lifted mankind by its own bootstraps to a higher rung of evolution.

It was an age of sharp contrasts. The old patterns of feudal culture were breaking up, and the new patterns of capitalism were being formed. In the turbulent interval before the old order gave way to the new, there were two cen-

turies of violence, upheaval, and readjustment. Old and new
stood side by side. Feudal estates bordered the thriving,
bustling towns, and industries shouldered the sheltering walls
of near-by monasteries. Medieval castles, massive, self-
sufficient, built for self-defence in a rude age,frowned darkly
down upon the open sunny terraces of Renaissance manors.
The sober-suited monk jostled the gaily-bedecked courtier,
and the bowman, still clad in crude leather, fought alongside
the arquebusier. In libraries, the hand-copied versions of
Aristotle in medieval Latin, of Augustine, Anselm, and
Aquinas rubbed bindings with magnificent printed editions
of Plato in Greek, Petrarch in Italian, Montaigne in French,
and Cervantes in Spanish. Rabelais lists some of the medieval dog-Latin books of St. Victor, masquerading them under
such jocular titles as *The Apology against Those who Allege
that the Pope's Mule eats only at the Hours;* these scholastic
trifles he contrasts with the modern books of his utopian
Abbey, which contains "fair great libraries in Greek, Latin,
Hebrew, French, Italian, and Spanish." In these, and in a
thousand other violent contrasts, can be seen the outward
signs of an inward rending of the fabric.

To the leaders of the Renaissance the Medieval elements
in their culture became identified with "the sorry scheme of
things," while the "heart's desire" was sought in a more
natural and human way of life. That the ideals for this
natural and human way were often rediscovered in the
classics, after fourteen centuries of comparative neglect, made
them seem no less new and modern. Ancient and modern
thinkers joined forces in a common onslaught against the
outworn modes of medievalism. As has so often been pointed
out, the closed and authoritarian system of the Middle Ages
was replaced by the open and relativistic world of modern
times. The closed geography of feudal Europe was pried
open, first by the Crusades, then by the discovery of new
trade routes, and finally by the world-wide explorations of
the great navigators. The flat two-dimensional earth became

a spheroid, three-dimensional world. The limited and static spatial theory of Ptolemy gave way to the dynamic helio-centric theory of Copernicus, Galileo, and Newton. Time, as well as space, was broadened. The development of chron-ology, the recovery of ancient monuments, and speculations about the future expanded the temporal scope of men's views. Economically, the closed and largely self-contained feudal estates were replaced by cities and towns, with the mutual interdependence that comes from the specialization of labor, till the whole medieval scheme of production was made over into the "free" system of commerce and industry. Politically, the structure of a Europe unified under the domination of the Church was replaced by a number of nationalistic states, each owing its strength and independence to the relative weakness of its neighboring states.

And, of course, thought changed too. Possibly the new conditions produced new ways of thinking; possibly new ways of thinking created these new conditions; more prob-ably, the two interacted. At any rate, during these two centuries entirely new attitudes arose. The more or less uni-fied body of scholastic thought, centering around the tradi-tional views of Aristotle, Augustine, and Aquinas, no longer commanded men's respect. Ecclesiasticism, which exercised over body, mind, and soul a rigid authoritarianism gave way before a new conception of individual freedom. Theology, which had been the handmaiden of the Church, was displaced by science, the handmaiden of industry. And the trivium and quadrivium, which had existed to serve theology, were recalled to their ancient office as *artes liberales,* the arts that serve to set men free. In general, the effort of the Middle Ages to determine the relation of man to God was replaced by a more modern attempt to determine man's relation to Nature. Hence these various new attitudes, diverse though they were, may conveniently be discussed in terms of Natur-alism.

Naturalism was not a new concept at the time of the Renaissance, for it had existed among the ancients; nor was it peculiar to the Renaissance, for it has survived long after other manifestations of the age have disappeared; nor can Naturalism offer a complete definition of the Renaissance, for, as we have already said, it was an incredibly complex age. Yet, in spite of all these limitations, it is still the most convenient single term to denote those intellectual attitudes which here concern us. Naturalism, as the word suggests, implied a more animal and less angelic acceptance of the pleasures of this world, more natural patterns of social behavior than were possible in the Middle Ages, a greater reliance upon native intelligence rather than faith, and a far greater interest in the methods and results of natural science, or the objective study of nature. Negatively, naturalism may best be understood as the opposite of supernaturalism. Positively, it implies the interpretation of all aspects of nature, including human activities, in terms of natural causes and by the aid of natural reason.

There were many outward signs of this naturalistic impulse. The delight in animal activity, the lavish display, the magnificent ceremonies of the Renaissance differ sharply from the repression, humility, and drab monastic round which was recommended, if not always practised, in medieval times. There was a new delight in the pagan pleasures of this world, and a new scorn for the asceticism and self-denial of the Middle Ages. Men's thoughts turned less to the rewards of an imagined heaven, and more toward the good things of this life. The festivals, frolics, pageants, masques, plays, the sudden flowering of pictorial art, of sculpture, of architecture, the lavish display in dress, the courtly manners, the elaborate ceremonials, such as that of the Field of the Cloth of Gold (1520), all were symbols of a new lust for life.

Inevitably there developed a different and more natural conception of human behavior. Actions were judged, not by their consonance with the Mosaic law nor by their probable effect upon eternal salvation, but by their immediate fruits. The medieval ideal is adumbrated by the cloistered monk, dedicated to the unworldly vows of poverty, chastity, and obedience, by the chaste nun or the saint, safe from the temptations of an evil world, by the theologian, dedicated to the study of God, or, occasionally, by the perfect knight, ruled like Roland by his chivalric fealty to his heavenly overlord. The Renaissance ideal is suggested in the polished courtier of Castiglione, the amoral prince of Machiavelli, the crowned poet Petrarch, or the omnivorous scholars Erasmus and Scaliger. These all sought, not the stifling of natural desires, but the satisfaction of them. Their goals were selfculture, political power, worldly fame, and the satisfaction of man's questing curiosity, rather than the attainment of an eternal reward. With this shift in aims, there was a corresponding change in men's judgments about social behavior. Desirable behavior ceased to be that enjoined by the Church and became that which was "natural" to a given situation and to an immediate goal.

The chosen instrument of naturalism was "natural" reason. Men became increasingly skeptical of supernatural revelation, whether gained through mystical intuition, through sacred Scripture, or through the divine infallibility of an alltoohuman Church. From acquiescent faith they turned to the unhampered light of their own native gifts. In this struggle for intellectual independence, they were immeasurably aided by the great Greek philosophers, historians, and scientists, who had interpreted the world directly through observation and through the exercise of natural reason. The pagan impulse to trust the senses, and the social imperative to satisfy natural desires, was paralleled by this new reliance upon natural reason, unaided by authority, tradition, or faith. Thus Descartes, in his famous phrase *cogito ergo sum*, made the very existence of man dependent upon this central activity, and the utopian writers agreed without exception that this was the one trustworthy instrument of improvement.

This reliance upon man's native intellect, quite distinct from that rationalism which Aquinas subordinated to faith, was to issue into the dominant rationalism of the succeeding centuries.

Pragmatically, the concepts of naturalism were justified by a phenomenal increase in knowledge. The achievements of the Renaissance in natural science, though less discussed than those in literature and the arts, were, under the circumstances, among the greatest triumphs of the age. Literature could boast, within a short span of time, of Petrarch, Boccaccio, Machiavelli, Ariosto, and Tasso, of Cervantes, Lope, and Calderon, of Camöens, of Rabelais, Ronsard, and Montaigne, of Marlowe, Spenser, Shakespeare, and Jonson; and art could boast an equally glorious roster. Yet science, starting almost from the first beginnings and hampered by long centuries of ignorance and obscurantism, produced some of the greatest names in the whole history of thought. Science became an international movement to which every nation contributed. Nicholas of Cusa and Kepler in Germany, Tycho Brahe in Denmark, Copernicus in Poland, Bacon, Harvey, and Newton in England, Descartes and Gassendi in France, and daVinci, Telesio, Bruno, and Galileo in Italy practically created science anew within little more than a century. Even here, of course, naturalism was tinctured with curious remnants of medievalism, as can be seen from the writings of these men. At the conclusion of Campanella's *Civitas Solis,* for example, the Grand Master exclaims:

> Oh, if you knew what our astrologers say of the coming age, and of our age, that has in it more history within a hundred years than all the world had in 4000 years before! of the wonderful inventions of printing and guns, and the use of the magnet, and how it all comes of Mercury, Mars, the Moon, and the Scorpion.

To which the sea captain properly replies, "Ah, well, they astrologize too much." Astrology and astronomy, alchemy

and chemistry, the old physics of Ptolemy and the new physics of Copernicus, the mystical nonsense of Paracelsus and
the close scientific observation of Harvey, all were included
in this complex age of transition. But as the old was sloughed
off, it became increasingly clear that naturalism, or the attempt to account for natural phenomena by natural causes,
was producing more results in science and technology in a
decade than scholasticism had produced in ten centuries.

This naturalistic movement, with its delight in natural
activity, its hedonistic ethics, its emphasis upon natural reason, and its phenomenal development in natural science, is
clearly reflected in the utopias of the Renaissance. Since
utopias are, by their very nature, compounded of revulsion
from present reality and attraction for a better world, they
are peculiarly fitted to express the conflicts of transitional
ages. Perhaps that is why our own war-torn era has seen
so many of them published within the past sixty years. In
the Renaissance, the outopic or negative aspect of these writings generally consists of a dislike for the medieval elements
of things as they are; the eutopic or positive aspect is closely
connected with naturalism.

Thus, in More, the first and greatest of the Renaissance
utopists, we find a natural delight in the senses and an almost
Epicurean ethics which postulates pleasure as the great aim
of human behavior. Since the Utopians, says Hythlodaye,
"define virtue to be living according to nature, so they imagine that nature prompts all people on to seek after pleasure
as the end of all they do." Their lives, consequently, are
devoted to fulfilling the natural demands of the human body
and intellect; that is, in the pursuit of food, social compan-
ionship, and intellectual activity. Although the Utopians
had no contact with European culture, they discovered, by
the exercise of natural reason alone, without revelation or
the authority of tradition, all the arts and sciences possessed
by Europe and carried them to a far higher level of development. These sciences, however, are devoted not solely to

the interpretation of God's manifestation in nature, but rather to the cause of human welfare. Thus agricultural chemistry, which increases natural produce and satisfies a fundamental desire of man's nature, had been carried to a high pitch of development.

The application of natural reason to human problems is shown most clearly, however, in the economic system devised by the Utopians. While Europe struggles under an un-natural system whereby the rich live off the poor, the Utopians have found the means for all men to live happily together. For More is among the first of the rational socialists. Un-troubled by tradition, by religious dogma, or by the dead weight of existing institutions, he employs the white light of reason to dissect the cause of human ills. He finds it in the institution of private property and in the corresponding political form of aristocracy, both of which

> are a conspiracy of the rich, who on pretence of managing the public only pursue their private end, and devise all the ways and arts they can find out, first that they may, without danger, preserve all that they have so ill acquired, and then that they may engage the poor to toil and labor for them at as low rates as possible, and oppress them as much as they please.

If this is his major quarrel with things as they are, his pro-posal for remoulding it nearer to the heart's desire is to abolish private property:

> I am persuaded that till property is taken away there can be no equitable or just distribution of things, nor can the world be happily governed; for as long as that is maintained, the greatest and the far best part of mankind will be still oppressed with a load of cares and anxieties.

His utopia is a commonwealth built up around the central economic principle of communism, where all the citizens labor for a common end, the common good. The ramifications of this central principle in all the walks of life, in the family, in education, in trade, and in war, are traced out in a natural series of cause and effects.

If More, with a wholly modern conception of the economic basis of human society, so clearly illustrates Renaissance naturalism, Rabelais, his great French contemporary, is even more illuminating. Rabelais is the naturalist *par excellence*. He revels in all the natural aspects of human life, its amenities and its obscenities, its low drunkenness and its high intoxication. His ethics is purely hedonistic, based on the daily enjoyment of the good things of this life, its food, its drink, its manifold experiences, and its opportunities for lust, love, and learning. Rabelais was one of the great rationalists of his day and ardently studied and supported natural sciences. Convinced that man is naturally good, and that this native excellence is corrupted only by bad institutions, he evokes a utopian environment where this natural goodness may have free play. The sorry scheme of things that he is in rebellion against is the medieval monastery, the very archetype of restrictive institution. Consequently he builds an ideal monastery wherein every rule is the precise opposite of those in real monasteries, and where the cardinal principle of action is the hedonistic injunction to follow one's own natural desires. Thus the Thelemites spend all their lives

> not in laws, statutes, or rules, but according to their own free will and pleasure . . . . for so had Gargantua established it. In all their rule and strictest tie of their order there was but this one clause to be observed
>
> #### Do What Thou Wilt
>
> Because men that are free, well born, well-bred, and conversant in honest companies, have naturally an instinct and spur that prompteth them unto virtuous actions, and withdraws them from vice. Those same men, when by base subjection and constraint they are brought under and kept down, turn aside

from that noble disposition, by which formerly they
were inclined to virtue.

Although the brief Abbey of Theleme gives the quintessence
of Rabelais' naturalism, it is wise to read the whole vast
volume to realize the force, the depth, and the vigor of this
major Renaissance movement. Rabelais' conception of man's
natural goodness, so sharply in opposition to that of his
strict contemporary, Calvin, was a dominant force in the
eighteenth century and appears as the basic philosophy behind our own naturalistic Declaration of Independence.

Naturalism was likewise the keynote of the utopian writing of Rabelais' compatriot, Montaigne. Like Rabelais,
Montaigne was steeped in the classics, and from them as
well as from the spirit of his own time, he drew the naturalistic concept that primitive man, living in a state of nature,
was better and happier than civilized man. His admired
Seneca had written:

> The first men and their immediate descendents fol-
> lowed nature, pure and uncorrupt . . . . How happy
> was the primitive age when the bounties of nature
> lay in common and were used promiscuously; nor
> had avarice and luxury disunited mortals and made
> them prey upon one another. They enjoyed all
> nature in common which thus gave them secure
> possession of the public wealth.

This primitivistic naturalism, somewhat akin to the native
goodness postulated by Rabelais, seemed to be borne out by
the recent discoveries of the Renaissance navigators. In the
Americas were found societies of men unacquainted with
the arts and vices of Europe; these "natural" men seemed no
less happy for their lack of civilization. Becoming acquainted
with some of these aborigines, Montaigne weaves together,
from fact and fantasy, a portrait of the noble savage which
serves at once as an attack against things as they are and a
justification for a more natural mode of life.

These people are wild in the sense in which we call

wild the fruits that nature has produced by herself
and in her ordinary progress; whereas in truth it is
those we have altered artificially and diverted from
the common order that we should rather call wild.
In the first we still see, in full life and vigor, the
genuine and most natural and useful virtues and
properties, which we have bastardized in the latter,
and only adapted to please our corrupt taste . . . .
Those nations, then, appear to me so far barbarous
in this sense, that their minds have been formed to
a very slight degree, and that they are still very
close to their original simplicity. They are still
ruled by the laws of Nature and very little corrupted by ours.

Montaigne's portrait and defense of a primitive or natural
utopia was read by Shakespeare, who appropriated it for a
celebrated passage in *The Tempest.*

If Rabelais and Montaigne exhibit the ethical naturalism
of their day, Campanella and Bacon mirror the rising power
of natural science. Of the two, Campanella is the more interested in education, Bacon in research, but both agree that
the method of science is that of rigorous observation of
natural phenomena and that the aim of science is to promote man's natural well-being. Campanella's utopia is a
curious compound of Platonism, medievalism, and modern
science, but his attitude toward education is essentially
rational and modern. By means of natural history exhibits,
his utopians are educated not in mere scholastic logic or
fruitless grammar, but in the objects of nature. From natural
objects, their thoughts rise to general scientific concepts, and
from these concepts they develop their philosophy and their
metaphysic. Hoh, the supreme ruler of the City of the Sun,
thus corresponds to the philosopher king of Plato, for he is
equipped to rule by having first learned all mathematics, all
the several sciences, and then philosophy. Campanella objects to medieval education on the grounds that

> you consider that man the most learned who knows
> most of grammar, or logic, or of Aristotle, or any
> other author. For such knowledge as this of yours,
> much servile labor and memory work are required
> so that a man is rendered unskilful, since he has con-
> templated nothing but the words of books and has
> given his mind with useless result to the considera-
> tion of the dead signs of things. Hence he knows
> not in what way God rules the universe, nor the
> ways and customs of nature and the nations.

Moreover, Campanella exhibits a wholly modern attitude
toward the mutual interdependence of all science in order to
form a complete educational scheme:

> he who knows only one science does not really
> know either that or the others, and he who is suited
> for only one science and has gathered his knowl-
> edge from books, is unlearned and unskilful. But
> this is not the case with intellects prompt and expert
> in every branch of knowledge and suitable for the
> consideration of natural objects, as it is necessary
> that our Hoh should be. Besides in our state the
> sciences are taught with a facility by which more
> scholars are turned out by us in one year than by
> you in ten or even fifteen.

Although Campanella's *Civitas Solis* is founded to some extent on the monastic way of life, it is in sharp revulsion
against medieval scholastic education, and it holds up as an
ideal a state that is communally organized for the welfare
of all through the technological use of science. This demands an educated citizenry, and Campenella's conception of
the aim of education, as the control of nature for man's
benefit, and of the means of education, as the study of natural phenomena with the use of visual aids, is an excellent
example of Renaissance naturalism.

Bacon is less concerned about mass education in the sciences and more interested in the training of research experts.

His *New Atlantis* is the fictional counterpart of his life-long writings in the cause of science. Opposed both to medieval scholasticism and to the contemporary emphasis upon classical literature, he wishes to tie man's natural reason down to the close observation of facts. For the gathering and inter-pretation of these facts he proposes an ideal institute for co-operative research in the natural sciences. This institu-tion, which foreshadowed the founding of scientific acade-mies some fifty years later, is

> sometimes called Salomon's House, and sometimes the College of the Six Days' Works, whereby I am satisfied that our excellent King had learned from the Hebrews that God had created the world and all that therein is within six days; and therefore he instituted that house for the finding out of the true nature of all things, whereby God might have the more glory in the workmanship of them, and men the more fruit in their use of them, did give it also that second name.

It is typical of the transitional nature of the Renaissance, with its mixture of old and new, of religion and naturalism, that God should get the glory, but men should enjoy the fruits. It carries one back to that very early naturalism of Homer when, in the tribal sacrifices, Zeus received the savor of the roasting flesh, but the warriors ate the meat. The savor of the Middle Ages still rises from these Renaissance utopias, but the meat is there.

Although these are the principal utopias of the period, they by no means exhaust the list. Many others, which also reflect the naturalism of the Renaissance, are no longer wide-ly read. One of the earliest was that of Gasparus Stiblimus, *Commentariolus de Eudaemonensium Republica* (1555). The best known is perhaps that of J. V. Andreae, *Christianopolis* (1619), which illustrates the spirit of the Protestant re-formation as well as that of naturalism. Another German utopia is that of S. Golt, *Nova Solyma* (1648). England,

with its heritage from More and Bacon, was particularly
rich in utopian literature during the seventeenth century.
Some of the better known works are Joseph Hall's *Mundus
Alter et Idem* (c.1605), Bishop Godwin's *The Man in the
Moone* (1630), which handed on the Lucianic tradition to
Cyrano de Bergerac, Samuel Hartlib's *Macaria* (1641), and
the still more famous *Oceana* of James Harrington (1656).
Some critics would also include among the utopias Thomas
Hobbes' great *Leviathan* (1651), and the work of Samuel
Hartlib's friend, John Milton's *The Readie and Easy Way
to Establish a Free Commonwealth* (1659), although strictly
these are political treatises. In France the most famous of
the seventeenth century utopias, Fenélon's *Telemaque,* appeared only in 1699, and cannot be considered a work of
the Renaissance.

The field of utopian literature is large, and largely has it
been commented upon. The most useful studies of the ideal
commonwealths of the Renaissance, J. Prys' *Der Staatsroman
des 16. und 17. Jahrhunderts und sein Erziehungsideal*
(Wurzburg, 1913), and G. E. Dermenghem's valuable treatise, *Thomas Morus et les Utopistes de la Renaissance* (Paris,
1927), are not yet available to the un-languaged reader. The
best general introductions to the field are the early discussion
by M. Kaufmann, *Utopias* (London, 1879), the readable
history by Lewis Mumford, *The Story of Utopias* (New
York, 1922), the scholarly treatise by J. O. Hertzler, *The
History of Utopian Thought* (New York, 1923), and the
sprightly little topographical tome by F. T. Russell, *Touring
Utopia* (New York, 1932). A good brief survey of the
British field is given in Harold Child's lecture, *Some English
Utopias,* reprinted in the transactions of the Royal Society
of Literature (XII, 1933). For background material, the
eminently readable work by H. W. Laidler, *A History of
Socialist Thought* (New York, 1927) should be consulted.

Yet, with the utopias as with all literature, the best introduction is in the works themselves. The interested student

should perhaps begin with those nearest his own time, with Huxley, Hudson, Wells, Anatole France, Howells, Twain, William Morris, and Bellamy, and work his way back, through the utopias of the romantic period, the eighteenth century, and the Renaissance, to those first, best, and most enduring of all ideal commonwealths, the *Republic* and the *Laws* of Plato.

F.R.W.

ADDITIONAL BIBLIOGRAPHY

Berneri, Marie L., *Journey Through Utopia*, New York, 1971

Bloch, Ernst, *A Philosophy of the Future*, New York, 1970

Buber, Martin, *Paths in Utopia*, New York, 1950

Cohn, Norman, *The Pursuit of the Millenium: Revolutionary Messianism in Medieval and Reformation Europe and Its Bearing on Modern Totalitarian Movements*, New York, 1961

Elliott, Robert C., *The Shape of Utopia: Studies in a Literary Genre*, Chicago, 1970

Giamatti, A. Bartlett, *The Earthly Paradise and the Renaissance Epic*, Princeton, 1966

Kateb, George, *Utopia*, New York, 1971

Kateb, George, *Utopia and Its Enemies*, New York, 1963

Lasky, Melvin J., *Utopias and Revolution*, Chicago, 1976

Levin, Harry, *The Myth of the Golden Age in the Renaissance*, Bloomington, Ind., 1969

Liljegren, Sten Bodvar, *Studies on the Origin and Early Tradition of English Utopian Fiction*, Uppsala, 1961

Mannheim, Karl, *Idealogy and Utopia: An Introduction to the Sociology of Knowledge*, New York, 1954

Manuel, Frank Edward, ed., *Utopias and Utopian Thought*, Boston, 1966

Manuel, Frank Edward, and Fritzie Prigohzy Manuel, *Utopian Thought in the Western World*, Cambridge, Mass., 1979

Molnar, Thomas Steven, *Utopias, the Perennial Heresy*, New York, 1967

Mumford, Lewis, *The Transformations of Man*, New York, 1956

Negley, Glenn Robert, *Utopian Literature: A Bibliography with a Supplementary Listing of Works Influential on Utopian Thought*, Lawrence, Kansas, 1977

Negley, Glenn Robert and J. Max Patrick, eds., *The Quest for Utopia*, New York, 1952

Polak, Frederick L., *The Image of the Future: Enlightening the Past, Orienting the Present, Forecasting the Future*, Dobbs Ferry, N.Y., 1961

Sanford, Charles L., *The Quest for Utopia*, Urbana, Ill., 1961

Rosenau, Helen, *The Ideal City: Its Architectural Evolution*, New York, 1974

Tod, Ian, and Michael Wheeler, *Utopia, an Illustrated History*, New York, 1978

For additional works on the individual authors see the back of each of the title pages.

A frutefull pleasaunt, and wittie
worke, of the beste state of a pub╱
lique weale, & of the newe yle, call╱
ed Utopia : written in Latine, by
the right worthie and famous Syr
Thomas More knyght, and trans╱
lated into Englishe by Raphe Ro╱
bynson, sometime fellowe of Cor╱
pus Christi College in Oxford, &
nowe by him at this seconde edi╱
tion newlie perused and corrected,
and also with divers notes in the
margent augmented ❧ ❧ ❧ ❧ ❧
Imprinted at London, by Abraham
Vele, dwellinge in Pauls church-
yarde, at the signe of the Lambe.

ADDITIONAL BIBLIOGRAPHY

Donner, Henry Wolfgang, *Introduction to Utopia*, London, 1946

Gibson, R.W., and J. Max Patrick, *Thomas More: A Preliminary Bibliography of His Works and of Moreana to the Year 1750*, New Haven, Conn., 1961

Hexter, J.H., *More's Utopia: The Biography of an Idea*, Westport, Conn., 1952

Reynolds, E.E., *The Field Is Won: The Life and Death of Saint Thomas More*, Milwaukee, Wisc., 1968

Overleaf: Title page of William Morris' Kelmscott Press edition of More's "Utopia", printed in Hammersmith, England, in 1893, and which uses the text of the second English edition of 1556.

SIR THOMAS MORE

Sir Thomas More (1478-1535), Lord Chancellor of England under Henry VIII, is now best remembered as a great humanist, as the author of *Utopia* (1516), and as a Catholic martyr. Educated at Oxford, at New Inn, and at Lincoln Inn, he early became acquainted with the most influential humanists of his time. Colet, Grocyn, and Linacre were among his teachers; Holbein painted him; Erasmus punned upon his name in his masterpiece, the *Encomium Moriae*, and dedicated the book to him. In general, the humanists sought, by re-introducing the study of Greek, Hebrew, and Latin, to broaden the medieval basis of knowledge and to enrich secular life by the pagan virtues of skepticism, moderation, tolerance, and rationalism. More's reputation as a scholar, his legal training, and his great abilities soon led him into politics. In 1504 he entered Parliament, rising steadily in the king's favor until, in 1529, he succeeded Wolsey as Lord Chancellor. Ironically, he who had preached religious toleration in his *Utopia,* now used his power to persecute heretics; more ironically still, he was himself accused of heresy and high treason, when he refused to take the oath of supremacy. For this, and for his unwillingness to forward the king's divorce from Catherine of Aragon, he was tried, convicted, and, after a year's imprisonment in the Tower, executed July 7, 1535. For his steadfast adherence to Rome, he was canonized four centuries later, in 1935.

More's many works exhibit the humanistic qualities of broad learning, witty skepticism, and searching rationalism. Among the more important of his writings are the translation, with Erasmus, of Lucian's *Dialogues* (1506), a task which deeply influenced his style and ideas; the translation,

from the Latin, of *The Lyfe of John Picus, Erle of Mirandula*
(1510), which served to introduce Platonism into the English Renaissance; the model *Historie of Richard the Third*
(1516); and the *Dyaloge of Comfort against Tribulacion*
(1533), a personal exhortation to philosophy written, like
that of Boethius, in prison. His masterpiece, however, is the
Utopia, or, to give it its full title, *Libellus vere aureus de
optimo Reipublicae statu deque nova insula Utopiae*. This
truly golden book was first conceived while More was serv-
ing in Antwerp. There he met Peter Giles (Aegidius), a
friend of Erasmus, and held with him the conversation that
opens the book. Although More owes much to Plato's
Republic, his leading ideas were formed from shrewd observation of the troubles of his time. The *Utopia* was first published in Latin at Louvain, in 1516, under the editorship of
Erasmus and in the same year as Erasmus' great edition of
the New Testament. Although the *Utopia* could not appear
in England because of its satire upon king and court, it was
quickly reprinted at Paris (1517), at Basle (1518), and at
Vienna, Florence, and Venice (1519). In 1551 the book
was translated into English by Ralphe Robynson. This
standard translation appears here in modernized form.

The best introduction to the humanists and their aims
is still that of Frederic Seebohm, *The Oxford Reformers*
(1867). The standard biography of More is by R. W
Chambers (1935), but students should also read the brief
life by More's son-in-law, William Roper, entitled, *The
Mirror of Virtue in Worldly Greatness; or the Life of Sir
Thomas More* (1626). A sympathetic little novel about
More's family is that by Anne Manning, *The Household of
Sir Thomas More* (1851). Although the *Utopia* is largely
self-explanatory, the excellent annotated editions by J. H. Lup-
ton (1895), Churton Collins (1904), and G. Sampson and
A. Guthkelch (1910) contain information of interest to the
advanced student, as does W. E. Campbell's analysis of
More's Utopia and His Social Teaching (1930).

UTOPIA

Book I

H ENRY the Eighth, the unconquered King of England,
a prince adorned with all the virtues that become
a great monarch, having some differences of no small
consequence with Charles the most serene prince of Castile, sent me into Flanders, as his ambassador, for treating
and composing matters between them. I was colleague
and companion to that incomparable man Cuthbert
Tonstal, whom the king with such universal applause
lately made Master of the Rolls; but of whom I will say
nothing; not because I fear that the testimony of a friend
will be suspected, but rather because his learning and
virtues are too great for me to do them justice, and so
well known, that they need not my commendations unless
I would, according to the proverb, "Show the sun with
a lantern." Those that were appointed by the prince to
treat with us met us at Bruges, according to agreement;
they were all worthy men. The Margrave of Bruges was
their head, and the chief man among them; but he that
was esteemed the wisest, and that spoke for the rest, was
George Temse, the Provost of Casselsee; both art and
nature had concurred to make him eloquent: he was very
learned in the law; and as he had a great capacity, so by
a long practice in affairs he was very dextrous at unrav-
elling them. After we had several times met without
coming to an agreement, they went to Brussels for some
days to know the prince's pleasure. And since our business would admit it, I went to Antwerp. While I was
there, among many that visited me, there was one that

was more acceptable to me than any other, Peter Giles, born at Antwerp, who is a man of great honor, and of a good rank in his town, though less than he deserves; for I do not know if there be anywhere to be found a more learned and a better bred young man: for as he is both a very worthy and a very knowing person, so he is so civil to all men, so particularly kind to his friends, and so full of candor and affection, that there is not perhaps above one or two anywhere to be found that is in all respects so perfect a friend. He is extraordinarily modest, there is no artifice in him; and yet no man has more of a prudent simplicity: his conversation was so pleasant and so innocently cheerful, that his company in a great measure lessened my longings to go back to my country, and to my wife and children, which an absence of four months had quickened very much. One day as I was returning home from Mass at St. Mary's, which is the chief church, and the most frequented of any in Antwerp, I saw him by accident talking with a stranger, who seemed past the flower of his age; his face was tanned, he had a long beard, and his cloak was hanging carelessly about him, so that by his looks and habit I concluded he was a seaman. As soon as Peter saw me, he came and saluted me; and as I was returning his civility, he took me aside, and pointing to him with whom he had been discoursing, he said, "Do you see that man? I was just thinking to bring him to you." I answered, "He should have been very welcome on your account." "And on his own too," replied he, "if you knew the man, for there is none alive that can give so copious an account of unknown nations and countries as he can do; which I know you very much desire." Then said I, "I did not guess amiss, for at first sight I took him for a seaman." "But you are much mistaken," said he, "for he has not sailed as a seaman, but as a traveller, or rather a philosopher. This Raphael, who from his family carries the name of Hythloday, is not ignorant of the Latin tongue, but is eminently learned in the Greek, having applied himself more particularly to that than to the former, because he had given himself much to philosophy, in which he knew that the Romans have left us nothing that is valuable, except what is to be found in Seneca and Cicero. He is a Portuguese by birth, and was so desirous of seeing the world, that he divided his estate among his brothers, run the same hazard as Americus Vesputius, and bore a share in three of his four voyages, that are now published, only he did not return with him in his last, but obtained leave of him almost by force, that he might be one of those twenty-four who were left at the farthest place at which they touched, in their last voyage to New Castle. The leaving him thus did not a little gratify one that was more fond of travelling than of returning home, to be buried in his own country; for he used often to say, that the way to heaven was the same from all places; and he that had no grave, had the heaven still over him. Yet this disposition of mind had cost him dear, if God had not been very gracious to him; for after he, with five Castilians, had travelled over many countries, at last, by some strange good fortune, he got to Ceylon, and from thence to Calicut, where he very happily found some Portuguese ships; and, beyond all men's expectations, returned to his native country." When Peter had said this to me, I thanked him for his kindness, in intending to give me the acquaintance of a man whose conversation he knew would be so acceptable; and upon that Raphael and I embraced each other. After these civilities were past which are usual with strangers upon their first meeting, we all went to my house, and entering into the garden, sat down on a green bank, and entertained one another in discourse. He told us, that when Vesputius had sailed away, he and his companions that stayed behind in New Castle, by degrees insinuated themselves into the affections of the people of the country, meeting often with them,

and treating them gently: and at last they not only lived
among them without danger, but conversed familiarly with
them; and got so far into the heart of the prince, whose
name and country I have forgot, that he both furnished
them plentifully with all things necessary, and also with
the conveniences of travelling; both boats when they went
by water, and wagons when they travelled over land: he
sent with them a very faithful guide, who was to introduce and recommend them to such other princes as they
had a mind to see: and after many days' journey, they
came to towns, and cities, and to commonwealths, that were
both happily governed and well peopled. Under the
equator, and as far as on both sides of it as the sun moves,
there lay vast deserts that were parched with the perpetual
heat of the sun; the soil was withered, all things looked
dismally, and all places were either quite uninhabited, or
abounded with wild beasts and serpents, and some few
men, that were neither less wild nor less cruel than the
beasts themselves. But as they went farther, a new scene
opened, all things grew milder, the air less burning, the
soil more verdant, and even the beasts were less wild: and
at last there were nations, towns, and cities, that had not
only mutual commerce among themselves, and with their
neighbors, but traded both by sea and land, to very remote countries. There they found the conveniences of
seeing many countries on all hands, for no ship went any
voyage into which he and his companions were not very
welcome. The first vessels that they saw were flat-
bottomed, their sails were made of reeds and wicker woven
close together, only some were of leather; but afterwards
they found ships made with rounded keels, and canvas
sails, and in all respects like our ships; and the seamen
understood both astronomy and navigation. He got wonderfully into their favor, by showing them the use of the
needle, of which till then they were utterly ignorant. They
sailed before with great caution, and only in summer-time,

but now they count all seasons alike, trusting wholly to the loadstone, in which they are perhaps more secure than safe; so that there is reason to fear that this discovery, which was thought would prove so much to their advantage, may by their imprudence become an occasion of much mischief to them. But it were too long to dwell on all that he told us he had observed in every place; it would be too great a digression from our present purpose: whatever is necessary to be told, concerning those wise and prudent institutions which he observed among civilized nations, may perhaps be related by us on a more proper occasion. We asked him many questions concerning all these things, to which he answered very willingly; only we made no inquiries after monsters, than which nothing is more common; for everywhere one may hear of ravenous dogs and wolves, and cruel man-eaters; but it is not so easy to find states that are well and wisely governed.

As he told us of many things that were amiss in those new-discovered countries, so he reckoned up not a few things from which patterns might be taken for correcting the errors of these nations among whom we live; of which an account may be given, as I have already promised, at some other time; for at present I intend only to relate those particulars that he told us of the manners and laws of the Utopians: but I will begin with the occasion that led us to speak of that commonwealth. After Raphael had discoursed with great judgment on the many errors that were both among us and these nations; had treated of the wise institutions both here and there, and had spoken as distinctly of the customs and government of every nation through which he had passed, as if he had spent his whole life in it; Peter being struck with admiration, said, "I wonder, Raphael, how it comes that you enter into no king's service, for I am sure there are none to whom you would not be very acceptable: for your learning and knowledge, both of men and things, is such, that you would not only

entertain them very pleasantly, but be of great use to
them, by the examples you could set before them, and the
advices you could give them; and by this means you
would both serve your own interest, and be of great use
to all your friends"—"As for my friends," answered he,
"I need not be much concerned, having already done for
them all that was incumbent on me; for when I was not
only in good health, but fresh and young, I distributed that
among my kindred and friends which other people do not
part with till they are old and sick; when they then unwillingly give that which they can enjoy no longer themselves.
I think my friends ought to rest contented with this, and
not to expect that for their sakes I should enslave myself
to any king whatsoever"—"Soft and fair," said Peter, "I
do not mean that you should be a slave to any king, but
only that you should assist them, and be useful to them."—
"The change of the word," said he, "does not alter the
matter."—"But term it as you will," replied Peter, "I do
not see any other way in which you can be so useful, both
in private and to your friends, and to the public, and by
which you can make your own condition happier."—"Happier!" answered Raphael, "is that to be compassed in a
way so abhorrent to my genius? Now I live as I will, to
which I believe few courtiers can pretend. And there are
so many that court the favor of great men, that there will
be no great loss if they are not troubled either with me
or with others of my temper." Upon this, said I, "I perceive, Raphael, that you neither desire wealth nor greatness; and indeed I value and admire such a man much
more than I do any of the great men in the world. Yet I
think you would do what would well become a generous
and philosophical a soul as yours is, if you would apply
your time and thoughts to public affairs, even though you
may happen to find it a little uneasy to yourself: and this
you can never do with so much advantage, as by being
taken into the counsel of some great prince, and putting

him on noble and worthy actions, which I know you would
do if you were in such a post; for the springs both of good
and evil flow from the prince, over a whole nation, as from
a lasting fountain. So much learning as you have, even
without practice in affairs, or so great a practice as you
have had, without any other learning, would render you
a very fit counsellor to any king whatsoever."—"You are
doubly mistaken," said he, "Mr. More, both in your opinion of me, and in the judgment you make of things: for as
I have not that capacity that you fancy I have; so, if I had
it, the public would not be one jot the better, when I had
sacrificed my quiet to it. For most princes apply themselves more to affairs of war than to the useful arts of
peace; and in these I neither have any knowledge, nor do
I much desire it: they are generally more set on acquiring
new kingdoms, right or wrong, than on governing well
those they possess. And among the ministers of princes,
there are none that are not so wise as to need no assistance,
or at least that do not think themselves so wise, that they
imagine they need none; and if they court any, it is only
those for whom the prince has much personal favor, whom
by their fawnings and flatteries they endeavor to fix to
their own interests: and indeed Nature has so made us,
that we all love to be flattered, and to please ourselves
with our own notions. The old crow loves his young, and
the ape her cubs. Now if in such a Court, made up of
persons who envy all others, and only admire themselves,
a person should but propose anything that he had either
read in history, or observed in his travels, the rest would
think that the reputation of their wisdom would sink, and
that their interest would be much depressed, if they could
run it down: and if all other things failed, then they would
fly to this, that such or such things pleased our ancestors,
and if were well for us if we could but match them. They
would set up their rest on such an answer, as a sufficient
confutation of all that could be said; as if it were a great

misfortune, that any should be found wiser than his ancestors; but though they willingly let go all the good things
that were among those of former ages, yet if better things
are proposed they cover themselves obstinately with this
excuse of reverence to past times. I have met with these
proud, morose, and absurd judgments of things in many
places, particularly once in England."—"Was you ever
there?" said I.—"Yes, I was," answered he, "and stayed
some months there, not long after the rebellion in the west
was suppressed with a great slaughter of the poor people
that were engaged in it."

"I was then much obliged to that reverend prelate,
John Morton, Archbishop of Canterbury, Cardinal, and
Chancellor of England: a man," said he, "Peter (for Mr.
More knows well what he was), that was not less vener-
able for his wisdom and virtues, than for the high character he bore. He was of a middle stature, not broken with
age; his looks begot reverence rather than fear; his conversation was easy, but serious and grave; he sometimes
took pleasure to try the force of those that came as suitors
to him upon business, by speaking sharply, though decently
to them, and by that he discovered their spirit and presence of mind, with which he was much delighted, when
it did not grow up to impudence, as bearing a great resemblance to his own temper; and he looked on such persons
as the fittest men for affairs. He spoke both gracefully
and weightily; he was eminently skilled in the law, had a
vast understanding, and a prodigious memory; and those
excellent talents with which Nature had furnished him,
were improved by study and experience. When I was in
England the king depended much on his counsels, and the
government seemed to be chiefly supported by him; for
from his youth he had been all along practiced in affairs;
and having passed through many traverses of fortune, he
had with great cost acquired a vast stock of wisdom, which
is not soon lost when it is purchased so dear. One day

when I was dining with him there happened to be at table
one of the English lawyers, who took occasion to run out
in a high commendation of the severe execution of justice
upon thieves, who, as he said, were then hanged so fast,
that there were sometimes twenty on one gibbet; and upon
that he said he could not wonder enough how it came to
pass, that since so few escaped, there were yet as many
thieves left who were still robbing in all places.   Upon
this, I took the boldness to speak freely before the Cardinal, said, there was no reason to wonder at the matter,
since this way of punishing thieves was neither just in
itself nor good for the public, for as the severity was too
great, so the remedy was not effectual; simple theft not being so great a crime that it ought to cost a man his life, no
punishment how severe soever being able to restrain those
from robbing who can find out no other way of livelihood.
'In this,' said I, 'not only you in England, but a great part
of the world imitate some ill masters that are readier to
chastise their scholars than to teach them.   There are
dreadful punishments enacted against thieves, but it were
much better to make such good provisions by which every
man might be put in a method how to live, and so be
preserved from the fatal necessity of stealing and of dying
for it.'—'There has been care enough taken for that,' said
he, 'there are many handicrafts, and there is husbandry,
by which they may make a shift to live unless they have a
greater mind to follow ill courses.'—'That will not serve
your turn,' said I, 'for many lose their limbs in civil or
foreign wars, as lately in the Cornish rebellion, and some
time ago in your wars with France, who being thus muti-
lated in the service of their king and country, can no
more follow their old trades, and are too old to learn new
ones: but since wars are only accidental things, and have
intervals, let us consider those things that fall out every
day.   There is a great number of noblemen among you,
that are themselves idle as drones, that subsist on other

men's labor, on the labor of their tenants, whom, to raise their revenues, they pare to the quick. This indeed is the only instance of their frugality, for in all other things they are prodigal, even to the beggaring of themselves: but besides this, they carry about with them a great number of idle fellows, who never learned any art by which they may gain their living; and these, as soon as either their lord dies, or they themselves fall sick, are turned out of doors; for your lords are readier to feed idle people, than to take care of the sick; and often the heir is not able to keep together so great a family as his predecessor did. Now when the stomachs of those that are thus turned out of doors, grow keen, they rob no less keenly; and what else can they do? for when, by wandering about, they have worn out both their health and their clothes, and are tattered, and look ghastly, men of quality will not entertain them, and poor men dare not do it; knowing that one who has been bred up in idleness and pleasure, and who was used to walk about with his sword and buckler, despising all the neighborhood with an insolent scorn, as far below him, is not fit for the spade and mattock: nor will he serve a poor man for so small a hire, and in so low a diet as he can afford to give him.' To this he answered, 'This sort of men ought to be particularly cherished, for in them consists the force of the armies for which we have occasion; since their birth inspires them with a nobler sense of honor, than is to be found among tradesmen or plowmen.'—'You may as well say,' replied I, 'that you must cherish thieves on the account of wars, for you will never want the one as long as you have the other; and as robbers prove sometimes gallant soldiers, so soldiers often prove brave robbers; so near an alliance there is between those two sorts of life. But this bad custom, so common among you, of keeping many servants, is not peculiar to this nation. In France there is yet a more pestiferous sort of people, for the whole country is full of soldiers, still

kept up in time of peace; if such a state of a nation can
be called a peace: and these are kept in pay upon the same
account that you plead for those idle retainers about noblemen; this being a maxim of those pretended statesmen
that it is necessary for the public safety, to have a good
body of veteran soldiers ever in readiness. They think
raw men are not to be depended on, and they sometimes
seek occasions for making war, that they may train up
their soldiers in the art of cutting throats; or as Sallust
observed, for keeping their hands in use, that they may
not grow dull by too long an intermission. But France has
learned to its cost, how dangerous it is to feed such beasts.
The fate of the Romans, Carthaginians, and Syrians, and
many other nations and cities, which were both overturned
and quite ruined by those standing armies, should make
others wiser: and the folly of this maxim of the French,
appears plainly even from this, that their trained soldiers
often find your raw men prove too hard for them; of
which I will not say much, lest you may think I flatter the
English. Every day's experience shows, that the mechanics
in the towns, or the clowns in the country, are not afraid
of fighting with those idle gentlemen, if they are not disabled by some misfortune in their body, or dispirited by extreme want, so that you need not fear that those well-
shaped and strong men (for it is only such that noblemen
love to keep about them, till they spoil them) who now
grow feeble with ease, and are softened with their effeminate manner of life, would be less fit for action if they were
well bred and well employed. And it seems very unreasonable, that for the prospect of a war, which you need never
have but when you please, you should maintain so many
idle men, as will always disturb you in time of peace, which
is ever to be more considered than war. But I do not
think that this necessity of stealing arises only from hence;
there is another cause of it more peculiar to England.'—
'What is that?' said the Cardinal.—'The increase of pas-

ture,' said I, 'by which your sheep, which are naturally
mild, and easily kept in order, may be said now to devour
men, and unpeople, not only villages, but towns; for where-
ever it is found that the sheep of any soil yield a softer
and richer wool than ordinary, there the nobility and gen-
try, and even those holy men the abbots, not contented
with the old rents which their farms yielded, nor thinking
it enough that they, living at their ease, do no good to the
public, resolve to do it hurt instead of good. They stop
the course of agriculture, destroying houses and towns,
reserving only the churches, and enclose grounds that they
may lodge their sheep in them. As if forests and parks
had swallowed up too little of the land, those worthy countrymen turn the best inhabited places in soltitudes; for
when an insatiable wretch, who is a plague to his country,
resolves to inclose many thousand acres of ground, the
owners, as well as tenants, are turned out of their possessions, by tricks, or by main force, or being wearied out
with all usage, they are forced to sell them. By which
means those miserable people, both men and women, married and unmarried, old and young, with their poor but
numerous families (since country business requires many
hands), are all forced to change their seats, not knowing
whither to go; and they must sell almost for nothing their
household stuff, which could not bring them much money,
even though they might stay for a buyer. When that little
money is at an end, for it will be soon spent; what is left
for them to do, but either to steal and so to be hanged
(God knows how justly), or to go about and beg? And if
they do this, they are put in prison as idle vagabonds;
while they would willingly work, but can find none that
will hire them; for there is no more occasion for country labor, to which they have been bred, when there is no arable
ground left. One shepherd can look after a flock, which
will stock an extent of ground that would require many
hands, if it were to be plowed and reaped. This likewise

in many places raises the price of corn. The price of
wool is also risen, that the poor people who were wont
to make cloth are no more able to buy it; and this likewise makes many of them idle. For since the increase of
pasture God has punished the avarice of the owners, by a
rot among the sheep, which has destroyed vast numbers of
them; to us it might have seemed more just had it fell on
the owners themselves. But suppose the sheep should increase ever so much, their price is not like to fall; since
though they cannot be called a monopoly, because they are
not engrossed by one person, yet they are in so few hands,
and these are so rich, that as they are not pressed to sell
them sooner than they have a mind to it, so they never do
it till they have raised the price as high as possible. And
on the same account it is, that the other kinds of cattle are
so dear, because many villages being pulled down, and all
country labor being much neglected, there are none who
make it their business to breed them. The rich do not
breed cattle as they do sheep, but buy them lean, and at low
prices; and after they have fattened them on their grounds,
sell them again at high rates. And I do not think that all
the inconveniences this will produce are yet observed; for
as they sell the cattle dear, so if they are consumed faster
than the breeding countries from which they are bought
can afford them, then the stock must decrease, and this
must needs end in great scarcity; and by these means this
your island, which seemed as to this particular the happiest
in the world, will suffer much by the cursed avarice of a
few persons; besides this, the rising of corn makes all people lessen their families as much as they can; and what can
those who are dismissed by them do, but either beg or rob?
And to this last, a man of a great mind is much sooner
drawn than to the former. Luxury likewise breaks in apace
upon you, to set forward your poverty and misery; there is
an excessive vanity in apparel, and great cost in diet; and
that not only in noblemen's families, but even among

tradesmen, among the farmers themselves, and among all ranks of persons. You have also many infamous houses, and besides those that are known, the taverns and ale-houses are no better; add to these, dice, cards, tables, foot-ball, tennis, and quoits, in which money runs fast away; and those that are initiated into them, must in the conclusion betake themselves to robbing for a supply. Banish these plagues, and give orders that those who have dis-peopled so much soil, may either rebuild the villages they have pulled down, or let out their grounds to such as will do it; restrain those engrossings of the rich, that are as bad almost as monopolies; leave fewer occasions to idleness; let agriculture be set up again, and the manufacture of the wool be regulated, that so there may be work found for those companies of idle people whom want forces to be thieves, or who now being idle vagabonds, or useless ser-vants, will certainly grow thieves at last. If you do not find a remedy to these evils, it is a vain thing to boast of your severity in punishing theft, which though it may have the appearance of justice, yet in itself is neither just nor con-venient. For if you suffer your people to be ill educated, and their manners to be corrupted from their infancy, and then punish them for those crimes to which their first edu-cation disposed them, what else is to be concluded from this, but that you first make thieves and then punish them?"

"While I was talking thus, the counsellor who was pres-ent had prepared an answer, and had resolved to resume all I had said, according to the formality of a debate, in which things are generally repeated more faithfully than they are answered; as if the chief trial to be made were of men's memories. 'You have talked prettily for a stranger,' said he, 'having heard of many things among us which you have not been able to consider well; but I will make the whole matter plain to you, and will first repeat in order all that you have said, then I will show how much your ignorance of our affairs has misled you, and will in the last place answer all your arguments. And that I may begin where I promised there were four things—' 'Hold your peace,' said the Cardinal, 'this will take up too much time; therefore we will at present ease you of the trouble of answering, and reserve it to our next meeting, which shall be to-morrow, if Raphael's affairs and yours can admit it. But, Raphael,' said he to me, 'I would gladly know upon what reason it is that you think theft ought not to be punished by death? Would you give way to it? Or do you propose any other punishment that will be more useful to the public? For since death does not restrain theft, if men thought their lives would be safe, what fear or force could restrain ill men? On the contrary, they would look on the mitigation of the punishment as an invitation to commit more crimes.' I answered, 'It seems to me a very unjust thing to take away a man's life for a little money; for nothing in the world can be of equal value with a man's life: and if it is said, that it is not for the money that one suffers, but for his breaking the law, I must say, extreme justice is an extreme injury; for we ought not to approve of these terrible laws that make the smallest offences capital, nor of that opinion of the Stoics, that makes all crimes equal, as if there were no difference to be made between the killing a man and the taking his purse, between which, if we examine things impartially, there is no likeness nor proportion. God has commanded us not to kill, and shall we kill so easily for a little money? But if one shall say, that by the law we are only forbid to kill any, except when the laws of the land allow of it; upon the same grounds, laws may be made in some cases to allow of adultery and perjury: for God having taken from us the right of disposing, either of our own or of other people's lives, if it is pretended that the mutual consent of man in making laws can authorize man-slaughter in cases in which God has given us no example, that it frees people from the obligation of the divine law, and so makes murder a lawful action; what is this, but to give a preference to human laws before the divine? And if this is once admitted, by the same rule men may in all other things put what restrictions they please upon the laws of God. If by the Mosaical law, though it was rough and severe, as being a yoke laid on an obstinate and servile nation, men were only fined, and not put to death for theft, we cannot imagine that in this new law of mercy, in which God treats us with the tenderness of a father, He has given us a greater license to cruelty than He did to the Jews. Upon these reasons it is, that I think putting thieves to death is not lawful; and it is plain and obvious that it is absurd, and of ill consequence to the commonwealth, that a thief and a murderer should be equally punished; for if a robber sees that his danger is the same, if he is convicted of theft as if he were guilty of murder, this will naturally incite him to kill the person whom otherwise he would only have robbed, since if the punishment is the same, there is more security, and less danger of discovery, when he that can best make it is put out of the way; so that terrifying thieves too much, provokes them to cruelty.

" 'But as to the question, what more convenient way of punishment can be found? I think it is much more easier to find out that, than to invent anything that is worse; why should we doubt but the way that was so long in use among the old Romans, who understood so well the arts of government, was very proper for their punishment? They condemned such as they found guilty of great crimes, to work their whole lives in quarries, or to dig in mines with chains about them. But the method that I liked best, was that which I observed in my travels in Persia, among the Polylerits, who are a considerable and well-governed people. They pay a yearly tribute to the King of Persia; but in all other respects they are a free nation, and governed by their own laws. They lie far from the sea, and are environed with hills; and being contented with the productions of their own country, which is very fruitful, they have

little commerce with any other nation; and as they, according to the genius of their country, have no inclination to enlarge their borders; so their mountains, and the pension
they pay to the Persian, secure them from all invasions.
Thus they have no wars among them; they live rather conveniently than with splendor, and may be rather called a
happy nation, than either eminent or famous; for I do not
think that they are known so much as by name to any
but their next neighbors. Those that are found guilty of
theft among them, are bound to make restitution to the
owner, and not as it is in other places, to the prince, for
they reckon that the prince has no more right to the stolen
goods than the thief; but if that which was stolen is no
more in being, then the goods of the thieves are estimated,
and restitution being made out of them, the remainder is
given to their wives and children: and they themselves are
condemned to serve in the public works, but are neither
imprisoned, nor chained, unless there happened to be some
extraordinary circumstances in their crimes. They go about
loose and free, working for the public. If they are idle or
backward to work, they are whipped; but if they work
hard, they are well used and treated without any mark of
reproach, only the lists of them are called always at night,
and then they are shut up. They suffer no other uneasiness,
but this of constant labor; for as they work for the public,
so they are well entertained out of the public stock, which
is done differently in different places. In some places, whatever is bestowed on them, is raised by a charitable contribu-
tion; and though this way may seem uncertain, yet so merciful are the inclinations of that people, that they are plentifully supplied by it; but in other places, public revenues
are set aside for them; or there is a constant tax of a poll-
money raised for their maintenance. In some places they
are set to no public work, but every private man that has
occasion to hire workmen, goes to the market-places and
hires them of the public, a little lower than he would do a

freeman: if they go lazily about their task, he may quicken
them with the whip. By this means there is always some
piece of work or other to be done by them; and beside their
livelihood, they earn somewhat still to the public. They all
wear a peculiar habit, of one certain color, and their hair
is cropped a littl above their ears, and a piece of one of
their ears is cut off. Their friends are allowed to give them
either meat, drink, or clothes, so they are of their proper
color; but it is death, both to the giver and taker, if they
give them money; nor is it less penal for any freeman to
take money from them, upon any account whatsoever: and
it is also death for any of these slaves (so they are called)
to handle arms. Those of every division of the country are
distinguished by a peculiar mark; which it is capital for
them to lay aside, to go out of their bounds, or to talk with
a slave of another jurisdiction; and the very attempt of an
escape is no less penal than an escape itself; it is death
for any other slave to be accessory to it; and if a freeman
engages in it he is condemned to slavery. Those that discover it are rewarded; if freemen, in money; and if slaves,
with liberty, together with a pardon for being accessory to
it; that so they might find their account, rather in repenting
of their engaging in such a design, than in persisting in it.

"These are their laws and rules in relation to robbery;
and it is obvious that they are as advantageous as they are
mild and gentle; since vice is not only destroyed, and
men preserved, but they are treated in such a manner as to
make them see the necessity of being honest, and of em-
ploying the rest of their lives in repairing the injuries they
have formerly done to society. Nor is there any hazard
of their falling back to their old customs: and so little
do travellers apprehend mischief from them, that they
generally make use of them for guides, from one jurisdiction to another; for there is nothing left them by which
they can rob, or be the better for it, since as they are
disarmed, so the very having of money is a sufficient con-

viction: and as they are certainly punished if discovered, so they cannot hope to escape; for their habit being in all the parts of it different from what is commonly worn, they cannot fly away, unless they would go naked, and even then their cropped ears would betray them. The only danger to be feared from them, is their conspiring against the government: but those of one division and neighborhood can do nothing to any purpose, unless a general conspiracy were laid amongst all the slaves of the several jurisdictions, which cannot be done, since they cannot meet or talk together; nor will any venture on a design where the concealment would be so dangerous, and the discovery so profitable. None are quite hopeless of recovering their freedom, since by their obedience and patience, and by giving good grounds to believe that they will change their manner of life for the future, they may expect at last to obtain their liberty: and some are every year restored to it, upon the good character that is given of them.—When I had related all this, I added, that I did not see why such a method might not be followed with more advantage, than could ever be expected from that severe justice which the counsellor magnified so much. To this he answered, that it could never take place in England, without endangering the whole nation. As he said this, he shook his head, made some grimaces, and held his peace, while all the company seemed of his opinion, except the Cardinal, who said that it was not easy to form a judgment of its success, since it was a method that never yet had been tried. 'But if,' said he, 'when the sentence of death was passed upon a thief, the prince would reprieve him for a while, and make the experiment upon him, denying him the privilege of a sanctuary; and then if it had a good effect upon him, it might take place; and if it did not succeed, the worst would be, to execute the sentence on the condemned persons at last. And I do not see,' added he, 'why it would be either unjust, inconvenient, or at all dangerous, to admit of such a delay: in my opinion, the vagabonds ought to be treated in the same manner; against whom, though we have made many laws, yet we have not been able to gain our end.' When the Cardinal had done, they all commended the motion, though they had despised it when it came from me; but more particularly commended what related to the vagabonds, because it was his own observation.

"I do not know whether it be worth while to tell what followed, for it was very ridiculous; but I shall venture at it, for as it is not foreign to this matter, so some good use may be made of it. There was a jester standing by, that counterfeited the fool so naturally, that he seemed to be really one. The jests which he offered were so cold and dull, that we laughed more at him than at them; yet sometimes he said, as it were by chance, things that were not unpleasant; so as to justify the old proverb, 'That he who throws the dice often, will sometimes have a lucky hit.' When one of the company had said, that I had taken care of the thieves, and the Cardinal had taken care of the vagabonds, so that there remained nothing but that some public provision might be made for the poor, whom sickness or old age had disabled from labor. 'Leave that to me,' said the fool, 'and I shall take care of them; for there is no sort of people whose sight I abhor more, having been so often vexed with them, and with their sad complaints; but as dolefully soever as they have told their tale, they could never prevail so far as to draw one penny from me: for either I had no mind to give them anything, or when I had a mind to do it, I had nothing to give them: and they now know me so well, that they will not lose their labor, but let me pass without giving me any trouble, because they hope for nothing, no more in faith than if I were a priest: but I would have a law made, for sending all these beggars to monasteries, the men to the Benedictines to be made lay-brothers, and the women to be nuns.' The Cardinal smiled, and approved of it in jest; but the rest liked it in earnest.

There was a divine present, who though he was a grave morose man, yet he was so pleased with this reflection that was made on the priests and the monks, that he began to play with the fool, and said to him, 'This will not deliver you from all beggars, except you take care of us friars.'— 'That is done already,' answered the fool, 'for the Cardinal has provided for you, by what he proposed for restraining vagabonds, and setting them to work, for I know no vaga- bonds like you.' This was well entertained by the whole company, who looking at the Cardinal, perceived that he was not ill pleased at it; only the friar himself was vexed, as may be easily imagined, and fell into such a passion, that he could not forbear railing at the fool, and calling knave, slanderer, backbiter, and son of perdition, and then cited some dreadful threatenings out of the Scriptures against him. Now the jester thought he was in his element, and laid about him freely. 'Good friar,' said he, 'be not angry, for it is written, "In patience possess your soul." '—The friar answered (for I shall give you his own words) 'I am not angry, you hangman; at least I do not sin in it, for the Psalmist says, "Be ye angry, and sin not." '—Upon this the Cardinal admonished him gently, and wished him to govern his passions. 'No, my lord,' said he, ' I speak not but from a good zeal, which is said, "The zeal of thy house hath eaten me up;" and we sing in our church, that those who mocked Elisha as he went up to the house of God, felt the effects of his zeal; which that mocker, that rogue, that scoundrel, will perhaps feel.'—'You do this perhaps with a good intention,' said the Cardinal; 'but in my opinion, it were wiser in you, and perhaps better for you, not to en- gage in so ridiculous a contest with a fool.'—'No, my lord,' answered he, 'that were not wisely done; for Solomon, the wisest of men, said. "Answer a fool according to his folly;" which I now do, and show him the ditch into which he will fall, if he is not aware of it; for if the many mockers of Elisha, who was but one bald man, felt the effect of his zeal,

what will become of one mocker of so many friars, among
whom there are so many bald men? We have likewise a
Bull, by which all that jeer us are excommunicated.'—
When the Cardinal saw that there was no end of this matter, he made a sign to the fool to withdraw, turned the discourse another way; and soon after rose from the table,
and dismissing us, went to hear causes.

"Thus, Mr. More, I have run out into a tedious story, of
the length of which I had been ashamed, if, as you earnestly begged it of me, I had not observed you to hearken to it,
as if you had no mind to lose any part of it. I might have
contracted it, but I resolved to give it to you at large, that
you might observe how those that despised what I had
proposed, no sooner perceived that the Cardinal did not
dislike it, but presently approved of it, fawned so on him,
and flattered him to such a degree, that they in good earnest applauded those things that he only liked in jest. And
from hence you may gather, how little courtiers would
value either me or my counsels."

To this I answered, "You have done me a great kindness
in this relation; for as everything has been related by you,
both wisely and pleasantly, so you have made me imagine
that I was in my own country, and grown young again, by
recalling that good Cardinal to my thoughts, in whose
family I was bred from my childhood: and though you are
upon other accounts very dear to me, yet you are the
dearer, because you honor his memory so much; but after
all this I cannot change my opinion; for I still think that if
you could overcome that aversion which you have to the
Courts of Princes, you might, by the advice which it is in
your power to give, do a great deal of good to mankind;
and this is the chief design that every good man ought to
propose to himself in living; for your friend Plato thinks
that nations will be happy, when either philosophers become kings, or kings become philosophers, it is no wonder
if we are so far from that happiness, while philosophers

will not think it their duty to assist kings with their councils."—"They are not so base-minded," said he, "but that
they would willingly do it: many of them have already done
it by their books, if those that are in power would but
hearken to their good advice. But Plato judged right, that
except kings themselves became philosophers, they who
from their childhood are corrupted with false notions,
would never fall in entirely with the councils of philosophers, and this he himself found to be true in the person of
Dionysius.

"Do not you think, that if I were about any king, pro-
posing good laws to him, and endeavoring to root out
all the cursed seeds of evil that I found in him, I should
either be turned out of his Court, or at least laughed at
for my pains? For instance, what could it signify if I were
about the King of France, and were called into his cabinet-
council, where several wise men, in his hearing, were pro-
posing many expedients; as by what arts and practices
Milan may be kept; and Naples, that had so oft slipped out
of their hands, recovered; how the Venetians, and after
them the rest of Italy, may be subdued; and then how
Flanders, Brabant, and all Burgundy, and some other kingdoms which he has swallowed already in his designs, may
be added to his empire. One proposes a league with the
Venetians, to be kept as long as he finds his account in it,
and that he ought to communicate councils with them, and
give them some share of the spoil, till his success makes
him need or fear them less, and then it will be easily taken
out of their hands. Another proposes the hiring the
Germans, and the securing the Switzers by pensions. Another proposes the gaining the Emperor by money, which
is omnipotent with him. Another proposes a peace with
the King of Arragon, and in order to cement it, the
yielding up the King of Navarre's pretensions. Another
thinks the Prince of Castile is to be wrought on, by the
hope of an alliance; and that some of his courtiers are to

be gained to the French faction by pensions. The hardest
point of all is what to do with England: a treaty of peace
is to be set on foot, and if their alliance is not to be depended on, yet is to be made as firm as possible; and they
are to be called friends, but suspected as enemies; therefore
the Scots are to be kept in readiness, to be let loose upon
England on every occasion: and some banished nobleman
is to be supported underhand (for by the league it cannot
be done avowedly) who has a pretension to the crown,
by which means that suspected prince may be kept in awe.
Now when things are in so great a fermentation, and so
many gallant men are joining councils, how to carry on
the war, if so mean a man as I should stand up, and wish
them to change all their councils, to let Italy alone, and
stay at home, since the kingdom of France was indeed
greater than could be well governed by one man; that
therefore he ought not to think of adding others to it: and
if after this, I should propose to them the resolutions of the
Achorians, a people that lie on the south-east of Utopia,
who long ago engaged in war, in order to add to the
dominions of their prince another kingdom, to which he
had some pretensions by an ancient alliance. This they
conquered, but found that the trouble of keeping it was
equal to that by which it was gained; that the conquered
people were always either in rebellion or exposed to foreign
invasions, while they were obliged to be incessantly at war,
either for or against them, and consequently could never
disband their army; that in the meantime they were oppressed with taxes, their money went out of the kingdom,
their blood was spilled for the glory of their king, without
procuring the least advantage to the people, who received
not the smallest benefit from it even in time of peace; and
that their manners being corrupted by a long war, robbery
and murders everywhere abounded, and their laws fell into
contempt; while their king, distracted with the care of two
kingdoms, was the less able to apply his mind to the in-

terests of either. When they saw this, and that there would
be no end to these evils, they by joint councils made an
humble address to their king, desiring him to choose which
of the two kingdoms he had the greatest mind to keep,
since he could not hold both; for they were too great a
people to be governed by a divided king, since no man
would willingly have a groom that should be in common
between him and another. Upon which the good prince
was forced to quit his new kingdom to one of his friends
(who was not long after dethroned), and to be contented
with his old one. To this I would add, that after all those
warlike attempts, the vast confusions, and the consumption
both of treasure and of people that must follow them; perhaps upon some misfortune, they might be forced to throw
up all at last; therefore it seemed much more eligible that
the king should improve his ancient kingdom all he could,
and make it flourish as much as possible; that he should
love his people, and be beloved of them; that he should live
among them, govern them gently, and let other kingdoms
alone, since that which had fallen to his share was big
enough, if not too big for him. Pray how do you think
would such a speech be heard?"—"I confess," said I, "I
think not very well."

"But what," said he, "if I should sort with another kind
of ministers, whose chief contrivances and consultations
were, by what art the prince's treasures might be increased.
Where one proposes raising the value of specie when the
king's debts are large, and lowering it when his revenues
were to come in, that so he might both pay much with a
little, and in a little receive a great deal: another proposes
a pretence of a war, that money might be raised in order to
carry it on, and that a peace be concluded as soon as that
was done; and this with such appearances of religion as
might work on the people, and make them impute it to the
piety of their prince, and to his tenderness for the lives of
his subjects. A third offers some old musty laws, that have

been forgotten by all the subjects, so they had been also broken by them; and proposes the levying the penalties of these laws, that as it would bring in a vast treasure, so there might be a very good pretence for it, since it would look like the executing a law, and the doing of justice. A fourth proposes the prohibiting of many things under severe penalties, especially such as were against the interest of the people, and then the dispensing with these prohibitions upon great compositions, to those who might find their advantage in breaking them. This would serve two ends, both of them acceptable to many; for as those whose avarice led them to transgress would be severely fined, so the selling licenses dear would look as if a prince were tender of his people, and would not easily, or at low rates, dispense with anything that might be against the public good. Another proposes that the judges must be made sure, that they may declare always in favor of the prerogative, that they must be often sent for to Court, that the king may hear them argue those points in which he is concerned; since how unjust soever any of his pretensions may be, yet still some one or other of them, either out of contradiction to others, or the pride of singularity, or to make their court, would find out some pretence or other to give the king a fair color to carry the point; for if the judges but differ in opinion, the clearest thing in the world is made by that means disputable, and truth being once brought in question, the king may then take advantage to expound the law for his own profit; while the judges that stand out will be brought over, either out of fear or modesty; and they being thus gained, all of them may be sent to the bench to give sentence boldly, as the king would have it; for fair pretences will never be wanting when sentence is to be given in the prince's favor. It will either be said that equity lies of his side, or some words in the law will be found sounding that way, or some forced sense will be put on them; and when all other things fail, the king's undoubted prerogative will be pre-

tended, as that which is above all law; and to which a religious judge ought to have a special regard.   Thus all consent to that maxim of Crassus, that a prince cannot have
treasure enough, since he must maintain his armies out of
it; that a king, even though he would, can do nothing un-
justly; that all property is in him, not excepting the very
persons of his subjects; and that no man has any other
property, but that which the king out of his goodness
thinks fit to leave him.   And they think it is the prince's
interest, that there be as little of this left as may be, as if
it were his advantage that his people should have neither
riches nor liberty; since these things make them less easy
and less willing to submit to a cruel and unjust government; whereas necessity and poverty blunts them, makes
them patient, beats them down, and breaks that height of
spirit, that might otherwise dispose them to rebel.   Now
what if after all these propositions were made, I should
rise up and assert, that such councils were both unbecoming a king, and mischievous to him: and that not only
his honor but his safety consisted more in his people's
wealth, than in his own; if I should show that they choose
a king for their own sake, and not for his; that by his
care and endeavors they may be both easy and safe; and
that therefore a prince ought to take more care of his people's happiness than of his own, as a shepherd is to take
more care of his flock than of himself.   It is also certain,
that they are much mistaken that think the poverty of a
nation is a means of public safety.   Who quarrel more than
beggars?   Who does more earnestly long for a change, than
he that is uneasy in his present circumstances?   And who
run to create confusion with so desperate a boldness, as
those who have nothing to lose, hope to gain by them?   If
a king should fall under such contempt or envy, that he
could not keep his subjects in their duty, but by oppression
and ill usage, and by rendering them poor and miserable,
it were certainly better for him to quit his kingdom, than

to retain it by such methods, as makes him while he keeps
the name of authority, lose the majesty due to it. Nor is
it so becoming the dignity of a king to reign over beggars,
as over rich and happy subjects. And therefore Fabricius,
a man of a noble and exalted temper, said, he would rather
govern rich men, than be rich himself; since for one man
to abound in wealth and pleasure, when all about him are
mourning and groaning, is to be a gaoler and not a king.
He is an unskilful physician, that cannot cure one disease
without casting his patient into another: so he that can
find no other way for correcting the errors of his people,
but by taking from them the conveniences of life, shows
that he knows not what it is to govern a free nation. He
himself ought rather to shake off his sloth, or to lay down
his pride; for the contempt or hatred that his people have
for him, takes its rise from the vices in himself. Let him
live upon what belongs to him, without wronging others,
and accommodate his expense to his revenue. Let him
punish crimes, and by his wise conduct let him endeavor
to prevent them, rather than be severe when he has suffered them to be too common; let him not rashly revive
laws that are abrogated by disuse, especially if they have
been long forgotten, and never wanted; and let him never
take any penalty for the breach of them, to which a judge
would not give way in a private man, but would look on
him as a crafty and unjust person for pretending to it.
To these things I would add, that law among the Macar-
ians, a people that lie not far from Utopia, by which their
king, on the day on which he begins to reign, is tied by
an oath confirmed by solemn sacrifices, never to have at
once above a thousand pounds of gold in his treasures, or
so much silver as is equal to that in value. This law, they
tell us, was made by an excellent king, who had more regard to the riches of his country than to his own wealth;
and therefore provided against the heaping up of so much
treasure, as might impoverish the people. He thought that

moderate sum might be sufficient for any accident; if either
the king had occasion for it against rebels, or the kingdom
against the invasion of an enemy; but that it was not
enough to encourage a prince to invade other men's rights,
a circumstance that was the chief cause of his making that
law. He also thought that it was a good provision for that
free circulation of money, so necessary for the course of
commerce and exchange: and when a king must distribute
all those extraordinary accessions that increase treasure
beyond the due pitch, it makes him less disposed to oppress his subjects. Such a king as this will be the terror
of ill men, and will be beloved by all the good.

"If, I say, I should talk of these or such like things, to
men that had taken their bias another way, how deaf would
they be to all I could say?"—"No doubt, very deaf," answered I; "and no wonder, for one is never to offer at propositions or advice that we are certain will not be entertained. Discourses so much out of the road could not avail
anything, nor have any effect on men whose minds were
prepossessed with different sentiments. This philosophical
way of speculation is not unpleasant among friends in a
free conversation, but there is no room for it in the Courts
of Princes where great affairs are carried on by authority."
—"That is what I was saying," replied he, "that there is
no room for philosophy in the Courts of Princes."—"Yes,
there is," said I, "but not for this speculative philosophy
that makes everything to be alike fitting at all times: but
there is another philosophy that is more pliable, that knows
its proper scene, accommodates itself to it, and teaches a
man with propriety and decency to act that part which
has fallen to his share. If when one of Plautus's comedies
is upon the stage and a company of servants are acting their
parts, you should come out in the garb of a philosopher,
and repeat out of 'Octavia's discourse of Seneca's to Nero,'
would it not be better for you to say nothing than by mixing things of such different natures to make an impertinent

tragi-comedy? For you spoil and corrupt the play that is
in hand when you mix with it things of an opposite nature, even though they are much better. Therefore go
through with the play that is acting the best you can, and
do not confound it because another that is pleasanter comes
into your thoughts. It is even so in a commonwealth, and
in the councils of princes; if ill opinions cannot be quite
rooted out, and you cannot cure some received vice according to your wishes, you must not therefore abandon
the commonwealth, for the same reasons you should not
forsake the ship in a storm because you cannot command
the winds. You are not obliged to assault people with
discourses that are out of their road, when you see that
their received notions must prevent your making an impression upon them. You ought rather to cast about and
to manage things with all the dexterity in your power, so
that if you are not able to make them go well they may be
as little ill as possible; for except all men were good everything cannot be right, and that is a blessing that I do not
at present hope to see." "According to your arguments,"
answered he, "all that I could be able to do would be to
preserve myself from being mad while I endeavored to cure
the madness of others; for if I speak truth, I must repeat
what I have said to you; and as for lying, whether a philosopher can do it or not, I cannot tell, I am sure I cannot do
it. But though these discourses may be uneasy and ungrateful to them, I do not see why they should seem foolish
or extravagant: indeed if I should either propose such
things as Plato has contrived in his commonwealth, or as
the Utopians practice in theirs, though they might seem
better, as certainly they are, yet they are so different from
our establishment, which is founded on property, there
being no such thing among them, that I could not expect
that it would have any effect on them; but such discourses
as mine, which only call past evils to mind and give warning of what may follow, have nothing in them that is

so absurd that they may not be used at any time, for they
can only be unpleasant to those who are resolved to run
headlong the contrary way; and if we must let alone everything as absurd or extravagant which by reason of the
wicked lives of many may seem uncouth, we must, even
among Christians, give over pressing the greatest part of
those things that Christ hath taught us, though He has
commanded us not to conceal them, but to proclaim on
the house-tops that which He taught in secret. The greatest parts of His precepts are more opposite to the lives of
the men of this age than any part of my discourse has been;
but the preachers seemed to have learned that craft to
which you advise me, for they observing that the world
would not willingly suit their lives to the rules that Christ
has given, have fitted His doctrine as if it had been a leaden
rule, to their lives, that so some way or other they might
agree with one another. But I see no other effect of this
compliance except it be that men become more secure in
their wickedness by it. And this is all the success that I
can have in a Court, for I must always differ from the
rest, and then I shall signify nothing; or if I agree with
them, I shall then only help forward their madness. I do
not comprehend what you mean by your casting about, or
by the bending and handling things so dextrously, that
if they go not well they may go as little ill as may be; for
in Courts they will not bear with a man's holding his peace
or conniving at what others do. A man must barefacedly
approve of the worst counsels, and consent to the blackest
designs: so that he would pass for a spy, or possibly for a
traitor, that did but coldly approve of such wicked practices: and therefore when a man is engaged in such a society, he will be so far from being able to mend matters
by his casting about, as you call it, that he will find no occasions of doing any good: the ill company will sooner
corrupt him, than be the better for him: or if notwithstanding all their ill company, he still remains steady and

innocent, yet their follies and knavery will be imputed to him; and by mixing counsels with them, he must bear his share of all the blame that belongs wholly to others.

"It was no ill simile by which Plato set forth the un-reasonableness of a philosopher's meddling with govern-ment. If a man, says he, was to see a great company run out every day into the rain, and take delight in being wet; if he knew that it would be to no purpose for him to go and persuade them to return to their houses, in order to avoid the storm, and that all that could be expected by his going to speak to them would be that he himself should be as wet as they, it would be best for him to keep within doors; and since he had not influence enough to correct other people's folly, to take care to preserve himself.

"Though to speak plainly my real sentiments, I must freely own, that as long as there is any property, and while money is the standard of all other things, I cannot think that a nation can be governed either justly or happily: not justly, because the best things will fall to the share of the worst men; nor happily, because all things will be divided among a few (and even these are not in all respects happy), the rest being left to be absolutely miserable. Therefore when I reflect on the wise and good constitution of the Utopians, among whom all things are so well governed, and with so few laws; where virtue hath its due reward, and yet there is such an equality, that every man lives in plenty; when I compare with them so many other nations that are still making new laws, and yet can never bring their con-stitution to a right regulation, where notwithstanding every one has his property; yet all the laws that they can invent have not the power either to obtain or preserve it, or even to enable men certainly to distinguish what is their own from what is another's; of which the many lawsuits that every day break out, and are eternally depending, give too plain a demonstration; when, I say, I balance all these things in my thoughts, I grow more favorable to Plato, and

do not wonder that he resolved not to make any laws for
such as would not submit to a community of all things: for
so wise a man could not but foresee that the setting all
upon a level was the only way to make a nation happy,
which cannot be obtained so long as there is property: for
when every man draws to himself all that he can compass,
by one title or another, it must needs follow, that how
plentiful soever a nation may be, yet a few dividing the
wealth of it among themselves, the rest must fall into indi-
gence. So that there will be two sorts of people among
them, who deserve that their fortunes should be interchanged; the former useless, but wicked and ravenous;
and the latter, who by their constant industry serve the
public more than themselves, sincere and modest men.
From whence I am persuaded, that till property is taken
away there can be no equitable or just distribution of
things, nor can the world be happily governed: for as long
as that is maintained, the greatest and the far best part of
mankind will be still oppressed with a load of cares and
anxieties. I confess without taking it quite away, those
pressures that lie on a great part of mankind may be made
lighter; but they can never be quite removed. For if
laws were made to determine at how great an extent in
soil, and at how much money every man must stop, to limit
the prince that he might not grow too great, and to restrain the people that they might not become too insolent,
and that none might factiously aspire to public employments, which ought neither to be sold, nor made burthen-
some by a great expense; since otherwice those that serve
in them would be tempted to reimburse themselves by
cheats and violence, and it would become necessary to find
out rich men for undergoing those employments which
ought rather to be trusted to the wise. These laws, I say,
might have such effects, as good diet and care might have
on a sick man, whose recovery is desperate: they might al-
lay and mitigate the disease, but it could never be quite

healed, nor the body politic be brought again to a good
habit, as long as property remains; and it will fall out as in
a complication of diseases, that by applying a remedy to
one sore, you will provoke another; and that which removes
the one ill symptom produces others, while the strengthening one part of the body weakens the rest."—"On the contrary," answered I, "it seems to me that men cannot live
conveniently, where all things are common: how can there
be any plenty, where every man will excuse himself from
labor? For as the hope of gain doth not excite him, so
the confidence that he has in other men's industry may
make him slothful: if people come to be pinched with want,
and yet cannot dispose of anything as their own; what
can follow upon this but perpetual sedition and bloodshed,
especially when the reverence and authority due to magistrates falls to the ground? For I cannot imagine how that
can be kept up among those that are in all things equal
to one another."—"I do not wonder," said he, "that it
appears so to you, since you have no notion, or at least no
right one, of such a constitution: but if you had been in
Utopia with me, and had seen their laws and rules, as I did,
for the space of five years, in which I lived among them;
and during which time I was so delighted with them, that
indeed I should never have left them, if it had not been
to make the discovery of that new world to the Europeans;
you would then confess that you had never seen a people so
well constituted as they."—"You will not easily persuade
me," said Peter, "that any nation in that new world is
better governed than those among us. For as our under-
standings are not worse than theirs, so our government,
if I mistake not, being more ancient, a long practice has
helped us to find out many conveniences of life: and some
happy chances have discovered other things to us, which
no man's understanding could ever have invented."—
"As for the antiquity, either of their government, or of
ours," said he, "you cannot pass a true judgment of it,

unless you had read their histories; for if they are to be
believed, they had towns among them before these parts
were so much as inhabited. And as for those discoveries,
that have been either hit on by chance, or made by ingenious men, these might have happened there as well as
here. I do not deny but we are more ingenious than they
are, but they exceed us much in industry and application.
They knew a little concerning us before our arrival among
them; they call us all by a general name of the nations that
lie beyond the Equinoctial Line; for their Chronicle men-
tions a shipwreck that was made on their coast 1,200 years
ago; and that some Romans and Egyptians that were in the
ship, getting safe ashore, spent the rest of their days
amongst them; and such was their ingenuity, that from this
single opportunity they drew the advantage of learning
from those unlooked-for guests, and acquired all the useful
arts that were then among the Romans, and which were
known to these shipwrecked men: and by the hints that
they gave them, they themselves found out even some of
those arts which they could not fully explain; so happily
did they improve that accident, of having some of our
people cast upon their shore. But if such an accident has
at any time brought any from thence into Europe, we
have been so far from improving it, that we do not so
much as remember it; as in after-times perhaps it will be
forgot by our people that I was ever there. For though
they from one such accident made themselves masters of all
the good inventions that were among us; yet I believe it
would be long before we should learn or put in practice any
of the good institutions that are among them. And this
is the true cause of their being better governed, and living
happier than we, though we come not short of them in
point of understanding or outward advantages."—Upon
this I said to him, "I earnestly beg you would describe that
island very particularly to us. Be not too short, but set
out in order all things relating to their soil, their rivers,

their towns, their people, their manners, constitutions, laws, and, in a word, all that you imagine we desire to know. And you may well imagine that we desire to know every‑ thing concerning them, of which we are hitherto ignorant." —"I will do it very willingly," said he, "for I have digested the whole matter carefully; but it will take up some time." —"Let us go then," said I, "first and dine, and then we shall have leisure enough." He consented. We went in and dined, and after dinner came back, and sat down in the same place. I ordered my servants to take care that none might come and interrupt us. And both Peter and I desired Raphael to be as good as his word. When he saw that we were very intent upon it, he paused a little to recollect himself, and began in this manner.

BOOK II

THE ISLAND of Utopia is in the middle two hundred miles broad, and holds almost at the same breadth over a great part of it; but it grows narrower towards both ends. Its figure is not unlike a crescent: between its horns, the sea comes in eleven miles broad, and spreads itself into a great bay, which is environed with land to the compass of about five hundred miles wide, and is well secured from winds. In this bay there is no great current, the whole coast is, as it were, one continued harbor, which gives all that live in the island great convenience for mutual commerce; but the entry into the bay, occasioned by rocks on the one hand, and shallows on the other, is very dangerous. In the middle of it there is one single rock which appears above water, and may therefore be easily avoided, and on the top of it there is a tower in which a garrison is kept, the other rocks lie under water and are very dangerous. The channel is known only to the natives, so that if any stranger should enter into the bay, without one of their pilots, he would run great danger of shipwreck, for even they themselves could not pass it safe, if some marks that are on the coast did not direct their way; and if these should be but a little shifted, any fleet that might come against them, how great soever it were, would be certainly lost. On the other side of the island there are likewise many harbors; and the coast is so fortified, both by nature and art, that a small number of men can hinder the descent of a great army. But they report (and there remains good marks of it to make it credible) that this was no island at first, but a part of the continent. Utopus that conquered it (whose name it still carries, for Abraxa was its first

41

name) brought the rude and uncivilized inhabitants into
such a good government, and to that measure of politeness,
that they now far excel all the rest of mankind; having
soon subdued them, he designed to separate them from the
continent, and to bring the sea quite round them. To
accomplish this, he ordered a deep channel to be dug fifteen
miles long; and that the natives might not think he treated
them like slaves, he not only forced the inhabitants, but
also his own soldiers, to labor in carrying it on. As he set
a vast number of men to work, he beyond all men's expectations brought it to a speedy conclusion. And his neighbors who at first laughed at the folly of the undertaking,
no sooner saw it brought to perfection, than they were
struck with admiration and terror.

There are fifty-four cities in the island, all large and well
built: the manners, customs, and laws of which are the
same, and they are all contrived as near in the same manner as the ground on which they stand will allow. The
nearest lie at least twenty-four miles distance from one
another, and the most remote are not so far distant, but
that a man can go on foot in one day from it, to that which
lies next it. Every city sends three of their wisest senators
once a year to Amaurot, to consult about their common
concerns; for that is chief town of the island, being situated
near the centre of it, so that it is the most convenient
place for their assemblies. The jurisdiction of every city
extends at least twenty miles: and where the towns lie
wider, they have much more ground: no town desires to
enlarge its bounds, for the people consider themselves
rather as tenants than landlords. They have built over all
the country, farmhouses for husbandmen, which are well
contrived, and are furnished with all things necessary for
country labor. Inhabitants are sent by turns from the
cities to dwell in them; no country family has fewer than
forty men and women in it, besides two slaves. There is a
master and mistress set over every family; and over thirty
families there is a magistrate. Every year twenty of this

family come back to the town, after they have stayed two years in the country; and in their room there are other twenty sent from the town, that they may learn country work from those that have been already one year in the country, as they must teach those that come to them the next from the town. By this means such as dwell in those country farms are never ignorant of agriculture, and so commit no errors, which might otherwise be fatal, and bring them under a scarcity of corn. But though there is every year such a shifting of the husbandmen, to prevent any man being forced against his will to follow that hard course of life too long; yet many among them take such pleasure in it, that they desire to continue it in many years. These husbandmen till the ground, breed cattle, hew wood, and convey it to the towns, either by land or water, as is most convenient. They breed an infinite multi- tude of chickens in a very curious manner; for the hens do not sit and hatch them, but vast number of eggs are laid in a gentle and equal heat, in order to be hatched, and they are no sooner out of the shell, and able to stir about, but they seem to consider those that feed them as their mothers, and follow them as other chickens do the hen that hatched them. They breed very few horses, but those they have are full of mettle, and are kept only for exercising their youth in the art of sitting and riding them; for they do not put them to any work, either of plowing or carriage, in which they employ oxen; for though their horses are stronger, yet they find oxen can hold out longer; and as they are not subjected to so many diseases, so they are kept upon a less charge, and with less trouble; and even when they are so worn out, that they are no more fit for labor, they are good meat at last. They sow no corn, but that which is to be their bread; for they drink either wine, cider, or perry, and often water, sometimes boiled with honey or liquorice, with which they abound; and though they know exactly how much corn will serve every town, and all that tract of country which belongs to it, yet they sow much more, and breed more cattle than are necessary for their consumption; and they give that overplus of which they make no use to their neighbors. When they want anything in the country which it does not produce, they fetch that from the town, without carrying anything in exchange for it. And the magistrates of the town take care to see it given them; for they meet generally in the town once a month, upon festival day. When the time of harvest comes, the magistrates in the country send to those in the towns, and let them know how many hands they will need for reaping the harvest; and the number they call for being sent to them, they commonly dispatch it all in one day.

OF THEIR TOWNS, PARTICULARLY AMAUROT

He that knows one of their towns, knows them all, they are so like one another, except where the situa-tion makes some difference. I shall therefore describe one of them; and none is so proper as Amaurot; for as none is more eminent, all the rest yielding in precedence to this, because it is the seat of their supreme council; so there was none of them better known to me, I having lived five years altogether in it.

It lies upon the side of a hill, or rather a rising ground; its figure is almost square, for from the one side of it, which shoots up almost to the top of the hill, it runs down in a descent for two miles to the river Anider; but it is a little broader the other way that runs along by the bank of that river. The Anider rises about eighty miles above Amaurot in a small spring at first; but other brooks falling into it, of which two are more considerable than the rest. As it runs by Amaurot, it is grown half a mile broad; but it still grows larger and larger, till after sixty miles course below it, it is lost in the ocean, between the town and the sea, and for some miles above the town, it ebbs and flows every six hours, with a strong current. The tide comes up for about thirty miles so full, that there is nothing but salt water in the river, the fresh water being driven back with its force; and above that, for some miles, the water is brackish; but a little higher, as it runs by the town, it is quite fresh; and when the tide ebbs, it continues fresh all along to the sea. There is a bridge cast over the river, not of timber, but of fair stone, consisting of many stately arches; it lies at that part of the town which is farthest from the sea, so that ships without any hindrance lie all along the side of the town. There is likewise another river that runs by it, which though it is not great, yet it runs pleasantly, for it rises out of the same hill on which the town stands, and so runs down through it, and falls into the Anider. The in- habitants have fortified the fountain-head of this river, which springs a little without the towns; that so if they should happen to be beseiged, the enemy might not be able to stop or divert the course of the water, nor poison it; from thence it is carried in earthen pipes to the lower streets; and for those places of the town to which the water of that small river cannot be conveyed, they have great cisterns for receiving the rain-water, which supplies the want of the other. The town is compassed with a high and thick wall, in which there are many towers and forts; there is also a broad and deep dry ditch, set thick with thorns, cast round three sides of the town, and the river is instead of a ditch on the fourth side. The streets are very convenient for all carriage, and are well sheltered from the winds. Their buildings are good, and are so uniform, that a whole side of a street looks like one house. The streets are twenty feet broad; there lie gardens behind all their houses; these are large but enclosed with buildings, that on all hands face the streets; so that every house has both a door to the street, and a back door to the garden. Their doors all have two leaves, which, as they are easily opened,

so they shut of their own accord; and there being no
property among them, every man may freely enter into any
house whatsoever. At every ten years end they shift their
houses by lots. They cultivate their gardens with great care,
so that they have both vines, fruits, herbs, and flowers in
them; and all is so well ordered, and so finely kept, that I
never saw gardens anywhere that were both so fruitful and
so beautiful as theirs. And this humor of ordering their
gardens so well, is not only kept up by the pleasure they
find in it, but also by an emulation between the inhabitants
of the several streets, who vie with each other; and there is
indeed nothing belonging to the whole town that is both
more useful and more pleasant. So that he who founded
the town, seems to have taken care of nothing more than of
their gardens; for they say, the whole scheme of the town
was designed at first by Utopus, but he left all that belonged to the ornament and improvement of it, to be added
by those that should come after him, that being too much
for one man to bring to perfection. Their records, that
contain the history of their town and state, are preserved
with an exact care, and run backwards 1,760 years. From
these it appears that their houses were at first low and
mean, like cottages, made of any sort of timber, and were
built with mud walls and thatched with straw. But now
their houses are three stories high: the fronts of them are
faced either with stone, plastering, or brick; and between
the facings of their walls they throw in their rubbish
Their roofs are flat, and on them they lay a sort of plaster,
which costs very little, and yet is so tempered that it is
not apt to take fire, and yet resists the weather more than
lead. They have great quantities of glass among them,
with which they glaze their windows. They use also in
their windows a thin linen cloth, that is so oiled or gummed
that it both keeps out the wind and gives free admission
to the light.

OF THEIR MAGISTRATES

Thirty families choose every year a magistrate, who
was anciently called the Syphogrant, but is now called
the Philarch; and over every ten Syphogrants, with the
families subject to them, there is another magistrate, who
was anciently called the Tranibor, but of late the Arch-
philarch. All the Syphogrants, who are in number two
hundred, choose the Prince out of a list of four, who are
named by the people of the four divisions of the city;
but they take an oath before they proceed to an election,
that they will choose him whom they think most fit for
the office. They give their voices secretly, so that it is
not known for whom every one gives his suffrage. The
Prince is for life, unless he is removed upon suspicion of
some design to enslave the people. The Tranibors are new
chosen every year, but yet they are for the most part continued. All their other magistrates are only annual. The
Tranibors meet every third day, and oftener if necessary,
and consult with the Prince, either concerning the affairs
of the state in general, or such private differences as may
arise sometimes among the people; though that falls out
but seldom. There are always two Syphogrants called
into the council-chamber, and these are changed every
day. It is a fundamental rule of their government, that
no conclusion can be made in anything that relates to the
public, till it has been first debated three several days in
their council. It is death for any to meet and consult concerning the state, unless it be either in their ordinary
council, or in the assembly of the whole body of the people.

These things have been so provided among them, that
the Prince and the Tranibors may not conspire together to
change the government, and enslave the people; and therefore when anything of great importance is set on foot, it is
sent to the Syphogrants; who after they have communi-
cated it to the families that belong to their divisions, and

have considered it among themselves, make report to the senate; and upon great occasions, the matter is referred to the council of the whole island. One rule observed in their council, is, never to debate a thing on the same day in which it is first proposed; for that is always referred to the next meeting, that so men may not rashly, and in the heat of discourse, engage themselves too soon, which might bias them so much, that instead of consulting the good of the public, they might rather study to support their first opinions, and by a perverse and preposterous sort of shame, hazard their country rather than endanger their own reputation, or venture the being suspected to have wanted foresight in the expedients that they at first proposed. And therefore to prevent this, they take care that they may rather be deliberate than sudden in their motions.

OF THEIR TRADES, AND MANNER OF LIFE

Agriculture is that which is so universally understood among them, that no person, either man or woman, is ignorant of it; they are instructed in it from their childhood, partly by what they learn at school, and partly by practice; they being led out often into the fields, about the town, where they not only see others at work, but are likewise exercised in it themselves. Besides agriculture, which is so common to them all, every man has some peculiar trade to which he applies himself, such as the manufacture of wool, or flax, masonry, smith's work, or carpenter's work; for there is no sort of trade that is in great esteem among them. Throughout the island they wear the same sort of clothes without any other distinction, except what is necessary to distinguish the two sexes, and the married and unmarried. The fashion never alters; and as it is neither disagreeable nor uneasy, so it is suited to the climate, and calculated both for their summers and winters. Every family makes their own clothes; but all among them, women as well as men, learn one or other of the trades formerly mentioned. Women, for the most part, deal in wool and flax, which suit best their weakness, leaving the ruder trades to the men. The same trades generally pass down from father to son, inclinations often following descent; but if any man's genius lies another way, he is by adoption translated into a family that deals in the trade to which he is inclined: and when that is to be done, care is taken not only by his father, but by the magistrate, that he may be put to a discreet and good man. And if after a person has learned one trade, he desires to acquire another, that is also allowed, and is managed in the same manner as the former. When he has learned both, he follows that which he likes best, unless the public has more occasion for the other.

The chief, and almost the only business of the Sypho-grants, is to take care that no man may live idle, but that every one may follow his trade diligently; yet they do not wear themselves out with perpetual toil, from morning to night, as if they were beasts of burden, which as it is indeed a heavy slavery, so it is everywhere the common course of life amongst all mechanics except the Utopians; but they dividing the day and night into twenty-four hours, appoint six of these for work; three of which are before dinner; and three after. They then sup, and at eight o'clock, counting from noon, go to bed and sleep eight hours. The rest of their time besides that taken up in work, eating and sleeping, is left to every man's discretion; yet they are not to abuse that interval to luxury and idleness, but must employ it in some proper exercise according to their various inclinations, which is for the most part reading. It is ordinary to have public lectures every morning before daybreak; at which none are obliged to appear but those who are marked out for literature; yet a great many, both men and women of all ranks, go to hear lectures of one sort or other, according to their inclinations. But if others, that are not made for contemplation, choose rather

to employ themselves at that time in their trades, as many
of them do, they are not hindered, but are rather commended, as men that take care to serve their country.
After supper, they spend an hour in some diversion, in
summer in their gardens, and in winter in the halls where
they eat; where they entertain each other, either with
music or discourse. They do not so much as know dice,
or any such foolish and mischievous games: they have,
however, two sorts of games not unlike our chess; the one
is between several numbers, in which one number, as it
were, consumes another: the other resembles a battle between the virtues and the vices, in which the enmity in
the vices among themselves, and their agreement against
virtue, is not unpleasantly represented; together with the
special oppositions between the particular virtues and
vices; as also the methods by which vice either openly
assaults or secretly undermines virtue; and virtue on the
other hand resists it. But the time appointed for labor
is to be narrowly examined, otherwise you may imagine,
that since there are only six hours appointed for work, they
may fall under a scarcity of necessary provisions. But it is
so far from being true, that this time is not sufficient for
supplying them with plenty of all things, either necessary
or convenient; that it is rather too much; and this you will
easily apprehend, if you consider how great a part of all
other nations is quite idle. First, women generally do little,
who are the half of mankind; and if some few women are
diligent, their husbands are idle: then consider the great
company of idle priests, and of those that are called religious men; add to these all rich men, chiefly those that
have estates inland, who are called noblemen and gentlemen, together with their families, made up of idle persons,
that are kept more for show than use; add to these, all
those strong and lusty beggars, that go about pretending
some disease, in excuse for their begging; and upon the
whole account you will find that the numbers of those by

whose labors mankind is supplied, is much less than you perhaps imagined. Then consider how few of those that work are employed in labors that are of real service; for we who measure all things by money, give rise to many trades that are both vain and superfluous, and serve only to support riot and luxury. For if those who work were employed only in such things as the conveniences of life require, there would be an such an abundance of them, that the prices of them would sink, that tradesmen could not be maintained by their gains; if all those who labor about useless things, were set to more profitable employments, and if all they that languish out their lives in sloth and idleness, every one of whom consumes as much as any two of the men that are at work, were forced to labor, you may easily imagine that a small proportion of time would serve for doing all that is either necessary, profitable, or pleasant to mankind, especially while pleasure is kept within its due bounds. This appears very plainly in Utopia, for there, in a great city, and in all the territory that lies round it, you can scarce find five hundred, either men or women, by their age and strength, are capable of labor, that are not engaged in it; even the Syphogrants, though excused by the law, yet do not excuse themselves, but work, that by their examples they may excite the industry of the rest of the people. The like exemption is allowed to those, who being recommended to the people by the priests, are by the secret suffrages of the Syphogrants privileged from labor, that they may apply themselves wholly to study; and if any of these fall short of those hopes that they seemed at first to give, they are obliged to return to work. And sometimes a mechanic, that so employs his leisure hours, as to make a considerable advancement in learning, is eased from being a tradesman, and ranked among their learned men. Out of these they choose their ambassadors, their priests, their Tranibors, and the Prince himself; anciently called their Barzenes, but is called of late their Ademus.

And thus from the great numbers among them that are neither suffered to be idle, nor to be employed in any fruit-less labor, you may easily make the estimate how much may be done in those few hours in which they are obliged to labor. But besides all that has already been said, it is to be considered that the needful arts among them are managed with less labor than anywhere else. The building or the repairing of houses among us employs many hands, because often a thriftless heir suffers a house that his father built to fall into decay, so that his successor must, at a great cost, repair that which he might have kept up with a small charge: it frequently happens, that the same house which one person built at a vast expense, is neglected by another, who thinks he has a more delicate sense of the beauties of architecture; and he suffering it to fall to ruin, builds another at no less charge. But among the Utopians, all things are so regulated that men very seldom build upon a new piece of ground; and are not only very quick in re-pairing their houses, but show their foresight in prevent-ing their decay: so that their buildings are preserved very long, with but little labor; and thus the builders to whom that care belongs are often without employment, except the hewing of timber and the squaring of stones, that the materials may be in readiness for raising a building very suddenly, when there is any occasion for it. As to their clothes, observe how little work is spent in them: while they are at labor, they are clothed with leather and skins, cast carelessly about them, which will last seven years; and when they appear in public they put on an upper garment, which hides the other; and these are all of one color, and that is the natural color of the wool. As they need less woollen cloth than is used anywhere else, so that which they make use of is much less costly. They use linen cloth more; but that is prepared with less labor, and they value cloth only by the whiteness of the linen, or by the clean-ness of the wool, without much regard to the fineness of

the thread: while in other places, four or five upper garments of woollen cloth, of different colors, and as many
vests of silk, will scarce serve one man; and while those
that are nicer think ten too few, every man there is content with one, which very often serves him two years.
Nor is there anything that can tempt a man to desire
more; for if he had them, he would neither be the warmer,
nor would he make one jot the better appearance for it.
And thus, since they are all employed in some useful labor,
and since they content themselves with fewer things, it
falls out that there is a great abundance of all things among
them: so that it frequently happens, that for want of other
work, vast numbers are sent out to mend the highways.
But when no public undertaking is to be performed, the
hours of working are lessened. The magistrates never
engage the people in unnecessary labor, since the chief
end of the constitution is to regulate labor by the necessities
of the public, and to allow all the people as much time
as is necessary for the improvement of their minds, in
which they think the happiness of life consists.

OF THEIR TRAFFIC

But it is now time to explain to you the mutual intercourse of this people, their commerce, and the rules by which
all things are distributed among them.

As their cities are composed of families, so their families
are made up of those that are nearly related to one another.
Their women, when they grow up, are married out; but all
the males, both children and grandchildren, live still in the
same house, in great obedience to their common parent,
unless age has weakened his understanding; and in that
case, he that is next to him in age comes in his room. But
lest any city should become either too great, or by accident
be dispeopled, provision is made that none of their cities
may become above six thousand families, besides those of

the country around it. No family may have less than ten, and more than sixteen persons in it; but there can be no determined number for the children under age. This rule is easily observed, by removing some of the children of a more fruitful couple to any other family that does not abound so much in them. By the same rule, they supply cities that do not increase so fast, from others that breed faster; and if there is any increase over the whole island, then they draw out a number of their citizens out of the several towns, and send them over to the neighboring con- tinent; where, if they find that the inhabitants have more soil than they can well cultivate, they fix a colony, taking the inhabitants into their society, if they are willing to live with them; and where they do that of their own accord, they quickly enter into their method of life, and conform to their rules, and this proves a happiness to both nations: for according to their constitution, such care is taken of the soil, that it becomes fruitful enough for both, though it might be otherwise too narrow and barren for any one of them. But if the natives refuse to conform themselves to their laws, they drive them out of these bounds which they mark out for themselves, and use force if they resist. For they account it a very just cause of war, for a nation to hinder others from possessing a part of that soil, of which they make no use, but which is suffered to lie idle and uncultivated; since every man has by the law of Nature a right to such a waste portion of the earth as is necessary for his subsistence. If an accident has so lessened the number of inhabitants of any of their towns, that it cannot be made up from the other towns of the island, without diminishing them too much, which is said to have fallen out but twice since they were first a people, when great numbers were carried off by the plague; the loss is then supplied by recalling as many as are wanted from their colonies; for they will abandon these, rather than suffer the towns in the island to sink too low.

But to return to their manner of living in society, the oldest man of every family, as has been already said, is its governor. Wives serve their husbands, and children their parents, and always the younger serves the elder. Every city is divided into four equal parts, and in the middle of each there is a market-place: what is brought thither, and manufactured by the several families, is carried from thence to houses appointed for that purpose, in which all things of a sort are laid by themselves; and thither every father goes and takes whatsoever he or his family stand in need of, without either paying for it, or leaving anything in exchange. There is no reason for giving a denial to any person, since there is such plenty of everything among them; and there is no danger of a man's asking for more than he needs; they have no inducements to do this, since they are sure that they shall always be supplied. (It is the fear of want that makes any of the whole race of animals either greedy or ravenous; but besides fear, there is in man a pride that makes him fancy it a particular glory to excel others in pomp and excess.) But by the laws of the Utopians, there is no room for this. Near these markets there are others for all sorts of provisions, where there are not only herbs, fruits, and bread, but also fish, fowl, and cattle. There are also, without their towns, places appointed near some running water, for killing their beasts, and for washing away their filth; which is done by their slaves: for they suffer none of their citizens to kill their cattle, because they think that pity and good-nature, which are among the best of those affections that born with us, are much impaired by the butchering of animals: nor do they suffer anything that is foul or unclean to be brought within their towns, lest the air should be infected by ill smells which might prejudice their health. In every street there are great halls that lie at an equal distance from each other, distinguished by particular names. The Syphogrants dwell in those that are set over thirty families, fifteen lying on one side of it,

and as many on the other. In these halls they all meet
and have their repasts. The stewards of every one of them
come to the market-place at an appointed hour; and according to the number of those that belong to the hall, they
carry home provisions. But they take more care of their
sick than of any others: these are lodged and provided
for in public hospitals: they have belonging to every town
four hospitals, that are built without their walls, and are so
large that they may pass for little towns: by this means, if
they had ever such a number of sick persons, they could
lodge them conveniently, and at such a distance, that such
of them as are sick of infectious diseases may be kept so
far from the rest that there can be no danger of contagion.
The hospitals are furnished and stored with all things that
are convenient for the ease and recovery of the sick; and
those that are put in them are looked after with such
tender and watchful care, and are so constantly attended by
their skilful physicians, that as none is sent to them against
their will, so there is scarce one in a whole town that, if he
should fall ill, would not choose rather to go thither than
lie sick at home.

After the steward of the hospitals has taken for the sick
whatsoever the physician prescribes, then the best things
that are left in the market are distributed equally among
the halls, in proportion to their numbers, only, in the first
place, they serve the Prince, the chief priest, the Tranibors,
the ambassadors, and strangers, if there are any, which
indeed falls out but seldom, and for whom there are houses
well furnished, particularly appointed for their reception
when they come among them. At the hours of dinner and
supper, the whole Syphogranty being called together by
sound of trumpet, they meet and eat together, except only
such as are in the hospitals, or lie sick at home. Yet after
the halls are served, no man is hindered to carry provisions
home from the market-place; for they know that none
does that but for some good reason; for though any that

will may eat at home, yet none does it willingly, since it is
both ridiculous and foolish for any to give themselves the
trouble to make ready an ill dinner at home, when there is
a much more plentiful one made ready for him so near
hand. All the uneasy and sordid services about these halls
are performed by their slaves; but the dressing and cooking
their meat, and the ordering their tables, belong only to
the women, all those of every family taking it by turns.
They sit at three or more tables, according to their number;
the men sit towards the wall, and the women sit on the
other side, that if any of them should be taken suddenly ill,
which is no uncommon case amongst women with child,
she may, without disturbing the rest, rise and go to the
nurse's room, who are there with the sucking children;
where there is always clean water at hand, and cradles in
which they may lay the young children, if there is occasion
for it, and a fire that they may shift and dress them before
it. Every child is nursed by its own mother, if death or
sickness does not intervene; and in that case the Syphogrants' wives find out a nurse quickly, which is no hard
matter; for any one that can do it offers herself cheerfully; for as they are much inclined to that piece of mercy,
so the child whom they nurse considers the nurse as its
mother. All the children under five years old sit among
the nurses, the rest of the younger sort of both sexes, till
they are fit for marriage, either serve those that sit at table;
or if they are not strong enough for that, stand by them in
great silence, and eat what is given them; nor have they
any other formality of dining. In the middle of the first
table, which stands across the upper end of the hall, sit the
Syphogrant and his wife; for that is the chief and most conspicuous place; next to him sit two of the most ancient, for
there go always four to a mess. If there is a temple within
that Syphogranty, the priest and his wife sit with the Syphogrant above all the rest: next them there is a mixture of
old and young, who are so placed, that as the young are

set near others, so they are mixed with the more ancient; which they say was appointed on this account, that the gravity of the old people, and the reverence that is due to them might restrain the younger from all indecent words and gestures. Dishes are not served up to the whole table at first, but the best are first set before the old, whose seats are distinguished from the young, and after them all the rest are served alike. The old men distribute to the younger any curious meats that happen to be set before them, if there is not such an abundance of them that the whole company may be served alike.

Thus old men are honored with a particular respect; yet all the rest fare as well as they. Both dinner and supper are begun with some lecture of morality that is read to them; but it is so short, that it is not tedious nor uneasy to them to hear it: from hence the old men take occasion to entertain those about them, with some useful and pleasant enlargements; but they do not engross the whole discourse so to themselves, during their meals, that the younger may not put in for a share: on the contrary, they engage them to talk, that so they may in that free way of conversation find out the force of every one's spirit, and observe his temper. They despatch their dinners quickly, but sit long at supper; because they go to work after the one, and are to sleep after the other, during which they think the stomach carries on the concoction more vigorously. They never sup without music; and there is always fruit served up after meat; while they are at table, some burn perfumes, and sprinkle about fragrant ointments and sweet waters: in short, they want nothing that may cheer up their spirits: they give them-selves a large allowance that way, and indulge themselves in all such pleasures as are attended with no inconvenience. Thus do those that are in the towns live together; but in the country, where they live at great distance, every one eats at home, and no family wants any necessary sort of provision, for it is from them that provisions are sent unto those that live in the towns.

OF THE TRAVELING OF THE UTOPIANS

If any man has a mind to visit his friends that live in some other town, or desires to travel and see the rest of the country, he obtains leave very easily from the Sypho-grant and Tranibors, when there is no particular occasion for him at home: such as travel, carry with them a passport from the Prince, which both certifies the license that is granted for travelling, and limits the time of their return. They are furnished with a wagon and a slave, who drives the oxen, and looks after them: but unless there are women in the company, the wagon is sent back at the end of the journey as a needless encumbrance: while they are on the road, they carry no provisions with them; yet they want nothing, but are everywhere treated as if they were at home. If they stay in any place longer than a night, every one follows his proper occupation, and is very well used by those of his own trade: but if any man goes out of the city to which he belongs, without leave, and is found ramb-ling without a passport, he is severely treated, he is pun-ished as a fugitive, and sent home disgracefully; and if he falls again into the like fault, is condemned to slavery. If any man has a mind to travel only over the precinct of his own city, he may freely do it with his father's permis-sion and his wife's consent; but when he comes into any of the country houses, if he expects to be entertained by them, he must labor with them and conform to their rules: and if he does this, he may freely go over the whole pre-cinct; being thus as useful to the city to which he belongs, as if he were still within it. Thus you see that there are no idle persons among them, nor pretences of excusing any from labor. There are no taverns, no alehouses nor stews among them; nor any other occasions of corrupting each other, of getting into corners, or forming themselves into parties: all men live in full view, so that all are obliged, both to perform their ordinary task, and to employ themselves well in their spare hours. And it is certain that a people thus ordered must live in great abundance of all things; and these being equally distributed among them, no man can want, or be obliged to beg.

In their great council at Amaurot, to which there are three sent from every town once a year, they examine what towns abound in provisions, and what are under any scarcity, that so the one may be furnished from the other; and this is done freely, without any sort of exchange; for according to their plenty or scarcity, they supply, or are supplied from one another; so that indeed the whole island is, as it were, one family. When they have thus taken care of their whole country, and laid up stores for two years, which they do to prevent the ill consequences of an unfavorable season, they order an exportation of the overplus, both of corn, honey, wool, flax, wood, wax, tallow, leather, and cattle; which they send out commonly in great quantities to other nations. They order a seventh part of all these goods to be freely given to the poor of the countries to which they send them, and sell the rest at moderate rates. And by this exchange, they not only bring back those few things that they need at home (for indeed they scarce need anything but iron), but likewise a great deal of gold and silver; and by their driving this trade so long, it is not to be imagined how vast a treasure they have got among them: so that now they do not much care whether they sell off their merchandise for money in hand, or upon trust. A great part of their treasure is now in bonds; but in all their contracts no private man stands bound, but the writing runs in the name of the town; and the towns that owe them money, raise it from those private hands that owe it to them, lay it up in their public chamber, or enjoy the profit of it till the Utopians call for it; and they choose rather to let the greatest part of it lie in their hands who make advantage of it, than to call for it themselves: but if they see that any of their other neighbors stand more in need of it, then they call it in and lend it to them: whenever they are engaged in war, which is the only occasion in which their treasure can be usefully employed, they make use of it themselves. In great extremities or sudden accidents they employ it in hiring foreign troops, whom they more willingly expose to danger than their own people: they give them great pay, knowing well that this will work even on their enemies, that it will engage them either to betray their own side, or at least desert it, and that it is the best means of raising mutual jealousies among them: for this end they have an incredible treasure; but they do not keep it as a treasure, but in such a manner as I am almost afraid to tell, lest you think it so extravagant, as to be hardly credible. This I have the more reason to apprehend, because if I had not seen it myself, I could not have been easily persuaded to have believed it upon any man's report.

It is certain that all things appear incredible to us, in proportion as they differ from own customs. But one who can judge aright, will not wonder to find, that since their constitution differs so much from ours, their value of gold and silver should be measured by a very different standard; for since they have no use for money among themselves, but keep it as a provision against events which seldom happen, and between which there are generally long intervening intervals; they value it no farther than it deserves, that is, in proportion to its use. So that it is plain, they must prefer iron either to gold or silver: for men can no more live without iron, than without fire or water; but Nature has marked out no use for the other metals, so essential as not easily to be disposed with. The folly of men has enhanced the value of gold and silver, because of their scarcity. Whereas, on the contrary, it is their opinion that Nature, as an indulgent parent, has freely given us all the best things in great abundance, such as water and earth, but has laid up and hid from us the things that are vain and useless.

If these metals were laid up in any tower in the kingdom, it would raise a jealousy of the Prince and Senate, and give birth to that foolish mistrust into which the people are apt to fall, a jealousy of their intending to sacrifice the interest of the public to their own private advantage. If they should work it into vessels, or any sort of plate, they fear that the people might grow too fond of it, and so be unwilling to let the plate be run down, if a war made it necessary to employ it in paying their soldiers. To prevent all these inconveniences, they have fallen upon an expedient, which as it agrees with their other policy, so is it very different from ours, and will scarce gain belief among us, who value gold so much, and lay it up so carefully. They eat and drink out of vessels of earth, or glass, which make an agreeable appearance though formed of brittle materials: while they make their chamber-pots and close-stools of gold and silver; and that not only in their public halls, but in their private houses: of the same metals they likewise make chains and fetters for their slaves; to some of which, as a badge of infamy, they hang an ear-ring of gold, and make others wear a chain or a coronet of the same metal; and thus they take care, by all possible means, to render gold and silver of no esteem. And from hence it is, that while other nations part with their gold and silver, as unwillingly as if one tore out their bowels, those of Utopia would look on their giving in all they possess of those metals, when there were any use for them but as the parting with a trifle, or as we would esteem the loss of a penny. They find pearls on their coast; and diamonds and carbuncles on their rocks; they do not look after them, but if they find them by chance, they polish them, and with them they adorn their children, who are delighted with them, and glory in them during their childhood; but when they grow to years, and see that none but children use such baubles, they of their own accord, without being bid by their parents, lay them aside; and would be as much ashamed to use them afterwards, as children among us, when they come to years, are of their puppets and other toys.

I never saw a clearer instance of the opposite impressions that different customs make on people, than I observed in the ambassadors of the Anemolians, who came to Amaurot when I was there. As they came to treat of affairs of great consequence, the deputies from several towns met together to wait for their coming. The ambassadors of the nations that lie near Utopia, knowing their customs, and that fine clothes are in no esteem among them, that silk is despised, and gold is a badge of infamy, use to come very modestly clothed; but the Anemolians lying more remote, and having had little commerce with them, understanding that they were coarsely clothed, and all in the same manner, took it for granted that they had none of those fine things among them of which they made no use; and they being a vain-glorious rather than a wise people, resolved to set themselves out with so much pomp, that they should look like gods, and strike the eyes of the poor Utopians with their splendor. Thus three ambassadors made their entry with an hundred attendants, all clad in garments of different color, and the greater part in silk; the ambassadors themselves, who were of the nobility of their country, were in cloth of gold, and adorned with massy chains, ear-rings and rings of gold: their caps were covered with bracelets set full of pearls and other gems: in a word, they were set out with all those things that, among the Utopians, were either the badges of slavery, the marks of infamy, or the playthings of children. It was not unpleasant to see, on the one side, how they looked big, when they compared their rich habits with the plain clothes of the Utopians, who were come out in great numbers to see them make their entry: and, on the other, to observe how much they were mistaken in the impression which they hoped this pomp would have made on them. It appeared so ridiculous a show to all that had never stirred out of their country, and had not seen the customs of other nations, that though they paid some reverence to those that were the most meanly clad, as if they had been the ambassadors, yet when they saw the ambassadors them' selves, so full of gold and chains, they looked upon them a slaves, and forbore to treat them with reverence. You might have seen the children, who were grown big enough to despise their playthings, and who had thrown away their jewels, call to their mothers, push them gently, and cry out, "See that great fool that wears pearls and gems, as if he were yet a child." While their mothers very inno' cently replied, "Hold your peace, this I believe is one of the ambassador's fools." Others censured the fashion of their chains, and observed that they were of no use; for they were too slight to bind their slaves, who could easily break them; and besides hung so loose about them, that they thought it easy to throw them away, and so get from them. But after the ambassadors had stayed a day among them, and saw so vast a quntity of gold in their houses, which was as much despised by them as it was esteemed in other nations, and beheld more gold and silver in the chains and fetters of one slave than all their ornaments amounted to, their plumes fell, and they were ashamed of all that glory for which they had formerly valued them' selves, and accordingly laid it aside; a resolution that they immediately took, when on their engaging in some free dis' course with the Utopians, they discovered their sense of such things and their other customs. The Utopians won' der how any man should be so much taken with the glaring doubtful lustre of a jewel or a stone, that can look up to a star, or to the sun himself; or how any should value him' self because his cloth is made of a finer thread: for how fine soever that thread may be, it was once no better than the fleece of a sheep, and that sheep was a sheep still for all its wearing it. They wonder much to hear that gold which in itself is so useless a thing, should be everywhere so much esteemed, that even men for whom it was made, and by whom it has its value, should yet be thought of less value than this metal. That a man of lead, who has no more sense than a log of wood, and is a bad as he is foolish, should have many wise and good men to serve him, only because he has a great heap of that metal; and that if it should happen that by some accident or trick of law (which sometimes produces as great changes as chance itself) all this wealth should pass from the master to the meanest varlet of his whole family, he himself would very soon become one of his servants, as if he were a thing that belonged to his wealth, and so were bound to follow its fortune. But they much more admire and detest the folly of those who when they see a rich man, though they neither owe him anything, nor are in any sort dependent on his bounty, yet merely because he is rich give him little less than divine honors; even though they know him to be so covetous and base-minded, that notwithstanding all his wealth, he will not part with one farthing of it to them as long as he lives.

These and such like notions has that people imbibed, partly from their education, being bred in a country whose customs and laws are opposite to all such foolish maxims, and partly from their learning and studies; for though there are but few in any town that are so wholly excused from labor as to give themselves entirely up to their studies, these being only such persons as discover from their child-hood an extraordinary capacity and disposition for letters; yet their children, and a great part of the nation, both men and women, are taught to spend those hours in which they are not obliged to work in reading: and this they do through the whole progress of life. They have all their learning in their own tongue, which is both a copious and pleasant language, and in which a man can fully express his mind. It runs over a great tract of many countries, but

it is not equally pure in all places. They had never so much
as heard of the names of any of those philosophers that are
so famous in these parts of the world, before we went
among them; and yet they had made the same discoveries
as the Greeks, both in music, logic, arithmetic, and geometry. But as they are almost in everything equal to the
ancient philosophers, so they far exceed our modern logi-
cians; for they have never yet fallen upon the barbarous
niceties that our youth are forced to learn in those trifling
logical schools that are among us; they are so far from
minding chimeras, and fantastical images made in the mind,
that none of them could comprehend what we meant when
we talked to them of a man in the abstract, as common to
all men in particular (so that though we spoke of him as a
thing that we could point at with our fingers, yet none
of them could perceive him), and yet distinct from every
one, as if he were some monstrous Colossus or giant. Yet
for all this ignorance of these empty notions, they knew
astronomy, and were perfectly acquainted with the motions
of the heavenly bodies, and have many instruments, well
contrived and divided, by which they very accurately
compute the course and positions of the sun, moon, and
stars. But for the cheat, of divining by the stars by their
oppositions or conjunctions, it has not so much as entered
into their thoughts. They have a particular sagacity,
founded upon much observation, in judging of the weather,
by which they know when they may look for rain, wind, or
other alterations in the air; but as to the philosophy of
these things, the causes of the saltness of the sea, of its ebb-
ing and flowing, and of the original and nature both of the
heavens and the earth; they dispute of them, partly as our
ancient philosophers have done, and partly upon some new
hypothesis, in which, as they differ from them, so they do
not in all things agree among themselves.

As to moral philosophy, they have the same disputes
among them as we have here: they examine what are

properly good both for the body and the mind, and whether any outward thing can be called truly good, or if that term belong only to the endowments of the soul. They inquire likewise into the nature or virtue and pleasure; but their chief dispute is concerning the happiness of a man, and wherei.1 it consists? Whether in some one thing, or in a great many? They seem, indeed, more inclinable to that opinion that places, if not the whole, yet the chief part of a man's happiness in pleasure; and, what may seem more strange, they make use of arguments even from religion, notwithstanding its severity and roughness, for the support of that opinion so indulgent to pleasure; for they never dis-pute concerning happiness without fetching some argu-ments from the principles of religion, as well as from natu-ral reason, since without the former they reckon that all our inquiries after happiness must be but conjectural and defective.

These are their religious principles, that the soul of man is immortal, and that God of His goodness has designed that it should be happy; and that He has therefore ap-pointed rewards for good and virtuous actions, and punish-ments for vice, to be distributed after this life. Though these principles of religion are conveyed down among them by tradition ,they think that even reason itself determines a man to believe and acknowledge them, and freely confess that if these were taken away no man would be so insensi-ble as not to seek after pleasure by all possible means, law-ful or unlawful; using only this caution, that a lesser pleas-ure might not stand in the way of a greater, and that no pleasure ought to be pursued that should draw a great deal of pain after it; for they think it the maddest thing in the world to pursue virtue, that is a sour and difficult thing; and not only to renounce the pleasures of life, but willingly to undergo much pain and trouble, if a man has no pros-pect of a reward. And what reward can there be for one that has passed his whole life, not only without pleasure,

but in pain, if there is nothing to be expected after death?
Yet they do not place happiness in all sorts of pleasures,
but only in those that in themselves are good and honest.
There is a party among them who place happiness in bare
virtue; others think that our natures are conducted by
virtue to happiness, as that which is the chief good of man.
They define virtue thus, that it is a living according to Nature, and think that we are made by God for that end;
they believe that a man then follows the dictates of Nature
when he pursues or avoids things according to the direction of reason; they say that the first dictate of reason is
the kindling in us a love and reverence for the Divine
Majesty, to whom we owe both all that we have, and all
that we can ever hope for. In the next place, reason di-
rects us to keep our minds as free from passion and as
cheerful as we can, and that we should consider ourselves
as bound by the ties of good-nature and humanity to use
our utmost endeavors to help forward the happiness of all
other persons; for there never was any man such a morose
and severe pursuer of virtue, such an enemy to pleasure
that though he set hard rules for men to undergo much
pain, many watchings, and other rigors, yet did not at the
same time advise them to do all they could, in order to relieve and ease the miserable, and who did not represent
gentleness and good-nature as amiable dispositions. And
from thence they infer that if a man ought to advance the
welfare and comfort of the rest of mankind, there being no
virtue more proper and peculiar to our nature, than to ease
the miseries of others, to free from trouble and anxiety, in
furnishing them with the comforts of life, in which pleasure consists, Nature much more vigorously leads them to do
all this for himself. A life of pleasure is either a real evil,
and in that case we ought not to assist others in their pursuit of it, but on the contrary, to keep them from it all we
can, as from that which is most hurtful and deadly; or it
is a good thing, so that we not only may, but ought to help

others to it, why then ought not a man to begin with him-self? Since no man can be more bound to look after the good of another than after his own; for Nature cannot direct us to be good and kind to others, and yet at the same time to be unmerciful and cruel to ourselves. Thus, as they define virtue to be living according to Nature, so they imagine that Nature prompts all people on to seek after pleasure, as the end of all they do. They also observe that in order to our supporting the pleasures of life, Nature inclines us to enter into society; for there is no man so much raised above the rest of mankind as to be the only favorite of Nature, who, on the contrary, seems to have placed on a level all those that belong to the same species. Upon this they infer that no man ought to seek his own conveniences so eagerly as to prejudice others; and there-fore they think that not only all agreements between pri-vate persons ought to be observed; but likewise that all those laws ought to be kept, which either a good prince has published in due form, or to which a people, that is neither oppressed with tyranny nor circumvented by fraud, has consented, for distributing those conveniences of life which afford us all our pleasures.

They think it is an evidence of true wisdom for a man to pursue his own advantages, as far as the laws allow it. They account it piety to prefer the public good to one's private concerns; but they think it unjust for a man to seek for pleasure, by snatching another man's pleasures from him. And on the contrary, they think it a sign of a gentle and good soul, for a man to dispense with his own advantage for the good of others; and that by this means a good man finds as much pleasure one way, as he parts with another; for as he may expect the like from others when he may come to need it, so if that should fail him, yet the sense of a good action, and the reflections that he makes on the love and gratitude of those whom he has so obliged, gives the mind more pleasure than the body could have found in that from which it had restrained itself. They are also persuaded that God will make up the loss of those small pleasures, with a vast and endless joy, of which religion easily convinces a good soul.

Thus upon an inquiry into the whole matter, they reckon that all our actions, and even all our virtues, terminate in pleasure, as in our chief end and greatest happiness; and they call every motion or state, either of body or mind, in which Nature teaches us to delight, a pleasure. Thus they cautiously limit pleasure only to those appetites to which Nature leads us; for they say that Nature leads us only to those delights to which reason as well as sense carries us, and by which we neither injure any other person, nor lose the possession of greater pleasures, and of such as draw no troubles after them; but they look upon those delights which men by a foolish, though common, mistake call pleasure, as if they could change as easily the nature of things as the use of words; as things that greatly obstruct their real happiness, instead of advancing it, because they so entirely possess the minds of those that are once captivated by them with a false notion of pleasure, that there is no room left for pleasures of a truer or purer kind.

There are many things that in themselves have nothing that is truly delightful; on the contrary, they have a good deal of bitterness in them: and yet from our perverse appetites after forbidden objects, are not only ranked among the pleasures, but are made even the greatest designs of life. Among those who pursue these sophisticated pleasures, they reckon such as I mentioned before, who think themselves really the better for having fine clothes; in which they think they are doubly mistaken, both in the opinion that they have of their clothes, and in that they have of themselves; for if you consider the use of clothes, why should a fine thread be thought better than a coarse one? And yet these men, as if they had some real advantages beyond others, and did not owe them wholly to their mistakes, look big, seem to fancy themselves to be more valuable, and imagine that a respect is due to them for the sake of a rich garment, to which they would not have pretended if they had been more meanly clothed; and even resent it as an affront, if that respect is not paid them. It is also a great folly to be taken with outward remarks of respect, which signify nothing: for what true or real pleasure can one man find in another's standing bare, or making legs to him? Will the bending another man's knees give ease to yours? And will the head's being bare cure the madness of yours? And yet it is wonderful to see how this false notion of pleasure bewitches many who delight themselves with the fancy of their nobility, and are pleased with this conceit, that they are descended from ancestors, who have been held for some successions rich, and who have had great possessions; for this is all that makes no-bility at present; yet they do not think themselves a whit less noble, though their immediate parents have left none of this wealth to them, or though they themselves have squandered it away. The Utopians have no better opinion of those who are much taken with gems and precious stones, and who account it a degree of happiness, next to a divine one, if they can purchase one that is very extra-ordinary; especially if it be of that sort of stones that is then in great request; for the same sort is not at all times universally of the same value; nor will men buy it unless it be dismounted and taken out of the gold; the jeweller is then made to give good security, and required solemnly to swear that the stone is true, that by such an exact caution a false one might not be bought instead of a true: though if you were to examine it, your eye could find no difference between the counterfeit and that which is true; so that they are all one to you as much as if you were blind. Or can it be thought that they who heap up an use-less mass of wealth, not for any use that it is to bring them, but merely to please themselves with the contemplation of

it, enjoy any true pleasure in it? The delight they find is
only a false shadow of joy. Those are no better whose error
is somewhat different from the former, and who hide it, out
of their fear of losing it; for what other name can fit the
hiding it in the earth, or rather the restoring it to it again,
it being thus cut off from being useful, either to its owner
or to the rest of mankind? And yet the owner having hid
it carefully, is glad, because he thinks he is now sure of it.
If it should be stole, the owner, though he might live perhaps ten years after the theft, of which he knew nothing,
would find no difference between his having or losing it;
for both ways it was equally useless to him.

Among those foolish pursuers of pleasure, they reckon
all that delight in hunting, in fowling, or gaming: of whose
madness they have only heard, for they have no such
things among them. But they have asked us, what sort of
pleasure is it that men can find in throwing the dice? For
if there were any pleasure in it, they think the doing of it
so often should give one a surfeit of it: and what pleasure
can one find in hearing the barking and howling of dogs,
which seem rather odious than pleasant sounds? Nor can
they comprehend the pleasure of seeing dogs run after a
hare, more than of seeing one dog run after another; for if
the seeing them run is that which gives the pleasure, you
have the same entertainment to the eye on both these occasions; since that is the same in both cases; but if the
pleasure lies in seeing the hare killed and torn by the dogs,
this ought rather to stir pity, that a weak, harmless and
fearful hare should be devoured by strong, fierce, and cruel
dogs. Therefore all this business of hunting is, among the
Utopians, turned over to their butchers; and those, as has
been already said, are all slaves; and they look on hunting
as one of the basest parts of a butcher's work: for they
account it both more profitable and more decent to kill
those beasts that are more necessary and useful to mankind;
whereas the killing and tearing of so small and miserable

an animal can only attract the huntsman with a false show of pleasure, from which he can reap but small advantage. They look on the desire of the bloodshed, even of beasts, as a mark of a mind that is already corrupted with cruelty, or that at least by the frequent returns of so brutal a pleasure must degenerate into it.

Thus, though the rabble of mankind look upon these, and on innumerable other things of the same nature, as pleasures; the Utopians, on the contrary, observing that there is nothing in them truly pleasant, conclude that they are not to be reckoned among pleasures: for though these things may create some tickling in the senses (which seems to be a true notion of pleasure,) yet they imagine that this does not arise from the thing itself, but from a depraved custom, which may so vitiate a man's taste, that bitter things may pass for sweet; as women with child think pitch or tallow taste sweeter than honey; but as a man's sense when corrupted, either by a disease or some ill habit, does not change the nature of other things, so neither can it change the nature of pleasure.

They reckon up several sorts of pleasures, which they call true ones: some belong to the body and others to the mind. The pleasures of the mind lie in knowledge, and in that delight which the contemplation of truth carries with it; to which they add the joyful reflections on a well-spent life, and the assured hopes of a future happiness. They divide the pleasures of the body into two sorts; the one is that which gives our senses some real delight, and is performed, either by recruiting nature, and supplying those parts which feed the internal heat of life by eating and drinking; or when nature is eased of any surcharge that oppresses it; when we are relieved from sudden pain, or that which arises from satisfying the appetite which Nature has wisely given to lead us to the propagation of the species. There is another kind of pleasure that arises neither from our receiving what the body requires, nor its being relieved

when overcharged, and yet by a secret, unseen virtue affects the senses, raises the passions, and strikes the mind
with generous impressions; this is the pleasure that arises
from music.   Another kind of bodily pleasure is that
which results from an undisturbed and vigorous constitution of body, when life and active spirits seem to actuate
every part.   This lively health, when entirely free from
all mixture of pain, of itself gives an inward pleasure, in-
dependent of all external objects of delight; and though
this pleasure does not so powerfully affect us, nor act so
strongly on the senses as some of the others, yet it may
be eteemed as the greatest of all pleasures, and almost all
the Utopians reckon it the foundation and basis of all the
other joys of life; since this alone makes the state of life
easy and desirable; and when this is wanting, a man is
really capable of no other pleasure.   They look upon freedom from pain, if it does not rise from perfect health, to be
a state of stupidity rather than of pleasure.   This subject
has been very narrowly canvassed among them; and it has
been debated whether a firm and entire health could be
called a pleasure or not?   Some have thought that there
was no pleasure but what was excited by some sensible
motion in the body.   But this opinion has been long ago
excluded from them, so that now they almost universally
agree that health is the greatest of all bodily pleasures;
and that as there is a pain in sickness, which is as opposite
in its nature to pleasure as sickness itself is to health; so
they hold, that health is accompanied with pleasure: and if
any should say that sickness is not really pain, but that it
only carries pain along with it, they look upon that as a
fetch of subtilty, that does not much alter the matter.   It is
all one, in their opinion, whether it be said that health is in
itself a pleasure, or that it begets a pleasure, as fire gives
heat; so it be granted, that all those whose health is entire
have a true pleasure in the enjoyment of it: and they
reason thus—what is the pleasure of eating, but that a

man's health which has been weakened, does, with the assistance of food, drive away hunger, and so recruiting itself
recovers its former vigor? And being thus refreshed, it
finds a pleasure in that conflict; and if the conflict is pleasure, the victory must yet breed a greater pleasure, except
we fancy that it becomes stupid as soon as it has obtained
that which it pursued, and so neither knows nor rejoices
in its own welfare. If it is said that health cannot be
felt, they absolutely deny it; for what man is in health
that does not perceive it when he is awake? Is there any
man that is so dull and stupid as not to acknowledge that
he feels a delight in health? And what is delight but
another name for pleasure?

But of all pleasures, they esteem those to be most valuable that lie in the mind; the chief of which arises out of
true virtue, and the witness of a good conscience. They
account health the chief pleasure that belongs to the body;
for they think that the pleasure of eating and drinking,
and all the other delights of sense, are only so far desirable
as they give or maintain health. But they are not pleasant
in themselves, otherwise than as they resist those impressions that our natural infirmities are still making upon us:
for as a wise man desires rather to avoid diseases than to
take a physic; and to be freed from pain, rather than to
find ease by remedies; so it is more desirable not to need
this sort of pleasure, than to be obliged to indulge it. If any
man imagines that there is a real happiness in these enjoy-
ments, he must then confess that he would be the happiest
of all men if he were to lead his life in perpetual hunger,
thirst, and itching, and by consequence in perpetual eating,
drinking, and scratching himself; which any one may easily
see would be not only a base, but a miserable state of life.
These are indeed the lowest of pleasures, and the least
pure; for we can never relish them, but when they are
mixed with the contrary pains. The pain of hunger must
give us the pleasure of eating; and here the pain out-

balances the pleasure; and as the pain is more vehement,
so it lasts much longer; for as it begins before the pleasure,
so it does not cease but with the pleasure that extinguishes
it, and both respire together. They think, therefore, none
of those pleasures are to be valued any further than as they
are necessary; yet they rejoice in them, and with due
gratitude acknowledge the tenderness of the great Author
of Nature, who has planted in us appetites, by which those
things that are necessary for our preservation are likewise
made pleasant to us. For how miserable a thing would life
be, if those daily diseases of hunger and thirst were to be
carried off by such bitter drugs as we must use for those
diseases that return seldomer upon us? And thus these
pleasant as well as proper gifts of Nature maintain the
strength and the sprightliness of our bodies.

They also entertain themselves with the other delights
let in at their eyes, their ears, and their nostrils, as the pleasant relishes and seasonings of life, which Nature seems to
have marked out peculiarly for man; since no other sort of
animals contemplates the figure and beauty of the universe;
nor is delighted with smells, any further than as they distinguish meats by them; nor do they apprehend the con-
cords or discords of sound; yet in all pleasures whatsoever
they take care that a lesser joy does not hinder a greater,
and that pleasure may never breed pain, which they think
always follows dishonest pleasures. But they think it madness for a man to wear out the beauty of his face, or the
force of his natural strength; to corrupt the sprightliness of
his body by sloth and laziness, or to waste it by fasting;
that it is madness to weaken the strength of his constitution, and reject the other delights of life; unless by renounc-
ing his own satisfaction, he can either serve the public or
promote the happiness of others, for which he expects a
greater recompense from God. So that they look on such
a course of life as the mark of a mind that is both cruel to
itself, and ungrateful to the Author of Nature, as if we

would not be beholden to Him for His favors, and therefore rejects all His blessings; as one who should afflict himself for the empty shadow of virtue; or for no better end
than to render himself capable of bearing those misfortunes
which possibly will never happen.

This is their notion of virtue and of pleasure; they think
that no man's reason can carry him to a truer idea of them,
unless some discovery from Heaven should inspire him with
sublimer notions. I have not now the leisure to examine
whether they think right or wrong in this matter: nor do I
judge it necessary, for I have only undertaken to give you
an account of their constitution, but not to defend all their
principles. I am sure, that whatsoever may be said of their
notions, there is not in the whole world either a better
people or a happier government: their bodies are vigorous
and lively; and though they are but of a middle stature, and
have neither the fruitfullest soil nor the purest air in the
world, yet they fortify themselves so well by their temperate
course of life, against the unhealthiness of their air, and by
their industry they so cultivate their soil, that there is nowhere to be seen a greater increase both of corn and cattle,
nor are there anywhere healthier men, and freer from diseases: for one may there see reduced to practice, not only
all the art that the husbandman employs in manuring and
improving an ill soil, but whole woods plucked up by the
roots, and in other places new ones planted, where there
were none before. Their principal motive for this is the
convenience of carriage, that their timber may be either
near their towns, or growing on the banks of the sea, or of
some rivers, so as to be floated to them; for it is a harder
work to carry wood at any distance over land, than corn.
The people are industrious, apt to learn, as well as cheerful
and pleasant; and none can endure more labor, when it is
necessary; but except in that case they love their ease.
They are unwearied pursuers of knowledge; for when we
had given them some hints of the learning and discipline of

the Greeks, concerning whom we only instructed them (for we know that there was nothing among the Romans, except their historians and their poets, that they would value much), it was strange to see how eagerly they were set on learning that language. We began to read a little of it to them, rather in compliance with their importunity, than out of any hopes of their reaping from it any great advantage. But after a very short trial we found they made such progress, that we saw our labor was like to be more successful than we could have expected. They learned to write their characters, and to pronounce their language so exactly, had so quick an apprehension, they remembered it so faithfully, and became so ready and correct in the use of it, that it would have looked like a miracle if the greater part of those whom we taught had not been men both of extraordinary capacity and of a fit age for instruction. They were for the greatest part chosen from among their learned men, by their chief council, though some studied it of their own accord. In three years' time they became masters of the whole language, so that they read the best of the Greek authors very exactly. I am indeed apt to think that they learned that language the more easily, from its having some relation to their own. I believe that they were a colony of the Greeks; for though their language comes nearer the Persian, yet they retain many names, both for their towns and magistrates, that are of Greek derivation. I happened to carry a great many books with me, instead of merchandise, when I sailed my fourth voyage; for I was so far from thinking of soon coming back, that I rather thought never to have returned at all, and I gave them all my books, among which were many of Plato's and some of Aritotle's works. I had also Theophrastus on Plants, which, to my great regret, was imperfect; for having laid it carelessly by, while we were at sea, a monkey had seized upon it, and in many places torn out the leaves. They have no books of grammar but Lascares, for I did not carry Theo-

dorus with me; nor have they any dictionaries but Hesi-
chius and Dioscorides. They esteem Plutarch highly, and
were much taken with Lucian's wit, and with his pleasant
way of writing. As for the poets, they have Aristophanes,
Homer, Euripides, and Sophocles of Aldus' edition; and for
historians Thucydides, Herodotus and Herodian. One of my
companions, Thricius Apinatus, happened to carry with
him some of Hippocrates' works, and Galen's Microtechne,
which they held in great estimation; for though there is no
nation in the world that needs physics so little as they do,
yet there is not any that honors it so much: they reckon the
knowledge of it one of the pleasantest and most profitable
parts of philosophy, by which, as they search into the secrets
of Nature, so they not only find this study highly agreeable,
but think that such inquiries are very acceptable to the
Author of Nature; and imagine that as He, like the inventors of curious engines amongst mankind, has exposed this
great machine of the universe to the view of the only creatures capable of contemplating it, so an exact and curious
observer, who admires His workmanship, is much more
acceptable to Him than one of the herd, who like a beast
incapable of reason, looks on this glorious scene with the
eyes of a dull and unconcerned spectator.

The minds of the Utopians when fenced with a love for
learning, are very ingenious in discovering all such arts as
are necessary to carry it to perfection. Two things they owe
to us, the manufacture of paper, and the art of printing: yet
they are not so entirely indebted to us for these discoveries, but that a great part of the invention was their own.
We showed them some books printed by Aldus, we ex-
plained to them the way of making paper, and the mystery
of printing; but as we had never practised these arts, we
described them in a crude and superficial manner. They
seized the hints we gave them, and though at first they
could not arrive at perfection, yet by making many essays
they at last found out and corrected all their errors, and

conquered every difficulty. Before this they only wrote on
parchment, on reeds, or on the barks of trees; but now they
have established the manufactures of paper, and set up
printing-presses, so that if they had but a good number of
Greek authors they would be quickly supplied with many
copies of them: at present, though they have no more than
those I have mentioned, yet by several impressions they
have multiplied them into many thousands. If any man
was to go among them that had some extraordinary talent,
or that by much travelling had observed the customs of
many nations (which made us to be so well received), he
would receive a hearty welcome; for they are very desirous
to know the state of the whole world. Very few go among
them on the account of traffic, for what can a man carry to
them but iron, or gold, or silver, which merchants desire
rather to export than import to a strange country: and as
for their exportation, they think it better to manage that
themselves than to leave it to foreigners, for by this means,
as they understand the state of the neighboring countries
better, so they keep up the art of navigation, which cannot
be maintained but by much practice.

OF THEIR SLAVES, AND OF THEIR MARRIAGES

They do not make slaves of prisoners of war, except
those that are taken in battle; nor of the sons of their
slaves, nor of those of other nations: the slaves among them
are only such as are condemned to that state of life for the
commission of some crime, or, which is more common, such
as their merchants find condemned to die in those parts to
which they trade, who they sometimes redeeem at low
rates; and in other places have them for nothing. They are
kept at perpetual labor, and are always chained, but with
this difference, that their own natives are treated much
worse than others; they are considered as more profligate
than the rest, and since they could not be restrained by the

advantages of so excellent an education, are judged worthy of harder usage. Another sort of slaves are the poor of the neighboring countries, who offer of their own accord to come and serve them; they treat these better, and use them in all other respects as well as their own countrymen, ex' cept their imposing more labor upon them, which is no hard task to those that have been accustomed to it; and if any of these have a mind to go back to their own country, which indeed falls out but seldom, as they do not force them to stay, so they do not send them away empty-handed.

I have already told you with what care they look after their sick, so that nothing is left undone than can contribute either to their ease or health: and for those who are taken with fixed and incurable diseases, they use all possible ways to cherish them, and to make their lives as comfortable as possible. They visit them often, and take great pains to make their time pass off easily: but when any is taken with a torturing and lingering pain, so that there is no hope, either of recovery or ease, the priests and magistrates come and exhort them, that since they are now unable to go on with the business of life, are become a burden to themselves and to all about them, and they have really outlived them' selves, they should no longer nourish such a rooted distem' per, but choose rather to die, since they cannot live but in much misery: being assured, that if they thus deliver them' selves from torture, or are willing that others should do it, they shall be happy after death. Since by their acting thus, they lose none of the pleasures, but only the troubles of life; they think they behave not only reasonably, but in a manner consistent with religion and piety; because they fol' low the advice given them by their priests, who are the ex' pounders of the will of God. Such as are wrought on by these persuasions, either starve themselves of their own accord, or take opium, and by that means die without pain. But no man is forced on this way of ending his life; and if they cannot be persuaded to it, this does not induce them to fail in their attendance and care of them; but as they believe that a voluntary death, when it is chosen upon such an authority, is very honorable, so if any man takes away his own life, without the approbation of the priests and the Senate, they give him none of the honors of a decent funeral, but throw his body into a ditch.

Their women are not married before eighteen, nor their men before two-and-twenty, and if any of them run into forbidden embraces before marriage they are severely punished, and the privilege of marriage is denied them, unless they can obtain a special warrant from the Prince. Such disorders cast a great reproach upon the master and mistress of the family in which they happen, for it is supposed that they have failed in their duty. The reason for punishing this so severely is, because they think that if they were not strictly restrained from all vagrant appetites, very few would engage in a state in which they venture the quiet of their whole lives, by being confined to one person, and are obliged to endure all the inconveniences with which it is accompanied. In choosing their wives they use a method that would appear to us very absurd and ridiculous, but it is constantly observed among them, and is accounted perfectly consistent with wisdom. Before marriage some grave matron presents the bride naked, whether she is a virgin or a widow, to the bridegroom; and after that some grave man presents the bridegroom naked to the bride. We indeed both laughed at this, and condemned it as very indecent. But they, on the other hand, wondered at the folly of the men of all other nations, who, if they were to buy a horse of a small value, are so cautious that they will see every part of him, and take off his saddle and all his other tackle, that there may be no secret ulcer hid under any of them; and that yet in the choice of a wife, on which depends the happiness or unhappiness of the rest of his life, a man should venture upon trust, and only see about a hand's-breadth of the face, all the rest of the body being covered, under which there may lie hid what may be contagious, as well as loathsome. All men are not so wise as to choose a woman only for her good qualities; and even wise men con- sider the body as that which adds not a little to the mind: and it is certain there may be some such deformity covered with the clothes as may totally alienate a man from his wife when it is too late to part with her. If such a thing is dis- covered after marriage, a man has no remedy but patience. They therefore think it is reasonable that there should be good provision made against such mischievous frauds.

There was so much the more reason for them to make a regulation in this matter, because they are the only people of those parts that neither allow of polygamy, nor of divorces, except in the case of adultery, or insufferable per- verseness; for in these cases the Senate dissolves the mar- riage, and grants the injured person leave to marry again; but the guilty are made infamous, and are never allowed the privilege of a second marriage. None are suffered to put away their wives against their wills, from any great calamity that may have fallen on their persons; for they look on it as the height of cruelty and treachery to abandon either of the married persons when they need most the tender care of their comfort and chiefly in the case of old age, which as it carries many diseases along with it, so it is a disease of itself. But it frequently falls out that when a married couple do not well agree, they by mutual consent separate, and find out other persons with whom they hope they may live more happily. Yet this is not done without obtaining leave of the Senate, which never admits of a divorce, but upon a strict inquiry made, both by the senators and their wives, into the grounds upon which it is desired; and even when they are satisfied concerning the reasons of it, they go on but slowly, for they imagine that too great easiness in granting leave for new marriages would very much shake the kindness of married people. They punish severely those that defile the marriage-bed. If both parties are married

they are divorced, and the injured persons may marry one
another, or whom they please; but the adulterer and the
adultress are condemned to slavery. Yet if either of the
injured persons cannot shake off the love of the married
person, they may live with them still in that state, but they
must follow them to that labor to which the slaves are condemned; and sometimes the repentance of the condemned,
together with the unshaken kindness of the innocent and
injured person, has prevailed so far with the Prince that he
has taken off the sentence; but those that relapse after they
are once pardoned are punished with death.

Their law does not determine the punishment for other
crimes; but that is left to the Senate, to temper it according
to the circumstances of the fact. Husbands have power to
correct their wives, and parents to chastise their children,
unless the fault is so great that a public punishment is
thought necessary for striking terror into others. For the
most part, slavery is the punishment even of the greatest
crimes; for as that is no less terrible to the criminals themselves than death, so they think the preserving them in a
state of servitude is more for the interest of the commonwealth than killing them; since as their labor is a greater
benefit to the public than their death could be, so the sight
of their misery is a more lasting terror to other men than
that which would be given by their death. If their slaves
rebel, and will not bear their yoke, and submit to the labor
that is enjoined them, they are treated as wild beasts that
cannot be kept in order, neither by a prison, nor by their
chains; and are at last put to death. But those who bear
their punishment patiently, and are so much wrought on
by that pressure that lies so hard on them that it appears
they are really more troubled for the crimes they have committed than for the miseries they suffer, are not out of hope
but that at last either the Prince will, by his perogative, or
the people by their intercession, restore them again to their
liberty, or at least very much mitigate their slavery. He

that tempts a married woman to adultery, is no less severely punished than he that commits it; for they believe that a deliberate design to commit a crime, is equal to the fact itself: since its not taking effect does not make the person that miscarried in his attempt at all the less guilty.

They take great pleasure in fools, and as it is thought a base and unbecoming thing to use them ill, so they do not think it amiss for people to divert themselves with their folly: and, in their opinion, this is a great advantage to the fools themselves: for if men were so sullen and severe as not at all to please themselves with their ridiculous behaviour and foolish sayings, which is all that they can do to recommend themselves to others, it could not be expected that they would be so well provided for, nor so tenderly used as they must otherwise be. If any man should reproach another for his being misshaped or imperfect in any part of his body, it would not at all be thought a reflection on the person so treated, but it would be accounted scandalous in him that had upbraided another with what he could not help. It is thought a sign of a sluggish and sordid mind not to preserve carefully one's natural beauty; but it is likewise infamous among them to use paint. They all see that no beauty recommends a wife so much to her husband as the probity of her life, and her obedience: for as some few are catched and held only by beauty, so all are attracted by the other excellences which charm all the world.

As they fright men from committing crimes by punishments, so they invite them to the love of virtue by public honors: therefore they erect statues to the memories of such worthy men as have deserved well of their country, and set these in their market-places, both to perpetuate the remembrance of their actions, and to be an incitement to their posterity to follow their example.

If any man aspires to any office, he is sure never to compass it: they all live easily together, for none of the magisrather to be called fathers, and by being really so, they well rather to be called fathers, and by being really so, the well deserve the name; and the people pay them all the marks of honor the more freely, because none are exacted from them. The Prince himself has no distinction, either of garments, or of a crown; but is only distinguished by a sheaf of corn carried before him; as the high priest is also known by his being preceded by a person carrying a wax light.

They have but few laws, and such is their constitution that they need not many. They very much condemn other nations, whose laws, together with the commentaries on them, swell up to so many volumes; for they think it is an unreasonable thing to oblige men to obey a body of laws that are both of such a bulk, and so dark as not to be read and understood by every one of the subjects.

They have no lawyers among them, for they consider them as a sort of people whose profession it is to disguise matters, and to wrest the laws; and therefore they think it is much better that every man should plead his own cause, and trust it to the judge, as in other places the client trusts it to a counsellor. By this means they both cut off many delays, and find out truth more certainly: for after the parties have laid open the merits of the cause, without those artifices which lawyers are apt to suggest, the judge examines the whole matter, and supports the simplicity of such well-meaning persons, whom otherwise crafty men would be sure to run down: and thus they avoid those evils which appear very remarkably among all those nations that labor under a vast load of laws. Every one of them is skilled in their law, for as it is a very short study, so the plainest meaning of which words are capable is always the sense of their laws. And they argue thus: all laws are promulgated for this end, that every man may know his duty; and therefore the plainest and most obvious sense of the words is that which ought to be put upon them; since a more refined exposition cannot be easily comprehended, and would only serve to make the laws become useless to the greater part of

mankind, and especially to those who need most the direction of them: for it is all one, not to make a law at all, or
to couch it in such terms that without a quick apprehension,
and much study, a man cannot find out the true meaning of
it; since the generality of mankind are both so dull, and so
much employed in their several trades, that they have
neither the leisure nor the capacity requisite for such an
inquiry.

Some of their neighbors, who are masters of their own
liberties, having long ago, by the assistance of the Utopians, shaken off the yoke of tyranny, and being much taken
with those virtues which they observe among them, have
come to desire that they would send magistrates to govern
them; some changing them every year, and others every
five years. At the end of their government they bring
them back to Utopia, with great expressions of honor and
esteem, and carry away others to govern in their stead. In
this they seem to have fallen upon a very good expedient
for their own happiness and safety; for since the good or
ill condition of a nation depends so much upon their magistrates, they could not have made a better choice than by
pitching on men whom no advantages can bias; for wealth
is of no use to them, since they must so soon go back to
their own country; and they being strangers among them,
are not engaged in any of their heats or animosities; and
it is certain that when public judicatories are swayed, either
by avarice or partial affections, there must follow a dissolu-
tion of justice, the chief sinew of society.

The Utopians call those nations that come and ask
magistrates from them, neighbors; but those to whom they
have been of more particular service, friends. And as all
other nations are perpetually either making leagues or
breaking them, they never enter into an alliance with any
state. They think leagues are useless things, and believe
that if the common ties of humanity do not knit men together, the faith of promises will have no great effect; and

they are the more confirmed in this by what they see
among the nations round about them, who are no strict
observers of leagues and treaties. We know how religiously they are observed in Europe, more particularly where the
Christian doctrine is received, among whom they are sacred
and inviolable. Which is partly owing to the justice and
goodness of the princes themselves, and partly to the reverence they pay to the popes; who as they are most religious
observers of their own promises, so they exhort all other
princes to perform theirs; and when fainter methods do
not prevail, they compel them to it by the severity of the
pastoral censure, and think that it would be the most indecent thing possible if men who are particularly distinguished by the title of the faithful, should not religiously
keep the faith of their treaties. But in that new-found
world, which is not more distant from us in situation than
the people are in their manners and course of life, there is
no trusting to leagues, even though they were made with all
the pomp of the most sacred ceremonies; on the contrary,
they are on this account the sooner broken, some slight
pretence being found in the words of the treaties, which are
purposely couched in such ambiguous terms that they can
never be so strictly bound but they will always find some
loophole to escape at; and thus they break both their
leagues and their faith. And this is done with such impudence, and those very men who value themselves on having
suggested these expedients to their princes, would with a
haughty scorn declaim against such craft, or to speak
plainer, such fraud and deceit, if they found private men
make use of it in their bargains, and would readily say that
they deserve to be hanged.

By this means it is, that all sort of justice passes in the
world for a low-spirited and vulgar virtue, far below the
dignity of royal greatness. Or at least, there are set up
two sorts of justice; the one is mean, and creeps on the
ground, and therefore becomes none but the lower part of

mankind, and so must be kept in severely by many re-
straints that it may not break out beyond the bounds that
are set to it. The other is the particular virtue of princes,
which as it is more majestic than that which becomes the
rabble, so take a freer compass; and thus lawful and unlawful are only measured by pleasure and interest. These
practices of the princes that lie about Utopia, who make so
little account of their faith, seem to be the reasons that determine them to engage in no confederacies; perhaps they
would change their mind if they lived among us; but yet
though treaties were more religiously observed, they would
still dislike the custom of making them; since the world has
taken up a false maxim upon it, as if there were no tie of
Nature uniting one nation to another, only separated perhaps by a mountain or a river, and that all were born in a
state of hostility, and so might lawfully do all that mischief
to their neighbors against which there is no provision made
by treaties; and that when treaties are made, they do not
cut off the enmity, or restrain the license of preying upon
each other, if by the unskilfulness of wording them there
are not effectual provisos made against them. They, on
the other hand, judge that no man is to be esteemed our
enemy that has never injured us; and that the partnership
of the human nature is instead of a league. And that kindness and good-nature unite men more effectually and with
greater strength than any agreements whatsoever; since
thereby the engagements of men's hearts become stronger
than the bond and obligation of words.

OF THEIR MILITARY DISCIPLINE

They detest war as a very brutal thing; and which, to
the reproach of human nature, is more practiced by
men than by any sort of beasts. They, in opposition to the
sentiments of almost all other nations, think that there is
nothing more inglorious than that glory that is gained by

war. And therefore though they accustom themselves
daily to military exercises and the discipline of war, in
which not only their men but their women likewise are
trained up, that in cases of necessity they may not be quite
useless; yet they do not rashly engage in war, unless it be
either to defend themselves, or their friends, from any
unjust aggressors; or out of good-nature or in compassion
assist an oppressed nation in shaking off the yoke of
tyranny. They indeed help their friends, not only in de-
fensive, but also in offensive wars; but they never do that
unless they had been consulted before the breach was
made, and being satisfied with the grounds on which they
went, they had found that all demands of reparation were
rejected, so that a war was unavoidable. This they think
to be not only just, when one neighbor makes an inroad
on another, by public order, and carry away the spoils;
but when the merchants of one country are oppressed in
another, either under pretense of some unjust laws, or by
the perverse wresting of good ones. This they count a
juster cause of war than the other, because those injuries
are done under some color of laws. This was the only
ground of that war in which they engaged with the
Nephelogetes against the Aleopolitanes, a little before our
time; for the merchants of the former having, as they
thought, met with great injustice among the latter, which,
whether it was in itself right or wrong, drew on a terrible
war, in which many of their neighbors were engaged; and
their keeness in carrying it on being supported by their
strength in maintaining it, it not only shook some very
flourishing states, and very much excited others, but after
a series of much mischief ended in the entire conquest and
slavery of the Aleopolitanes, who though before the war
they were in all respects much superior to the Nephelogetes,
were yet subdued; but though the Utopians had assisted
them in the war, yet they pretended to no share of the
spoil.

But though they so vigorously assist their friends in obtaining reparation for the injuries they have received in affairs of this nature, yet if any such fraud was committed against themselves, provided not violence was done to their persons, they would only on their being refused satisfaction forbear trading with such people. This is not because they consider their neighbors more than their own citizens; but since their neighbors trade every one upon his own stock, fraud is a more sensible injury to them than it is to the Utopians, among whom the public in such a case only suffers. As they expect nothing in return for the merchandises they export but that in which they so much abound, and is of little use to them, the loss does not much affect them; they think therefore it would be too severe to revenge a loss attended with so little inconvenience either to their lives, or their subsistence, with the death of many persons; but if any of their people is either killed or wounded wrongfully, whether it be done by public authority or only by private men, as soon as they hear of it they send ambassadors, and demand that the guilty persons may be delivered up to them; and if that is denied, they declare war; but if it be complied with, the offenders are condemned either to death or slavery.

They would be both troubled and ashamed of a bloody victory over their enemies, and think it would be as foolish a purchase as to buy the most valuable goods at too high a rate. And in no victory do they glory so much as in that which is gained by dexterity and good conduct, without bloodshed. In such cases they appoint public triumphs, and erect trophies to the honor of those who have succeeded; for then do they reckon that a man acts suitably to his nature when he conquers his enemy in such a way as that no other creature but a man could be capable of, and that is by the strength of his understanding. Bears, lions, boars, wolves, and dogs, and all other animals employ their bodily force one against another, in which as many of them are superior to men, both in strength and fierceness, so they are all subdued by his reason and understanding.

The only design of the Utopians in war is to obtain that by force, which if it had been granted them in time would have prevented the war; or if that cannot be done, to take so severe a revenge on those that have injured them that they may be terrified from doing the like for the time to come. By these ends they measure all their designs, and manage them so that it is visible that the appetite of fame or vain-glory does not work so much on them as a just care of their own security.

As soon as they declare war, they take care to have a great many schedules, that are sealed with their common seal, affixed in the most conspicuous places of their enemies' country. This is carried secretly, and done in many places all at once. In these they promise great rewards to such as shall kill the prince, and lesser in proportion to such as shall kill any other persons, who are those on whom, next to the prince himself, they cast the chief balance of the war. And they double the sum to him that, instead of killing the person so marked out, shall take him alive and put him in their hands. They offer not only indemnity, but rewards, to such of the persons themselves that are so marked, if they will act against their countrymen: by this means those that are named in their schedules become not only distrustful of their fellow-citizens, but are jealous of one another, and are much distracted by fear and danger; for it has often fallen out that many of them, and even the Prince himself, have been betrayed by those in whom they have trusted most: for the rewards that the Utopians offer are so unmeasurably great, that there is no sort of crime to which men cannot be drawn by them. They consider the risk that those run who undertake such services, and offer a recompense proportioned to the danger; not only a vast deal of gold, but great revenues in lands, that lie among other nations that are their friends, where they may go and enjoy them very securely; and they observe the promises they make of this kind very religiously. They very much approve of this way of corrupting their enemies, though it appears to others to be base and cruel; but they look on it as a wise course, to make an end of what would be other-wise a long war, without so much as hazarding one battle to decide it. They think it likewise an act of mercy and love to mankind to prevent the great slaughter of those that must otherwise be killed in the progress of the war, both on their own side and on that of their enemies, by the death of a few that are most guilty; and that in so doing they are kind even to their enemies, and pity them no less than their own people, as knowing that the greater part of them do not engage in the war of their own accord, but are driven into it by the passions of their prince.

If this method does not succeed with them, then they sow seeds of contention among their enemies, and animate the prince's brother, or some of the nobility, to aspire to the crown. If they cannot disunite them by domestic broils, then they engage their neighbors against them, and make them set on foot some old pretensions, which are never wanting to princes when they have occasion for them. These they plentifully supply with money, though but very sparingly with any auxiliary troops: for they are so tender of their own people, that they would not willingly ex-change one of them, even with the prince of their enemies' country.

But as they keep their gold and silver only for such an occasion, so when that offers itself they easily part with it, since it would be no inconvenience to them though they should reserve nothing of it to themselves. For besides the wealth that they have among them at home, they have a vast treasure abroad, many nations round about them being deep in their debt: so that they hire soldiers from all places for carrying on their wars, but chiefly from the Zapolets, who live five hundred miles east of Utopia. They

are a rude, wild, and fierce nation, who delight in the woods
and rocks, among which they are born and bred up. They
are hardened both against heat, cold and labor, and know
nothing of the delicacies of life. They do not apply themselves to agriculture, nor do they care either for their
houses or their clothes. Cattle is all that they look after;
and for the greatest part they live either by hunting, or
upon rapine; and are made, as it were, only for war. They
watch all opportunities of engaging in it, and very readily
embrace such as are offered them. Great numbers of them
will frequently go out, and offer themselves for a very low
pay, to serve any that will employ them: they know none
of the arts of life, but those that lead to the taking it away;
they serve those that hire them, both with much courage
and great fidelity; but will not engage to serve for any determined time, and agree upon such terms, that the next
day they may go over to the enemies of those whom they
serve, if they offer them a greater encouragement: and will
perhaps return to them the day after that, upon a higher
advance of their pay. There are few wars in which they
make not a considerable part of the armies on both sides:
so it often falls out that they who are related, and are hired
in the same country, and so have lived long and familiarly
together, forgetting both their relations and former friendship, kill one another upon no other consideration that that
of being hired to it for a little money, by princes of different interests; and such a regard have they for money, that
they are easily wrought on by the difference of one penny
a day to change sides. So entirely does this avarice influence them; and yet this money, which they value so
highly, is of little use to them; for what they purchase thus
with their blood, they quickly waste on luxury, which
among them is but of a poor and miserable form.

This nation serves the Utopians against all people whatsoever, for they pay higher than any other. The Utopians
hold this for a maxim, that as they seek out the best sort of

men for their own use at home, so they make use of this worst sort of men for the consumption of war, and there- fore they hire them with the offers of vast rewards, to expose themselves to all sorts of hazards, out of which the greater part never returns to claim their promises. Yet they make them good most religiously to such as escape. This animates them to adventure again, whenever there is occa- sion for it; for the Utopians are not at all troubled how many of these happen to be killed, and reckon it a service done to mankind if they could be a means to deliver the world from such a lewd and vicious sort of people, that seem to have run together as to the drain of human nature. Next to these they are served in their wars with those upon whose account they undertake them, and with the auxiliary troops of their other friends, to whom they join a few of their own people, and send some men of eminent and ap- proved virtue to command in chief. There are two sent with him, who during his command are but private men, but the first is to succeed him if he should happen to be either killed or taken; and in case of the like misfortune to him, the third comes in his place; and thus they provide against ill events, that such accidents as may befall their generals may not endanger their armies. When they draw out troops of their own people, they take such out of every city as freely offer themselves, for none are forced to go against their wills, since they think that if any man is pressed that wants courage, he will not only act faintly, but by his cowardice dishearten others. But if an invasion is made on their country they make use of such men, if they have good bodies, though they are not brave; and either put them aboard their ships or place them on the walls of their towns, that being so posted they may find no opportunity of flying away; and thus either shame, the heat of action, or the im- possibility of flying, bears down their cowardice; they often make a virtue of necessity and behave themselves well, be- cause nothing else is left them. But as they force no man

to go into any foreign war against his will, so they do not
hinder those women who are willing to go along with their
husbands; on the contrary, they encourage and praise them,
and they often stand next their husbands in the front of the
army.   They also place together those who are related,
parents and children, kindred, and those that are mutually
allied, near one another; that those whom Nature has inspired with the greatest zeal for assisting one another, may
be the nearest and readiest to do it; and it is matter of
great reproach if husband or wife survive one another, or if
a child survive his parents, and therefore when they come
to be engaged in action they continue to fight to the last
man, if their enemies stand before them.   And as they use
all prudent methods to avoid the endangering their own
men, and if it is possible let all the action and danger fall
upon the troops they hire, so if it becomes necessary for
themselves to engage, they then charge with as much courage as they avoided it before with prudence: nor is it a fierce
charge at first, but it increases by degrees; and as they continue in action, they grow more obstinate and press harder
upon the enemy, insomuch that they will much sooner die
than give ground; for the certainty that their children will
be well looked after when they are dead, frees them from
all that anxiety concerning them which often masters men
of great courage; and thus they are animated by a noble
and invincible resolution.   Their skill in military affairs
increases their courage; and the wise sentiments which,
according to the laws of their country are instilled into
them in their education, give additional vigor to their
minds: for as they do not undervalue life so as prodigally
to throw it away, they are not so indecently fond of it as
to preserve it by base and unbecoming methods.   In the
greatest heat of action, the bravest of their youth, who
have devoted themselves to that service, single out the general of their enemies, set on him either openly or by ambus-
cade, pursue him everywhere, and when spent and wearied

out, are relieved by others, who never give over the pursuit; either attacking him with close weapons when they can get near him, or with those which wound at a distance, when others get in between them; so that unless he secures himself by flight, they seldom fail at last to kill or to take him prisoner. When they have obtained a victory, they kill as few as possible, and are much more bent on taking many prisoners than on killing those that fly before them; nor do they ever let their men so loose in the pursuit of their enemies, as not to retain an entire body still in order; so that if they have been forced to engage the last of their battalions before they could gain the day, they will rather let their enemies all escape than pursue them, when their own army is in disorder; remembering well what has often fallen out to themselves, that when the main body of their army has been quite defeated and broken, when their enemies imagining the victory obtained, have let themselves loose into an irregular pursuit, a few of them that lay for a reserve, waiting a fit opportunity, have fallen on them in their chase, and when straggling in disorder and apprehensive of no danger, but counting the day their own, have turned the whole action, and wresting out of their hands a victory that seemed certain and undoubted, while the vanquished have suddenly become victorious.

It is hard to tell whether they are more dextrous in laying or avoiding ambushes. They sometimes seem to fly when it is far from their thoughts; and when they intend to give ground, they do it so that it is very hard to find out their design. If they see they are ill posted, or are like to be overpowered by numbers, they then either march off in the night with great silence, or by some stratagem delude their enemies: if they retire in the daytime, they do it in such order, that it is no less dangerous to fall upon them in a retreat than in a march. They fortify their camps with a deep and large trench, and throw up the earth that is dug out of it for a wall; nor do they employ only their slaves in

this, but the whole army works at it, except those that are
then upon the guard; so that when so many hands are at
work, a great line and a strong fortification is finished in so
short a time that it is scarce credible. Their armour is
very strong for defence, and yet is not so heavy as to make
them uneasy in their marches; they can even swim with it.
All that are trained up to war, practice swimming. Both
horse and foot make great use of arrows, and are very
expert. They have no swords, but fight with a pole-axe
that is both sharp and heavy, by which they thrust or strike
down an enemy. They are very good at finding out warlike machines, and disguise them so well, that the enemy
does not perceive them till he feels the use of them; so
that he cannot prepare such a defence as would render
them useless; the chief consideration had in the making
them, is that they may be easily carried and managed.

If they agree to a truce, they observe it so religiously
that no provocations will make them break it. They never
lay their enemies' country waste, nor burn their corn, and
even in their marches they take all possible care that neither
horse nor foot may tread it down, for they do not know
but that they may have use for it themselves. They hurt
no man whom they find disarmed, unless he is a spy.
When a town is surrendered to them, they take it into their
protection: and when they carry a place by storm, they
never plunder it, but put those only to the sword that
opposed the rendering of it up, and make the rest of the
garrison slaves, but for the other inhabitants, they do them
no hurt; and if any of them had advised a surrender, they
give them good rewards out of the estates of those that
they condemn, and distribute the rest among their auxiliary
troops, but they themselves take no share of the spoil.

When a war is ended, they do not oblige their friend to
reimburse their expenses; but they obtain them of the
conquered, either in money, which they keep for the next
occasion, or in lands, out of which a constant revenue is to

be paid them; by many increases, the revenues which they draw out from several countries on such occasions, is now risen to above 700,000 ducats a year. They send some of their own people to receive these revenues, who have orders to live magnificently, and like princes, by which means they consume much of it upon the place; and either bring over the rest to Utopia, or lend it to that nation in which it lies. This they most commonly do, unless some great occasion, which falls out but very seldom, should oblige them to call for it all. It is out of these lands that they assign rewards to such as they encourage to adventure on desperate attempts. If any prince that engages in war with them is making preparations for invading their coun- try, they prevent him, and make his country the seat of the war; for they do not willingly suffer any war to break in upon their island; and if that should happen, they would only defend themselves by their own people, but would not call for auxiliary troops to their assistance.

OF THE RELIGIONS OF THE UTOPIANS

There are several sorts of religions, not only in differ- ent parts of the island, but even in every town; some worshipping the sun, others the moon, or one of the plan- ets: some worship such men as have been eminent in for- mer times for virtue, or glory, not only as ordinary deities, but as the supreme God: yet the greater and wiser sort of them worship none of these, but adore one eternal, invis- ible, infinite, and incomprehensible Deity; as a Being that is far above all our apprehensions, that is spread over the whole universe, not by His bulk, but by His power and virtue; Him they call the Father of All, and acknowledge that the beginnings, the increase, the progress, the vicissi- tudes, and the end of all things come only from Him; nor do they offer divine honors to any but to Him alone. And indeed, though they differ concerning other things, yet all agree in this, that they think there is one supreme Being that made and governs the world, whom they call in the language of their country Mithras. They differ in this, that one thinks the God whom he worships is this supreme Being, and another thinks that his idol is that God; but they all agree in one principle, that whoever is this supreme Being, He is also that great Essence to whose glory and majesty all honors are ascribed by the consent of all nations.

By degrees, they fall off from the various superstitions that are among them, and grow up to that one religion that is the best and most in request; and there is no doubt to be made but that all the others had vanished long ago, if some of those who advised them to lay aside their superstitions had not met with some unhappy accident, which being considered as inflicted by Heaven, made them afraid that the God whose worship had like to have been abandoned, had interposed, and revenged themselves on those who despised their authority.

After they had heard from us an account of the doctrine, the course of life, and the miracles of Christ, and of the wonderful constancy of so many martyrs, whose blood, so willingly offered up by them, was the chief concern of spreading their religion over a vast number of nations; it is not to be imagined how inclined they were to receive it. I shall not determine whether this proceeeded from any secret inspiration of God, or whether it was because it seemed so favorable to that community of goods, which is an opinion so particular as well as so dear to them; since they perceived that Christ and His followers lived by that rule, and that it was still kept up in some communities among the sincerest sort of Christians. From whichsoever of these motives it might be, true it is that many of them came over to our religion, and were initiated into it by baptism. But as two of our number were dead, so none of the four that survived were in priest's orders; we therefore could not baptize them; so that to our great regret they could not partake of the other sacraments, that can only be administered by priests; but they are instructed concerning them, and long most vehemently for them. They have had great disputes among themselves, whether one chosen by them to be a priest would not be thereby qualified to do all the things that belong to that character, even though he had no authority derived from the Pope; and they seemed to be resolved to choose some for that employment, but they had not done it when I left them.

Those among them that have not received our religion, do not fright any from it, and use none ill that goes over to it; so that all the while I was there, one man was only punished on this occasion. He being newly baptized, did, notwithstanding all that we can say to the contrary, dispute publicly concerning the Christian religion with more zeal than discretion; and with so much heat, that he not only preferred our worship to theirs, but condemned all their rites as profane; and cried out against all that adhered to them, as impious and sacrilegious persons, that were to be damned to everlasting burnings. Upon his having frequently preached in this manner, he was seized, and after trial he was condemned to banishment, not for having disparaged their religion, but for his inflaming the people to sedition: for this is one of their most ancient laws, that no man ought to be punished for his religion. At the first constitution of their government, Utopos having understood that before his coming among them the old inhabitants had been engaged in great quarrels concerning religion, by which they were so divided among themselves, that he found it an easy thing to conquer them, since instead of uniting their forces against him, every different party in religion fought by themselves; after he had subdued them, he made a law that every man might be of what religion he pleased, and might endeavor to draw others to it by the force of argument, and by amicable and modest ways, but without bitterness against those of other opinions; but that he ought to

use no other force but that of persuasion, and was neither
to mix with it reproaches nor violence; and such as did otherwise were to be condemned to banishment or slavery.

This law was made by Utopus, not only for preserving
the public peace, which he saw suffered much by daily contentions and irreconcilable heats, but because he thought
the interest of religion itself required it. He judged it not
fit to determine anything rashly, and seemed to doubt
whether those different forms of religion might not all
come from God, who might inspire men in a different manner, and be pleased with this variety; he therefore thought
it indecent and foolish for any man to threaten and terrify
another to make him believe what did not appear to him
to be true. And supposing that only one religion was
really true, and the rest false, he imagined that the native
force of truth would at last break forth and shine bright,
if supported only by the strength of argument, and attended to with a gentle and unprejudiced mind; while, on
the other hand, if such debates were carried on with violence and tumults, as the most wicked are always the most
obstinate, so the best and most holy religion might be
choked with superstition, as corn is with briars and thorns;
he therefore left men wholly to their liberty, that they
might be free to believe as they should see cause; only
he made a solemn and severe law against such as should
so far degenerate from the dignity of human nature as to
think that our souls died with our bodies, or that the
world was governed by chance, without a wise overruling
Providence: for they all formerly believed that there was a
state of rewards and punishments to the good and bad after
this life; and they now look on those that think otherwise
as scarce fit to be counted men, since they degrade so noble
a being as the soul, and reckon it no better than a beast's:
thus they are far from looking on such men as fit for human
society, or to be citizens of a well-ordered commonwealth;
since a man of such principles must needs, as oft as he dares

do it, despise all their laws and customs: for there is no
doubt to be made that a man who is afraid of nothing but
the law, and apprehends nothing after death, will not scru-
ple to break through all the laws of his country, either by
fraud or force, when by this means he may satisfy his appetites. They never raise any that hold these maxims,
either to honors or offices, nor employ them in any public
trust, but despise them, as men of base and sordid minds:
yet they do not punish them, because they lay this down
as a maxim that a man cannot make himself believe anything he pleases; nor do they drive any to dissemble their
thoughts by threatenings, so that men are not tempted to
lie or disguise their opinions; which being a sort of fraud,
is abhorred by the Utopians. They take care indeed to
prevent their disputing in defence of these opinions, especially before the common people; but they suffer, and
even encourage them to dispute concerning them in private with their priests and other grave men, being confident
that they will be cured of those mad opinions by having
reason laid before them. There are many among them that
run far to the other extreme, though it is neither thought
an ill nor unreasonable opinion, and therefore is not at
all discouraged. They think that the souls of beasts are
immortal, though far inferior to the dignity of the human
soul, and not capable of so great a happiness. They are
almost all of them very firmly persuaded that good men
will be infinitely happy in another state; so that though
they are compassionate to all that are sick, yet they lament
no man's death, except they see him loth to depart with
life; for they look on this as a very ill presage, as if the
soul, conscious to itself of guilt, and quite hopeless, was
afraid to leave the body, from some secret hints of ap-
proaching misery. They think that such a man's appearance before God cannot be acceptable to Him, who being
called on, does not go out cheerfully, but is backward
and unwilling, and is, as it were, dragged to it. They are

struck with horror when they see any die in this manner,
and carry them out in silence and with sorrow, and praying God that He would be merciful to the errors of the departed soul, they lay the body in the ground; but when any
die cheerfully, and full of hope, they do not mourn for
them, but sing hymns when they carry out their bodies,
and commending their souls very earnestly to God: their
whole behavior is then rather grave than sad, they burn
the body and set up a pillar where the pile was made, with
an inscription to the honor of the deceased. When they
come from the funeral, they discourse of his good life and
worthy actions, but speak of nothing oftener and with
more pleasure than of his serenity at the hour of death.
They think such respect paid to the memory of good men
is both the greatest incitement to engage others to follow
their example, and the most acceptable worship that can be
offered them; for they believe that though by the imper-
fection of human sight they are invisible to us, yet they
are present among us, and hear those discourses that pass
concerning themselves. They believe it inconsistent with
the happiness of departed souls not to be at liberty to be
where they will, and do not imagine them capable of the
ingratitude of not desiring to see those friends with whom
they lived on earth in the strictest bonds of love and kindness: besides they are persuaded that good men after death
have these affections and all other good dispositions increased rather than diminished, and therefore conclude
that they are still among the living, and observe all they
say or do. From hence they engage in all their affairs
with the greater confidence of success, as trusting to their
protection; while this opinion of the presence of their
ancestors is a restraint that prevents their engaging in ill
designs.

They despise and laugh at auguries, and the other vain
and superstitious ways of divination, so much observed
among other nations; but have great reverence for such

miracles as cannot flow from any of the powers of Nature, and look on them as effects and indications of the presence of the supreme Being, of which they say many instances have occurred among them; and that sometimes their public prayers, which upon great and dangerous occasions they have solemnly put up to God, with assured confidence of being heard, have been answered in a miraculous manner.

They think the contemplating God in His works, and the adoring Him for them, is a very acceptable piece of worship to Him.

There are many among them, that upon a motive of religion neglect learning, and apply themselves to no sort of study; nor do they allow themselves any leisure time, but are perpetually employed, believing that by the good things that a man does he secures to himself that happiness that comes after death. Some of these visit the sick; others mend highways, cleanse ditches, repair bridges, or dig turf, gravel, or stones. Others fell and cleave timber, and bring wood, corn, and other necessaries on carts into their towns. Nor do these only serve the public, but they serve even private men, more than the slaves themselves do; for if there is anywhere a rough, hard, and sordid piece of work to be done, from which many are frightened by the labor and loathsomeness of it, if not the despair of accomplishing it, they cheerfully, and of their own accord, take that to their share; and by that means, as they ease others very much, so they afflict themselves, and spend their whole life in hard labor; and yet they do not value themselves upon this, nor lessen other people's credit to raise their own; but by their stooping to such servile employments, they are so far from being despised, that they are so much the more esteemed by the whole nation.

Of these there are two sorts; some live unmarried and chaste, and abstain from eating any sort of flesh; and thus weaning themselves from all the pleasures of the present

life, which they account hurtful, they pursue, even by the
hardest and painfullest methods possible, that blessedness
which they hope for hereafter; and the nearer they approach to it, they are the more cheerful and earnest in their
endeavors after it. Another sort of them is less willing to
put themselves to much toil, and therefore prefer a married
state to a single one; and as they do not deny themselves
the pleasure of it, so they think the begetting of children is
a debt which they owe to human nature and to their
country; nor do they avoid any pleasure that does not
hinder labor, and therefore eat flesh so much the more
willingly, as they find that by this means they are the more
able to work; the Utopians look upon these as the wiser
sect, but they esteem the others as the most holy. They
would indeed laugh at any man, who from the principles of
reason would prefer an unmarried state to a married, or a
life of labor to an easy life; but they reverence and admire
such as do it from the motives of religion. There is
nothing in which they are more cautious than in giving
their opinion positively concerning any sort of religion.
The men that lead those severe lives are called in the
language of their country Brutheskas, which answers to
those we call religious orders.

Their priests are men of eminent piety, and therefore
they are but few, for there are only thirteen in every town,
one for every temple; but when they go to war, seven of
these go out with their forces, and seven others are chosen
to supply their room in their absence; but these enter again
upon their employment when they return; and those who
served in their absence attend upon the high-priest, till
vacancies fall by death; for there is one set over all the rest.
They are chosen by the people as the other magistrates are,
by suffrages given in secret, for preventing of factions; and
when they are chosen they are consecrated by the college of
priests. The care of all sacred things, the worship of God,
and an inspection into the manners of the people, are com-

mitted to them. It is a reproach to a man to be sent for by any of them, or for them to speak to him in secret, for that always gives some suspicion. All that is incumbent on them is only to exhort and admonish the people; for the power of correcting and punishing ill men belongs wholly to the Prince and to the other magistrates. The severest thing that the priest does, is the excluding those that are desperately wicked from joining in their worship. There is not any sort of punishment more dreaded by them than this, for as it loads them with infamy, so it fills them with secret horrors, such is their reverence to their religion; nor will their bodies be long exempted from their share of trouble; for if they do not very quickly satisfy the priests of the truth of their repentance, they are seized on by the Senate, and punished for their impiety. The education of youth belongs to the priests, yet they do not take so much care of instructing them in letters as in forming their minds and manners aright; they use all possible methods to infuse very early into the tender and flexible minds of children such opinions as are both good in themselves and will be useful to their country. For when deep impressions of these things are made at that age, they follow men through the whole course of their lives, and conduce much to preserve the peace of the government, which suffers by nothing more than by vices that rise out of ill opinions. The wives of their priests are the most extraordinary women of the whole country; sometimes the women themselves are made priests, though that falls out but seldom, nor are any but ancient widows chosen into that order.

None of the magistrates have greater honor paid them than is paid the priests; and if they should happen to commit any crime, they would not be questioned for it. Their punishment is left to God, and to their own consciences; for they do not think it lawful to lay hands on any man, how wicked soever he is, that has been in a peculiar manner dedicated to God; nor do they find any great inconvenience in this, both because they have so few priests, and because these are chosen with much caution, so that it must be a very unusual thing to find one who merely out of regard to his virtue, and for his being esteemed a singularly good man, was raised up to so great a dignity, degenerate into corruption and vice. And if such a thing should fall out, for man is a changeable creature, yet there being few priests, and these having no authority but what rises out of the respect that is paid them, nothing of great consequence to the public can proceed from the indemnity that the priests enjoy.

They have indeed very few of them, lest greater numbers sharing in the same honor might make the dignity of that order which they esteem so highly to sink in its reputation. They also think it difficult to find out many of such an exalted pitch of goodness, as to be equal to that dignity which demands the exercise of more than ordinary virtues. Nor are the priests in greater veneration among them than they are among their neighboring nations, as you may imagine by that which I think gives occasion for it.

When the Utopians engage in battle, the priests who accompany them to the war, apparelled in their sacred vestments, kneel down during the action, in a place not far from the field; and lifting up their hands to heaven, pray, first for peace, and then for victory to their own side, and particularly that it may be gained without the effusion of much blood on either side; and when the victory turns to their side, they run in among their own men to restrain their fury; and if any of their enemies see them, or call to them, they are preserved by that means; and such as can come so near them as to touch their garments, have not only their lives, but their fortunes secured to them; it is upon this account that all the nations round about consider them so much, and treat them with such reverence, that they have been often no less able to preserve their own people from the fury of their enemies, than to save their enemies from their rage; for it has sometimes fallen out, that when their armies have been in disorder, and forced to fly, so that their enemies were running upon the slaughter and spoil, the priests by interposing have sep, arated them from one another, and stopped the effusion of more blood; so that by their mediation a peace has been concluded on very reasonable terms; nor is there any nation about them so fierce, cruel, or barbarous as not to look upon their persons as sacred and inviolable.

The first and the last day of the month, and of the year, is a festival. They measure their months by the course of the moon, and their years by the course of the sun. The first days are called in their language the Cynemernes, and the last the Trapemernes; which answers in our language to the festival that begins, or ends the season.

They have magnificent temples, that are not only nobly built, but extremely spacious; which is the more necessary, as they have so few of them; they are a little dark within, which proceeds not from any error in the architecture, but is done with design; for their priests think that too much light dissipates the thoughts, and that a more moderate degree of it both recollects the mind and raises devotion. Though there are many different forms of religion among them, yet all these, how various soever, agree in the main point, which is the worshipping the Divine Essence; and therefore there is nothing to be seen or heard in their temples in which the several persuasions among them may not agree; for every sect performs those rites that are peculiar to it, in their private houses, nor is there anything in the public worship that contradicts the particular ways of those different sects. There are no images for God in their temples, so that every one may represent Him to his thoughts, according to the way of his religion; nor do they call this one God by any other name but that of Mithras, which is the common name by which they all express the Divine Essence, whatsoever otherwise they think it to be; nor are there any prayers among them but such as every one of them may use without prejudice to his own opinion.

They meet in their temples on the evening of the festival that concludes a season: and not having yet broke their fast, they thank God for their good success during that year or month, which is then at an end; and the next day being that which begins the new season, they meet early in their temples, to pray for the happy progress of all their affairs during that period upon which they then enter. In the festival which concludes the period, before they go to the temple, both wives and children fall on their knees before their husbands or parents, and confess everything in which they have either erred or failed in their duty, and beg pardon for it. Thus all little discontents in families are removed, that they may offer up their devotions with a pure and serene mind; for they hold it a great impiety to enter upon them with disturbed thoughts, or with a consciousness of their bearing hatred or anger in their hearts to any person whatsoever; and think that they should become liable to severe punishments if they presumed to offer sacrifices without cleansing their hearts, and reconciling all their differences. In the temples, the two sexes are separated, the men go to the right hand, and the women to the left; and the males and females all place themselves before the head master or mistress of that family to which they belong; so that those who have the government of them at home may see their deportment in public; and they intermingle them so, that the younger and the older may be set by one another; for if the younger sort were all set together, they would perhaps trifle away that time too much in which they ought to beget in themselves that religious dread of the supreme Being, which is the greatest and almost the only incitement to virtue.

They offer up no living creature in sacrifice, nor do they think it suitable to the divine Being, from whose bounty it

is that these creatures have derived their lives, to take
pleasure in their deaths, or the offering up their blood.
They burn incense and other sweet odors, and have a
great number of wax lights during their worship; not out of
any imagination that such oblations can add anything to the
divine Nature, which even prayers cannot do; but as it is a
harmless and pure way of worshipping God, so they think
those sweet savors and lights, together with some other
ceremonies, by a secret and unaccountable virtue, elevate
men's souls, and inflame them with greater energy and
cheerfulness during the divine worship.

All the people appear in the temples in white garments,
but the priest's vestments are parti-colored, and both the
work and colors are wonderful. They are made of no rich
materials, for they are neither embroidered nor set with
precious stones, but are composed of the plumes of several
birds, laid together with so much care and so neatly, that
the true value of them is far beyond the costliest materials.
They say that in the ordering and placing those plumes
some dark mysteries are represented, which pass down
among their priests in a secret tradition concerning them;
and that they are as hieroglyphics, putting them in mind of
the blessings that they have received from God, and of
their duties both to Him and to their neighbors. As soon
as the priest appears in those ornaments, they all fall pros-
trate on the ground, with so much reverence and so deep a
silence that such as look on cannot but be struck with it, as
if it were the effect of the appearance of a Diety. After
they have been for some time in this posture, they all stand
up, upon a sign given by the priest, and sing hymns to the
honor of God, some musical instruments playing all the
while. These are quite of another form than those used
among us: but as many of them are much sweeter than
ours, so others are made use of by us. Yet in one thing
they very much exceed us; all their music, both vocal and
instrumental, is adapted to imitate and express the passions,

and is so happily suited to every occasion, that whether the
subject of the hymn be cheerful or formed to soothe or
trouble the mind, or to express grief or remorse, the music
takes the impression of whatever is represented, affects and
kindles the passions, and works the sentiments deep into
the hearts of the hearers. When this is done, both priests
and people offer up very solemn prayers to God in a set
form of words; and these are so composed, that whatsoever
is pronounced by the whole assembly may be likewise applied by every man in particular to his own condition; in
these they acknowledge God to be the author and governor
of the world, and the fountain of all the good they receive,
and therefore offer up to Him their thanksgiving; and in
particular bless Him for His goodness in ordering it so,
that they are born under the happiest government in the
world, and are of a religion which they hope is the truest of
all others: but if they are mistaken, and if there is either a
better government or a religion more acceptable to God,
they implore His goodness to let them know it, vowing that
they resolve to follow Him whithersoever He leads them.
But if their government is the best, and their religion the
truest, then they pray that He may fortify them in it, and
bring all the world both to the same rules of life, and to the
same opinions concerning himself; unless, according to the
unsearchableness of His mind, He is pleased with a variety
of religions. Then they pray that God may give them an
easy passage at last to himself; not presuming to set limits to
Him, how early or late it should be; but if it may be wished
for, without derogating from His supreme authority, they
desire to be quickly delivered, and to be taken to himself,
though by the most terrible kind of death, rather than to be
detained long from seeing Him by the most prosperous
course of life. When this prayer is ended, they all fall
down again upon the ground, and after a little while they
rise up, go home to dinner, and spend the rest of the day
in diversion or military exercises.

Thus I have described to you, as particularly as I could, the constitution of that commonwealth, which I do not only think the best in the world, but indeed the only common-wealth that truly deserves that name. In all other places it is visible, that while people talk of a commonwealth, every man only seeks his own wealth; but there, where no man has any property, all men zealously pursue the good of the public: and, indeed, it is no wonder to see men act so differently; for in other commonwealths, every man knows that unless he provides for himself, how flourishing soever the commonwealth may be, he must die of hunger; so that he sees the necessity of preferring his own concerns to the public; but in Utopia, where every man has a right to every-thing, they all know that if care is taken to keep the public stores full, no private man can want anything; for among them there is no unequal distribution, so that no man is poor, none in necessity; and though no man has anything, yet they are all rich; for what can make a man so rich as to lead a serene and cheerful life, free from anxieties; neither apprehending want himself, nor vexed with the endless complaints of his wife? He is not afraid of the misery of his children, nor is he contriving how to raise a portion for his daughters, but is secure in this, that both he and his wife, his children and grandchildren, to as many genera-tions as he can fancy, will all live both plentifully and hap-pily; since among them there is no less care taken of those who were once engaged in labor, but grow afterwards unable to follow it, than there is elsewhere of these that continue still employed. I would gladly hear any man com-pare the justice that is among them with that of all other nations; among whom, may I perish, if I see anything that looks either like justice or equity: for what justice is there in this, that a nobleman, a goldsmith, a banker, or any other man, that either does nothing at all, or at best is employed in things that are of no use to the public, should live in great luxury and splendor, upon what is so ill acquired; and a mean man, a carter, a smith, or a plowman, that works harder even than the beasts themselves, and is employed in labors so necessary, that no commonwealth could hold out a year without them, can only earn so poor a livelihood, and must be led so miserable a life, that the condition of the beasts is much better than theirs? For as the beasts do not work constantly, so they feed almost as well, and with more pleasure; and have no anxiety about what is to come, whilst these men are depressed by a barren and fruitless employment, and tormented with the apprehensions of want in their old age; since that which they get by their daily labor does but maintain them at present, and is consumed as fast as it comes in, there is no overplus left to lay up for old age.

Is not that government both unjust and ungrateful, that is so prodigal of its favors to those that are called gentlemen, or goldsmiths, or such others who are idle, or live either by flattery, or by contriving the arts of vain pleasure; and on the other hand, takes no care of those of a meaner sort, such as plowmen, colliers, and smiths, without whom it could not subsist? But after the public has reaped all the advantage of their service, and they come to be oppressed with age, sickness, and want, all their labors and the good they have done is forgotten; and all the recompense given them is that they are left to die in great misery. The richer sort are often endeavoring to bring the hire of laborers lower, not only by their fraudulent practices, but by the laws which they procure to be made to that effect; so that though it is a thing most unjust in itself, to give such small rewards to those who deserve so well of the public, yet they have given those hardships the name and color of justice, by procuring laws to be made for regulating them.

Therefore I must say that, as I hope for mercy, I can have no other notion of all the other governments that I see or know, than that they are a conspiracy of the rich, who on pretence of managing the public only pursue their private ends, and devise all the ways and arts they can find out; first, that they may, without danger, preserve all that they have so ill acquired, and then that they may engage the poor to toil and labor for them at as low rates as possible, and oppress them as much as they please. And if they can but prevail to get these contrivances established by the show of public authority, which is considered as the representative of the whole people, then they are accounted laws. Yet these wicked men after they have, by a most insatiable covetousness, divided that among themselves with which all the rest might have been well supplied, are far from that happiness that is enjoyed among the Utopians: for the use as well as the desire of money being extinguished, much anxiety and great occasions of mischief is cut off with it. And who does not see that the frauds, thefts, robberies, quarrels, tumults, contentions, seditions, murders, treacheries, and witchcrafts, which are indeed rather punished than restrained by the severities of law, would all fall off, if money were not any more valued by the world? Men's fears, solicitudes, cares, labors, and watchings, would all perish in the same moment with the value of money: even poverty itself, for the relief of which money seems most necessary, would fall. But, in order to the apprehending this aright, take one instance.

Consider any year that has been so unfruitful that many thousands have died of hunger; and yet if at the end of that year a survey was made of the granaries of all the rich men that have hoarded up the corn, it would be found that there was enough among them to have prevented all that consumption of men that perished in misery; and that if it had been distributed among them, none would have felt the terrible effects of that scarcity; so easy a thing would it be to supply all the necessities of life, if that blessed thing called money, which is pretended to be invented for procuring them, was not really the only thing that obstructed their being procured!

I do not doubt but rich men are sensible of this, and that they well know how much a greater happiness it is to want nothing necessary than to abound in many super-fluities, and to be rescued out of so much misery than to abound with so much wealth; and I cannot think but the sense of every man's interest, added to the authority of Christ's commands, who as He was infinitely wise, knew what was best, and was not less good in discovering it to us, would have drawn all the world over to the laws of the Utopians, if pride, that plague of human nature, that source of so much misery, did not hinder it; for this vice does not measure happiness so much by its own conveniences as by the miseries of others; and would not be satisfied with being thought a goddess, if none were left that were miser-able, over whom she might insult. Pride thinks its own happiness shines the brighter by comparing it with the misfortunes of other persons; that by displaying its own wealth, they may feel their poverty the more sensibly. This is that infernal serpent that creeps into the breasts of mortals, and possesses them too much to be easily drawn out; and therefore I am glad that the Utopians have fallen upon this form of government, in which I wish that all the world could be so wise as to imitate them; for they have indeed laid down such a scheme and foundation of policy, that as men live happily under it, so it is like to be of great continuance; for they having rooted out of the minds of their people all the seeds both of ambition and faction, there is no danger of any commotion at home; which alone has been the ruin of many states, that seemed otherwise to be well secured; but as long as they live in peace at home, and are governed by such good laws, the envy of all their neighboring princes, who have often though in vain at-tempted their ruin, will never be able to put their state into any commotion or disorder.

When Raphael had thus made an end of speaking, though many things occurred to me, both concerning the manners and laws of that people, that seemed very absurd, as well as their way of making war, as in their notions of religion and divine matters; together with several other particulars, but chiefly what seemed the foundation of all the rest, their living in common, without the use of money, by which all nobility, magnificence, splendor, and majesty, which, according to the common opinion, are the true ornaments of a nation, would be quite taken away; yet since I perceived that Raphael was weary, and was not sure whether he could easily bear contradiction, remembering that he had taken notice of some who seemed to think they were bound in honor to support the credit of their own wisdom, by finding out something to censure in all other men's inventions, besides their own; I only commended their constitution, and the account he had given of it in general; and so taking him by the hand, carried him to supper, and told him I would find out some other time for examining this subject more particularly, and for discoursing more copiously upon it; and indeed I shall be glad to embrace an opportunity of doing it. In the meanwhile, though it must be confessed that he is both a very learned man, and a person who has obtained a great knowledge of the world, I cannot perfectly agree to everything he has related; however, there are many things in the Commonwealth of Utopia that I rather wish, than hope, to see followed in our governments.

Comment Gargantua fiſt baſtir pour le Moyne l'abbaye de Theleme. Chapitre. 1.

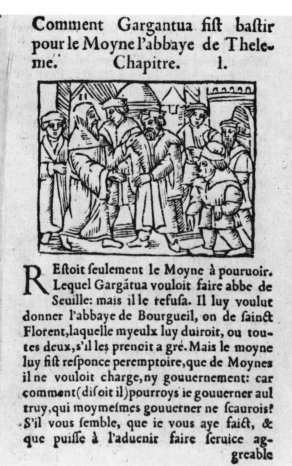

REſtoit ſeulement le Moyne à pouruoir. Lequel Gargátua vouloit faire abbe de Seuille: mais il le refuſa. Il luy voulut donner l'abbaye de Bourgueil, on de ſainĉt Florent, laquelle myeulx luy duiroit, ou toutes deux, s'il les prenoit a gré. Mais le moyne luy fiſt reſponce peremptoire, que de Moynes il ne vouloit charge, ny gouuernement: car comment (diſoit il) pourroys ie gouuerner aul truy, qui moymeſmes gouuerner ne ſcaurois? S'il vous ſemble, que ie vous aye faiĉt, & que puiſſe à l'aduenir faire ſeruice aggreable

From Rabelais' "La plaisante & joyeuse histoyre", Valence, 1547

THE ABBEY OF THELEME

by

FRANCOIS RABELAIS

ADDITIONAL BIBLIOGRAPHY

Bakhtin, Mikhail M., *Rabelais and His World,* tr. by Helene Iswolsky, Cambridge, Mass., 1971

Green, Thomas M., *Rabelais: A Study in Comic Courage,* Englewood Cliffs, N.J., 1970

Powys, J.C., *Rabelais,* London, 1948

Willcocks, M.P., *Laughing Philosopher,* New York, 1951

Wyndham Lewis, D.B., *Doctor Rabelais,* London, 1957

FRANCOIS RABELAIS

Francois Rabelais (c.1495-1553), the greatest humorist and satirist in modern literature, was, like More, an outstanding scholar and humanist. Born in Touraine toward the close of the fifteenth century, his education was both medieval and modern, conducted, as it was, in the monasteries of the Franciscan and Benedictine orders and in the eminent universities of Paris, Bourges, and Montpellier. His appetite for learning was omnivorous; he studied Greek, Latin, Hebrew, and apparently some Arabic, as well as most of the European languages of his day. He was trained in theology, in law, and in medicine, and is said, by popular tradition, to have practiced human dissection at a time when such anatomical antics were severely condemned. Although frequently in danger of attack for his radical ideas, his satire on the Church, and his broad humor, he successfully evaded prosecution, thanks to his friends in high places, and pursued his career of lecturing, traveling, and writing. His wit and learning brought him the acquaintance of Pierre Amy, Erasmus, Budé, and Etienne Dolet. Like them he strove to renew the classics and to transfer into modern literature some of the old wine of the ancients.

Rabelais lives, and will always live, by his one great book, the confused, confusing, chaotic, muddled, glorious, witty volume containing the inestimable deeds of Gargantua and his enormous offspring Pantagruel. This prose romance, which evolved throughout Rabelais' life, was still incomplete at his death. Characteristically, the second book, *Pantagruel,* appeared first in 1532, whereas the first book, *Gargantua,* appeared next, in 1534. Further adventures of Rabelais' huge, lusty, earthy, humane hero were recounted in three subsequent books (III, 1546; IV, 1552; and V, 1562, 1564).

More than sixty editions are said to have appeared in the
sixteenth century alone, and the book has continued for four
hundred years to rank with the comedies of Aristophanes
and Moliére, the novels of Petronius, Cervantes, Sterne,
Dickens, and Gogol, and the miscellaneous writings of
Browne, Swift, and Voltaire as one of the humorous master-
pieces of all literature. The key to Rabelais' humor lies in
his gross and earthy naturalism, in his delight in the common elements of life, and in his belief in the native goodness
of man. His famous motto, "Rire est le propre de l'homme,"
suggests that man is properly the laughing animal, and that
it is his duty, his right, and his privilege to laugh at, and
with, his fellow humans. This comic spirit, as well as his
belief in the natural goodness of man, is well exemplified in
the Utopian Abbey of Theleme, with which Gargantua
rewards the heroic deeds of his favorite drinking, tumbling,
fighting, swearing, mighty monk, Friar John. The abbey,
which is described in the closing chapters of Book I, is built
upon principles the precise opposite of those which obtained
in the monastaries where Rabelais spent, or mis-spent, part
of his youth; it is both a satire upon medieval ethical and
religious restrictions and a glorification of the new develop-
ments in architecture, learning, dress, manners, and abilities
of the Renaissance.

Good studies of the little that is known of Rabelais are
contained in the biographies of A. Tilley (1907), and Samuel Putnam (1928), while for those who read French easily
the standard work by Paul Stapfer (1889), and the delightful little study by Anatole France (1928) may profitably be
consulted. The recent edition of Rabelais' Complete Works
by Nock and Wilson (1931), and the modern translations by
Putnam (1929) and W. F. Smith (1935), contain valuable
introductions and notes. The seventeenth-century translation by Urquhart and Motteux (1653, 1708) has become so
justly famous in the English-speaking world that it is here
reprinted verbatim

THE ABBEY OF THELEME

HOW GARGANTUA CAUSED TO BE BUILT FOR THE MONK THE ABBEY OF THELEME

THERE was left only the monk to provide for, whom Gargantua would have made abbot of Sevillé, but he refused it. He would have given him the abbey of Bourgueil, or of Sanct Florent, which was better, or both if it pleased him. But the monk gave him a very peremptory answer, that he would never take upon him the charge nor 'government of monks. "For how shall I be able," said he, "to rule over others, that have not power or command over myself? If you think I have done you, or may hereafter do you any acceptable service, give me leave to found an abbey after my own mind and fancy." The notion pleased Gargantua very well, who thereupon offered him all the country of Theleme by the river of Loire, till within two leagues of the great forest of Porthaut. The monk then requested Gargantua, to institute his religious order contrary to all others. "First then," said Gargantua, "you must not build a wall about your convent, for all other abbeys are strongly walled and mured about." "See," said the monk, "and without cause, where there is mur before and mur behind, there is store of murmur, envy, and mutual conspiracy."

Moreover, seeing there are certain convents in the world, whereof the custom is, if any woman came (I mean chaste and honest women) they immediately sweep the ground which they have trod upon. Therefore was it ordained, that if any man or woman, entered into religious orders, should by chance come within this new abbey, all the rooms should be thoroughly washed and cleansed, through which they had passed. And because in all other monastaries and nunneries all is compassed, limited, and regulated by hours, it was decreed, that in this new structure there should be neither clock nor dial, but that, according to the opportunities and incident occasions, all their hours should be disposed of. "For," said Gargantua, "the greatest loss of time that I know, is, to count the hours. What good comes of it? Nor can there be any greater dotage in the world, than for one to guide and direct his courses by the sound of a bell, and not by his own judgment and discretion."

Item, because at that time they put no women into nunneries, but such as were either purlbind, blinkards, lame, crooked, illfavoured, mis-shapen, fools, senseless, spoiled, or corrupt; nor encloistered any men, but those that were either sickly, subject to defluxions, ill-bred louts, simple sots, or peevish trouble-houses. "But to the purpose," said the monk; "a woman that is neither fair nor good, to what use serves she?" "To make a nun of," said Gargantua. "Yea," said the monk, "and to make shirts and smocks." Therefore was it ordained, that into this religious order should be admitted no women that were not fair, well featured, and of a sweet disposition; nor men that were not comely, personable, and well-conditioned.

Item, because in the convents of women, men come not but underhand, privily, and by stealth; it was therefore enacted, that in this house there shall be no women in case there be not men nor men in case there be not women.

Item, because both men and women that are received into religious orders, after the expiring of their novitiate, or probation year, were constrained and forced perpetually to stay there all the days of their life; it was therefore ordered, that all whatever, men or women, admitted within this abbey, should have full leave to depart with peace and contentment, whensoever it should seem good to them so to do.

Item, for that the religious men and women did ordin-
arily make three vows, to wit, those of chastity, poverty,
and obedience; it was therefore constituted and appointed,
that in this convent they might be honorably married,
that they might be rich, and live at liberty. In regard of
the legitimate time of the persons to be initiated, and years
under and above which they were not capable of reception,
the women were to be admitted from ten till fifteen, and
the men from twelve to eighteen.

HOW THE ABBEY OF THE THELEMITES
WAS BUILT AND ENDOWED

For the fabric and furniture of the abbey Gargantua
caused to be delivered out, in ready money, seven and
twenty hundred thousand eight hundred and one, and
thirty of those golden rams of Berrie, which have a sheep
stamped on the one side, and a flowered cross on the other.
And for every year, until the whole work was completed,
he allotted threescore and nine thousand crowns of the
sun, and as many of the seven stars, to be charged all upon
the receipt of the custom. For the foundation and maintenance thereof for ever, he settled a perpetual fee-farm-
rent of three and twenty hundred, threescore and nine
thousand, five hundred and fourteen rose-nobles, exempt
from all homage, fealty, service, or burden whatsoever, and
payable every year at the gate of the abbey; and of this,
by letters patent, passed a very good grant.

The architecture was in a figure hexagonal, and in such
a fashion that in every one of the six corners there was
built a great round tower of threescore feet in diameter;
and were all of a like form and bigness. Upon the north
side ran along the river of Loire, on the bank whereof was
situated the tower called Arctic. Going towards the east,
there was another, called Calaer; the next following Anatole; the next Mesembrine; the next Hesperia, and the last

Criere. Every tower was distant from the other the space
of three hundred and twelve paces. The whole edifice
was everywhere six stories high, reckoning the cellar under-
ground for one. The second was arched after the fashion
of a basket-handle. The rest were cieled with pure wains-
coat, flourished with Flanders fret-work, in the form of the
foot of a lamp; and covered above with fine slates, with
an indorsement of lead, carrying the antique figures of little
puppets, and animals of all sorts, notably well suited to one
another, and gilt, together with the gutters, which jetting
without the walls, from betwixt the cross bars in a diagonal
figure, painted with gold and azure, reached to the very
ground, where they ended into great conduit pipes, which
carried all away unto the river from under the house.

This same building was a hundred times more sumptu-
ous and magnificent than ever was Bonnivet, Chambourg,
or Chantilly. For there were in it nine thousand, three
hundred, and two and thirty chambers; every one whereof
had a withdrawing room, a handsome closet, a wardrobe,
an oratory, and neat passage, leading into a great and spacious hall. Between every tower, in the midst of the said
body of building, there was a pair of winding stairs, whereof the steps were part of porphyry, part of Numidian stone,
and part of serpentine marble; each of those steps being
two and twenty feet in length, and three fingers thick, and
the just number of twelve betwixt every rest or landing-
place. In every resting-place were two fair antique arches,
where the light came in; and by those they went into a
cabinet closet), made even with, and of the breadth of the
said winding, and then reascending above the roofs of the
house ending conically in a pavillion. By that vize, or
winding, they entered on every side into a great hall, and
from the halls into the chambers. From the Arctic tower
unto the Criere, were the fair great libraries in Greek,
Latin, Hebrew, French, Italian, and Spanish, respectively
distributed in their several cantons, according to the di-

versity of these languages. In the midst there was a wonderful winding stair, the entry whereof was without the
house, in a vault or arch, six fathoms broad. It was made
in such symmetry and largeness that six men-at-arms, with
their lances in their rests, might together in a breast ride
all up to the very top of all the palace. From the tower
Anatole to the Mesembrine were spacious galleries, all
colored over and painted with the ancient prowesses, histories, and descriptions of the world. In the midst thereof
there was likewise such another ascent and gate, as we said
there was on the river side. Upon that gate was written,
in great antique letters, that which followeth.

THE INSCRIPTION SET UPON THE GREAT
GATE OF THELEME

Here enter not, religious boobies, sots,
Imposters, sniveling hypocrites, bigots;
Dark-brain distorted owls, worse than the Huns
Or Ostrogots, fore-runners of baboons;
Curs'd snakes, dissembling varlets, seeming sancts,
Slipshod caffards, beggars pretending wants;
Fomentors of divisions and debates,
Elsewhere, not here, make sale of your deceits.

   Your filthy trumperies,
   Stuff'd with pernicious lies.
    (Not worth a bubble)
    Would only trouble
   Our earthly Paradise.
   Your filthy trumperies.

Here enter not attorneys, barraters,
Nor bridle-champion-law practitioners;
Clerks, commissaries, scribes, nor pharisees,
Wilful disturbers of the people's ease,
Judges, destroyers, with an unjust breath,

That, like dogs, worry honest men to death.
We want not your demurrers, nor your pleas;
So at the gibbet go and seek your fees.
We are not for attendance or delays;
But would with ease and quiet pass our days.
   Law-suits, debates, and wrangling
   Hence are exil'd and jangling.
    Here we are very
    Frolic and merry,
   And free from all intangling
   Law-suits, debates, and wrangling.

Here enter not base pinching userers,
Pelf-lickers, everlasting gatherers;
Gold-graspers, coin-gripers, gulpers of mists,
With harpy-griping claws, who, tho' your chests
Vast sums of money should to you afford,
Would nevertheless be adding to the hoard:
And yet not be content; ye clutch-fist dastards,
Insatiable friends, and Pluto's bastards;
Greedy devourers, chichy, sneak-bill rogues;
Hell-mastiffs gnaw your bones, you rav'nous dogs.
   You beastly looking fellows,
   Reason doth plainly tell us,
    That we should not
    To you allot
   Room here, but at the gallows;
   You beastly looking fellows.

Here enter not, unsociable wight,
Humorsome churl, by day, nor yet by night.
No grumbling oaf, none of the sharping trade,
No huff-cap squire, or brother of the blade.
A tartar bred, or in Alsatia wars,
The ruffian comes not hither with his bears,
Elsewhere for shelter scour, ye bully-rocks.

And rogues, that rot with infamy and pox.
>Grace, honor, praise, delight,
>Here sojourn day and night,
>>Sound bodies, lin'd
>>With a good mind,
>Do here pursue with might
>Grace, honor, praise, delight.

Here enter you and welcome from our hearts,
All noble sparks, endow'd with gallant parts.
This is the glorious place which nobly shall
Afford sufficient to content you all;
Were you a thousand, here you shall not want
For anything; for what you ask, we grant.
The brave, the witty, here we entertain,
And, in a word, all worthy gentlemen,
>Men of heroic breasts
>Shall taste here of the feasts,
>>Both privily
>>And civilly
>All you are welcome guests,
>Men of heroic breasts.

Here enter you, pure, honest, faithful, true,
Expounders of the Scriptures, old and new;
Whose glosses do not the plain truth disguise,
And with false light distract or blind our eyes.
Here shall we find a safe and warm retreat,
When Error beats about and spreads her net.
Strange doctrines here must neither reap nor sow,
Just Faith and Charity together grow.
In short, confounded be their first device,
Who are the holy Scriptures' enemies.
>Here in the holy word
>Trust all, with one accord;
>>It will some help afford:

Tho' you be knight or lord,
You may find shield and sword,
Here in the holy word.

Here enter ladies all, of high degree,
Of goodly shape, of humor gay and free;
Of lovely looks, of sprightly flesh and blood:
Here take, here choose, here settle your abode.
The gent, the brisk, the fair, whoever comes,
With eyes that sparkle, or whose beauty blooms,
This bower is fashion'd by a gentle knight,
Ladies, for you, and innocent delight.

This is design'd a place
For every charming grace;
The witty and the fair
Hither may all repair;
For every lovely face
This is design'd a place.

WHAT MANNER OF DWELLING THE
THELEMITES HAD

In the middle of the lower court there was a stately fountain of fair alabaster; upon the top thereof stood the three Graces, with their cornucopias, and did jet out the water at their breasts, mouth, ears, eyes, and other open passages of the body. The inside of the buildings in this lower court, stood upon great pillars of cassydony stone, and porphyry marble, made arch-ways, after a goodly antique fashion: within those were spacious galleries, long and large, adorned with curious pictures, the horns of bucks and unicorns; with rhinoceroses, water-horses, called hippopotames; the teeth and tusks of elephants, and other things well worth the beholding. The lodging of the ladies took up all from the tower Arctic unto the gate Mesembrine. The men possessed the rest. Before the said lodging of

the ladies, that they might have their recreation between
the two first towers, on the outside were placed the tilt-
yard, the theatre and natatory, with most admirable baths
in three stages, situated above one another, well furnished
with all necessary accommodations and store of myrtle-
water. By the river side was a fine pleasure-garden, and in
the midst of that a labyrinth. Between the two towers
were the courts for tennis and the baloon. Towards the
tower Criere stood the orchard, full of all fruit-trees, set
and ranged in a quincuncial order. At the end of that was
the great park, abounding with all sorts of venison. Betwixt the third couple of towers were the butts and marks
for shooting with a snap-work gun, an ordinary bow for
common archers, or with a cross-bow. The office-houses
were without the tower of Hesperia, of one story high.
The stables were beyond the offices, and before them stood
the falconry, managed by ostridge-keepers and falconers,
very expert in the art. And it was yearly supplied and
furnished by the Candians, Venetians, and Sarmates with
all sorts of most excellent hawks, eagles, gerfalcons, gosse-
hawks, sacres, laniers, falcons, spar-hawks, marlins, and all
other kinds of them; so gentle and perfectly well manned,
that flying of themselves sometimes from the castle, for
their own disport, they would not fail to catch whatever
they encountered. The venery, where the beagles and
hounds were kept, was a little farther off drawing towards
the park.

All the halls, chambers, and closets, or cabinets, were
richly hung with tapestry, and hangings of divers sorts,
according to the variety of the seasons of the year. All
the pavements and floors were covered with green cloth;
the beds were all embroidered. In every back chamber or
withdrawing room, there was a looking-glass of pure crystal, set in a frame of fine gold, garnished all about with
pearls, and was of such greatness, that it would represent
to the full the whole lineaments and proportion of the per-

son that stood before it.   At the going out of the halls,
which belong to the ladies' lodgings, were the perfumers
and trimmers, through whose hands the gallants passed
when they were to visit the ladies.   These sweet artificers
did every morning furnish the ladies' chambers with the
spirit of roses, orange-flower water, and angelica; and to
each of them gave a little precious casket, vaporing forth
the most odoriferous exhalations of the choicest aromatical
scents.

HOW THE MEN AND WOMEN OF THE
RELIGIOUS ORDER OF THELEME
WERE APPARELLED

The ladies at the foundation of this order were apparelled after their own pleasure and liking; but since that, of
their own accord and free-will, they have reformed themselves; their accoutrements were in manner as followeth.
They wore stockings of scarlet crimson, or ingrained purple die, which reached just three inches above the knee,
having a list beautified with exquisite embroideries, and
rare incisions of the cutter's art; their garters were of the
color of their bracelets, and circled the knee a little, both
over and under: their shoes, pumps, and slippers, were
either of red, violet, or crimson velvet, pinked and jagged
like lobsters' wadles.

Next to their smock they put on the pretty kirtle or
vasquin of pure silk amblet; above that went the taffety
or tabby vardingale, of white, red, tawny, grey, or of any
other color: above this taffety petticoat they had another
of cloth, of tissue or brocade, embroidered with fine gold,
and interlaced with needle-work, or as they thought good,
and according to the temperature and disposition of the
weather, had their upper coats of satin, damask, or velvet,
and those either orange, tawny, green, ash-colored, blue,
yellow, bright, red, crimson, or white, and so forth; or had

them of cloth of gold, cloth of silver, or some other choice stuff, enriched with purple, or embroidered according to the dignity of the festival days and times wherein they wore them.

Their gowns, being still correspondent to the season, were either of cloth of gold, frizzled with a silver-raised work; of red satin, covered with gold purple; of tabby or taffety, white, blue, black, tawny, &c., of silk serge, silk amblet, velvet, cloth of silver, silver tissue, cloth of gold, gold wire, figured velvet, or figured satin, tinselled and overcast with golden threads, in divers variously purfled draughts.

In summer, some days, instead of gowns, they wore light handsome mantles, made either of the stuff of the aforesaid attire, or like Moresco rugs, of violet velvet frizzled, with a raised work of gold upon silver purl; or with a knotted cord work of gold embroidery, everywhere garnished with little Indian pearls. They always carried a fair pannache or plume of feathers of the color of their muff, bravely adorned and tricked out with glistering spangles of gold. In the winter time they had their taffety gowns, of all colors, as above-named: And those lined with the rich furrings of hind-wolves or speckled lynxes, black-spotted weasels, martlet-skins of Calabria, sables and other costly furs of inestimable value. Their beads, rings, bracelets, collars, carcanets, and neck chains, were all of precious stones, such as carbuncles, rubies, baleus, diamonds, sapphires, emeralds, tourquoises, garnets, agates, berilles, and excellent margarites. Their head-dressing also varied with the season of the year, according to which they decked themselves. In winter it was of the French fashion; in the spring of the Spanish; in summer of the fashion of Tuscany, except only upon the holidays and Sundays, at which time they were accoutered in the French mode, because they accounted it more honorable, and better befitting the garb of a matronal pudicity.

The men were apparelled after their fashion. Their
stockings were of tamine or of cloth serge, of white, black,
scarlet, or some other ingrained color. Their breeches
were of velvet, of the same color with their stockings, or
very near, embroidered and cut according to their fancy.
Their doublet was of cloth of gold, of cloth of silver, of
velvet, satin, damask, taffeties, &c., of the same colors,
cut, embroidered, and suitably trimmed up in perfection.
The points were of silk of the same colors; the tags were
of gold well enamelled. Their coats and jerkins were of
cloth of gold, cloth of silver, gold tissue, or velvet embroidered, as they saw fit. Their gowns were every whit as
costly as those of the ladies. Their girdles were of silk,
of the color of their doublets. Every one had a gallant
sword by his side, the hilt and handle whereof were gilt,
and the scabbard of velvet of the color of his breeches,
with a chape of gold, and pure goldsmith's work. The dagger was of the same. Their caps or bonnets were of black
velvet, adorned with jewels and buttons of gold; upon that
they wore a white plume, most prettily and minion-like
parted by so many rows of gold spangles, at the end whereof hung dangling in a more sparkling resplendency, fair
rubies, emeralds, diamonds, &c., but there was such a sym-
pathy betwixt the gallants and the ladies, that every day
they were apparelled in the same livery. And that they
might not miss, there were certain gentlemen appointed to
tell the youths every morning, what vestments the ladies
would on that day wear; for all was done according to the
pleasure of the ladies. In these so handsome cloaths and
habiliments so rich, think not that either one or the other
of either sex did waste any time at all; for the masters of
the wardrobes had all their raiments and apparels so ready
for every morning and the chamber ladies were so well
skilled, that in a trice they would be dressed, and completely in their clothes from head to foot. And to have
these accoutrements with the more conveniency, there was

about the wood of Theleme a row of houses of the extent of half a league, very neat and cleanly, wherein dwelt the goldsmiths, lapidaries, jewellers, embroiderers, taylors, gold-drawers, velvet-weavers, tapestry-makers, and upholsterers, who wrought there every one in his own trade, and all for the aforesaid jolly friars and nuns of the new stamp. They were furnished with matter and stuff from the hands of the Lord Nausiclete, who every year brought them seven ships from the Perlas and Cannibal islands, laden with ingots of gold, with raw silk, with pearls, and precious stones. And if any unions (pearls) began to grow old, and lose somewhat of their natural whiteness and lustre, those by their art did renew, by tendering them to eat to some pretty cocks, as they used to give casting unto hawks.

HOW THE THELEMITES WERE GOVERNED AND OF THEIR MANNER OF LIVING

All their life was spent not in laws, statutes, or rules, but according to their own free will and pleasure. They rose out of their beds when they thought good; they did eat, drink, labor, sleep, when they had a mind to it, and were disposed for it. None did awake them, none did offer to constrain them to eat, drink, nor do any other thing; for so had Gargantua established it. In all their rule and strictest tie of their order, there was but this one clause to be observed:

DO WHAT THOU WILT

Because men that are free, well-born, well-bred, and conversant in honest companies, have naturally an instinct and spur that prompteth them into virtuous actions, and withdraws them from vice, which is called honor. Those same men, when by base subjection and constraint they are brought under and kept down, turn aside from that noble disposition, by which they formerly were inclined to virtue, to shake off that bond of servitude, wherein they are so tyrannously enslaved; for it is agreeable to the nature of man to long after things forbidden, and to desire what is denied us. By this liberty they entered into a very laud-able emulation, to do all of them what they saw did please one. If any of the gallants or ladies should say, "Let us drink," they would all drink. If any one of them said, "Let us play," they all played. If one said, "Let us go a walking into the fields," they went all. If it were to go a hawking, or a hunting, the ladies mounted upon dainty well-paced nags, seated in a stately palfrey saddle, carried on their lovely fists miniardly begloved every one of them, either a sparhawk, or a laneret, or a marlin, and the young gallants carried the other kinds of hawks. So nobly were they taught, that there was neither he nor she amongst them, but could read, write, sing, play upon several musical instruments, speak five or six several languages, and com-pose in them all very quaintly, both in verse and prose. Never were seen so valiant knights, so noble and worthy, so dextrous and skilful both on foot and horseback, more brisk and lively, more nimble and quick, or better handling all manner of weapons, than were there. Never were seen ladies so proper and handsome, so miniard and dainty, less froward, or more ready with their hand, and with their needle, in every honest and free action belonging to that sex, than were there. For this reason, when the time came that any man of the said abbey, either at the request of his parents or for some other cause, had a mind to go out of it, he carried along with him one of the ladies, namely, her whom he had before that chosen for his mistress, and they were married together. And if they had formerly in Theléme lived in good devotion and amity, they did con-tinue therein, and increase it to a greater height in their state of matrimony; and did entertain that mutual love till the very last day of their life, in no less vigor and fervency than at the very day of their wedding . . . .

OF THE CANNIBALS

by

MICHEL DE MONTAIGNE

and

GONZALO'S SPEECH

from

THE TEMPEST

by

WILLIAM SHAKESPEARE

ADDITIONAL BIBLIOGRAPHY

Frame, D.M. *Montaigne's Discovery of Man,* New York, 1955

Sayce, Richard A., *The Essays of Montaigne: A Critical Exploration,* Evanston, Ill., 1972

Tannenbaum, S.A. *Michel Eyquem de Montaigne: A Concise Bibliography,* New York, 1942

Taylor, George Coffin, *Shakespeare's Debt to Montaigne,* Cambridge, Mass., 1925

Tetel, Marcel, *Montaigne,* New York, 1974

MICHEL DE MONTAIGNE
AND WILLIAM SHAKESPEARE

Michel de Montaigne (1533-1592), the first and foremost essayist in all literature, was born at Eyquem near Perigord in the same year that saw the death of Erasmus and the birth of Pantagruel. Montaigne's father had made a sufficient fortunte from trade to give his son a sound education. After a thorough tutoring in Latin, which made it a more familiar tongue than his native French, he studied classics at Bordeaux and law at Toulouse. Much of his life was occupied with public duties, as counsellor at Bordeaux, as a soldier under Francis I, and as a courtier. However, shortly after 1571 he was able to retire and devote himself to his beloved books. His favorites, as he tells us, were Plutarch and Seneca, the two ancients who came closest to discovering the personal essay. That discovery, however, was reserved for him.

Although Montaigne published other books, among them the translation of the *Theologia naturalis* of Raymond de Sabunde (1569), a rationalistic treatise which greatly deepened his own skepticism, and an edition of the works of his deceased humanist friend, Etienne de la Boetie, he lives in literature entirely through the ninety-three rambling discourses which established the familiar essay as a literary genre and which still remain unsurpassed. The first two books of *Essais* appeared in 1580; the third, together with revisions of the previous books, followed in 1588. The keynote of these agnostic essays is struck in Montaigne's famous phrase, "Que scay je," and in the skeptical remark: "I determine nothing; I do not comprehend things; I suspend judgment; I examine." One among these delightful discourses, that entitled *Des Cannibals*, skeptically examines the pretensions of his own civilization by comparing it to that of the South American native. His own he finds, as he says elsewhere,

based upon a "commonly accepted state of morality so un-
natural, especially as regards inhumanity and treachery,
which are to me the worst of all sins, that I have not the
heart to think of them without horror." The primitive society
of the Brazilians he finds so "natural" that it surpasses his
own in many points. This primitivistic concept, that pre-
civilized man is possessed of natural virtues which civilization has obscured, perverted, or destroyed, was to play a
large part in subsequent thought. Montaigne treats the concept in his usual loose and casual style, but from his discussion emerges a utopian way of life quite different from that
of More, Rabelais, Campanella, Bacon, Andreae, and other
Renaisssance writers.

Shakespeare, who became acquainted with Montaigne's
essays in the contemporary translation by Florio, borrowed
both the idea and, in some places, the language itself, for
the celebrated speech of Gonzalo in *The Tempest*. Shakespeare treats lightly and satirically what Montaigne evidently
considered a serious and significant contrast between natural
man and debased civilized man, but the essential idea remains
the same.

Books about Montaigne are legion. The student may
profitably consult Edward Dowden's *Montaigne* (1905), the
interesting volume by Marvin Lowenthal, *The Autobiogra-
phy of Michel de Montaigne* (1935), and the recent critical
selection by André Gide (1939). Emerson's appreciative
essay, included in *Representative Men* (1850) is well worth
reading, and Walter Pater's novel, *Gaston de Latour* (1896),
contains an interesting reconstruction of the period together
with a literary portrait of Montaigne. For Shakespeare's in-
debtedness, both to the *Essais* in general and to *Des Cannibals* in particular, J. M. Robertson's, *Montaigne and Shakespeare* (1897), is a standard work. Montaigne has frequently
been translated; the most famous version is that of Florio
(1603), which was used by Shakespeare, and which appears
here with some changes and with the omission of some irrele-
vant material.

OF THE CANNIBALS

I HAD living with me for a long time a man who had
lived for ten or twelve years in that other world
which was discovered in our century, in that place where
Villegaignon landed,[1] which he called Antarctic France.
This discovery of an unbounded country seems to me
worthy of consideration . . . This man I had was a simple
and ignorant fellow; hence the more fit to give true
evidence; for your sophisticated men are more curious
observers, and take in more things but they gloss them;
to lend weight to their interpretations and induce your
belief, they cannot help altering their story a little . . . .
From what I have heard of that nation, I can see nothing
barbarous or uncivilized about it, except that we all call
barbarism that which does not fit in with our usages. And
indeed we have no other level of truth and reason but the
example and model of the opinions and usages of the
country we live in. There we always see the perfect religion, the perfect government, the perfect and accomplished
manner of doing all things. Those people are wild in the
sense in which we call wild the fruits that Nature has
produced by herself and in her ordinary progress; whereas
in truth it is those we have altered artificially and diverted
from the common order, that we should rather call wild.
In the first we still see, in full life and vigor, the genuine
and most natural and useful virtues and properties, which
we have bastardized in the latter, and only adapted to

---

[1] In Brazil, in 1557.

please our corrupt taste. And yet in some of the uncultivated fruits of those countries there is a delicacy of flavor
that is excellent even to our taste, and rivals even our own.
It is not reasonable that art should gain the point of honor
over our great and powerful mother Nature. We have so
overburdened the beauty and richness of her works with
our inventions, that we have quite smothered her. And
yet, wherever she shines in her purity, she marvellously
puts to shame our vain and trivial efforts,

> Uncared, unmarked the ivy blossoms best;
> Midst desert rocks the ilex clusters still;
> And sweet the wild bird's untaught melody.
>
> —Propertius

Those nations, then, appear to me so far barbarous in
this sense, that their minds have been formed to a very
slight degree, and that they are still very close to their
original simplicity. They are still ruled by the laws of
Nature, and very little corrupted by ours; but they are still
in such a state of purity, that I am sometimes vexed that
they were not known earlier, at a time when there were
men who could have appreciated them better than we do.

I am sorry that Lycurgus and Plato had no knowledge
of them, for it seems to me that what we have learned by
contact with those nations surpasses not only all the beautiful colors in which the poets have depicted the golden
age, and all their ingenuity in inventing a happy state of
man, but also the conceptions and desires of Philosophy
herself. They were incapable of imagining so pure and
native a simplicity, as that which we see by experience;
nor could they have believed that human society could have
been maintained with so little human artifice and solder.
This is a nation, I should say to Plato, which has no
manner of traffic; no knowledge of letters; no science of
numbers; no name of magistrate or statesman; no use for
slaves; neither wealth nor poverty; no contracts; no suc-

cessions; no partitions; no occupation but that of idleness; only a general respect of parents; no clothing; no agricul' ture; no metals; no use of wine or corn. The very words denoting falsehood, treachery, dissimulation, avarice, envy, detraction, pardon, unheard of.[2] How far removed from this perfection would he find the ideal republic he imagined! *Men newly come from the hands of the gods.* (Seneca).

These manners first by nature taught. (Virgil.)

For the rest, they live in a region with a very agreeable and very temperate climate, so that, according to my wit' nesses, a sick man is rarely seen; and they assured me that they had never seen any man shaking with palsy, or with dripping eyes, toothless, or bent with age. They are settled along the sea-coast, and closed in on the land side by large and high mountains, the land between them and the sea extending for a hundred leagues or thereabouts. They have great abundance of fish and flesh, which bear no resemblance to ours, and they eat them roasted without any other preparation. The first man who brought a horse thither, although he had associated with them on several previous voyages, so horrified them in the riding posture, that they shot him dead with arrows before recognizing him.

Their buildings are very long, capable of holding two or three hundred souls, covered with the bark of tall trees, the strips resting by one end on the ground, and leaning to and supporting one another at the top, after the man' ner of some of our barns, the coverings of which slope down to the ground and serve as side-walls. They have a wood so hard that they can cut with it, of which they make their swords and gridirons to roast their meat. Their

---

[2] This is the passage which Shakespeare, through Florio's translation, reproduced almost word for word in *The Tempest,* Act II, sc. 1.

beds are made of cotton tissue, suspended from the roof
like those in our ships, each one having his own: for the
women sleep apart from their husbands.

They rise with the sun and eat immediately after rising,
for the whole day: for they have no other meal. They
drink nothing with that meal, like some other Eastern peo-
ples of whom Suidas tells us, who drank apart from eating;
but they drink several times a day, and to excess. Their
drink is made of some root, and is of the color of our
claret wines, and they only drink it warm. This beverage
will keep only two or three days; it has a slightly pungent
taste, is anything but heady, good for the stomach, and
laxative for such as are not used to it, but a very pleasant
drink for those who are. For bread they use a certain
white material resembling preserved coriander. I have tried
some of it: it is sweet but rather tasteless.

The whole day is spent in dancing. The younger men
hunt animals with bows. Some of the women meanwhile
spend their time warming their drink, which is their chief
duty. One of the old men, in the morning before they
begin to eat, preaches to the whole barnfull of people in
common, walking from one end to the other, repeating the
same words several times, until he has finished the round
(for the buildings are quite a hundred paces in length).
He recommends only two things, valor against the enemy
and love to their wives. And they never fail to stress this
obligation, which forms their refrain, 'that it is they who
keep their wine warm and seasoned.'

In several places, among others in my house, may be
seen the formation of their beds, of their ropes, their
wooden swords and bracelets, with which they cover their
wrists in battle, and large canes open at one end, by the
sound of which they keep the time and rhythm of their
dances. The are close shaven all over, and remove their
hair much more neatly than we do, although their razors
are only made of wood or stone. They believe the soul to

be immortal, and that those who have deserved well of the gods are lodged in that part of the heaven where the sun rises, and those who are damned in the west.

They have some kind of priest and prophet, who very seldom appears among the people, having his dwelling in the mountains. On his arrival there is a great feast and a solemn assemble of several villages (each barn, as I have described it, forms a village, and they are about a French league distant one from the other). This prophet speaks to them in public, exhorting them to virtue and their duty; but their whole ethical science comprises only these two articles: an unfaltering courage in war and affection to their women. This man foretells things to come, and the issue they are to expect from their enterprises; urges them to war, or holds them back; but he does so on the under-standing that, where he fails to prophesy correctly, and if things turn out otherwise than he has predicted, he is cut into a thousand pieces if he is caught, and condemned for a false prophet. For that reason he who has once mis-calculated is seen no more.

Divination is a gift of God, wherefore to abuse it ought to be regarded as a punishable imposture. Among the Scythians, when the prophets fail to hit the mark, they are laid, shackled hand and foot, on a little cart filled with heather and drawn by oxen, on which they were burned. They who take in hand such matters as depend on the conduct of human capacity are to be excused if they do their best. But those others who come and delude us with assurances of an extraordinary faculty that is beyond our ken, should they not be punished when they fail to carry out what they promise, and for the temerity of their im-posture?

They have their wars with the nations beyond their mountains, further back on the mainland, to which they go quite naked, with no other weapons but bows or wooden swords pointed at one end, after the fashion of the tongues

of our boar-spears. It is marvellous with what obstinacy they
fight their battles, which never end but in massacre and
bloodshed: for of routs and terrors they know not even
the meaning. Each man brings back as a trophy the head
of the enemy he has slain, and fixes it over the entrance to
his dwelling. After treating his prisoner well for a considerable time, and giving him all that hospitality can devise,
his captor convokes a great gathering of his acquaintance.
He ties a cord to one of his prisoner's arms, holding him
at some distance for fear of being hurt, and gives the other
arm to be held in the same way by his best friend; and
these two, in the presence of the whole assembly, dispatch
him with their swords. This done, they roast and eat him
in common, and send bits of him to their absent friends.
Not, as one might suppose, for nourishment, as the ancient
Scythians used to do, but to signify an extreme revenge.

And that it is so, may be seen from this: having perceived that the Portuguese, who had allied themselves with
their adversaries, inflicted a different kind of death on their
prisoners, which was to bury them up to the waist, shoot
the upper part of the bodies full of arrows, and afterwards
to hang them; they imagined that these people of another
world (seeing that they had sown the knowledge of a great
many vices among their neighbors, and were much greater
masters than themselves in every kind of wickedness) had
some reason for adopting this kind of vengeance, and that
it must be more painful than their own; wherefore they
began to give up their old method, and followed this one.

I am not so much concerned that we should remark on
the horrible barbarity of such acts, as that, whilst rightly
judging their errors, we should be so blind to our own. I
think there is more barbarity in eating a live than a dead
man, in tearing on the rack and torturing the body of a
man still full of feeling, in roasting him piecemeal and giving him to be bitten and mangled by dogs and swine (as
we have not only read, but seen within fresh memory, not

between old enemies, but between neighbors and fellow citizens, and, what is worse, under the cloak of piety and religion), than in roasting and eating him after he is dead . . . . We may therefore well call these people barbarians in respect to the rules of reason, but not in respect to ourselves, who surpass them in every kind of barbarity.

Their warfare is entirely noble and generous, and is as fair and excusable as can be expected in that human disease: their only motive being a zeal for valor. They do not strive to conquer new territory, for they still enjoy that luxuriance of nature which provides them, without labor and pains, with all necessary things in such abundance, that they have no need to enlarge their borders. They are still in that happy state of not desiring more than their natural needs demand: all that is over and above it is for them superfluity.

They generally call each other, if of the same age, brothers; if younger, children; and the old men are fathers to all the others. These latter leave to their heirs in common the full and undivided possession of their property without any but that pure title that Nature gives to her creatures, by bringing them into the world. If their neighbors cross the mountain to attack them, and gain the victory over them, the acquisition of the victor is the glory and advantage of having proved himself the superior in valor and virtue, for otherwise they have no needs for the spoils of the vanquished; and so they return to their own country, where they have no want of any necessaries, nor even of that great portion, which is to know how to enjoy happily their condition, and be content with it. These do the same in their turn. They ask of their prisoners no other reason but a confession and acknowledgment of being vanquished. But you will not find one in a whole century who would not rather die than yield, either by word or look, one tittle of an invincible greatness of courage; not one who would not rather be killed and eaten than even pray to be spared. They are very liberal in their treatment of their prisoners, in order to make life the more dear to them, and usually entertain them with threats of their impending death, the torments they will suffer, the preparations made to that end, the cutting up of their limbs, and the banquet that will be made at their expense. All this is done with the sole purpose of extorting from them a weak or spiritless word, or to give them a desire to escape, in order to gain the advantage of having terrified them and shaken their firmness. For indeed; if rightly taken, therein alone lies the real victory:

> The victor's wreath no triumphs more attest
> Than when the foe's subjection is confest.
> —Claudian

. . . . To return to our narrative. Far from giving in, in spite of all they suffer, these prisoners, on the contrary, during the two or three months that they are held in captivity, bear a cheerful countenance; they urge their captors to hasten to put them to the proof, defy them, insult them, reproach them with their cowardice and the number of battles lost against their own countrymen.

I have a song composed by a prisoner, which contains this outburst: 'Come boldly, every one of you, and assemble together to dine off me, for you shall at the same time eat your fathers and grandfathers, whose flesh has served to feed and nourish this body. These muscles, this flesh and these veins are yours, poor fools that you are: can you not see that they still contain the substance of your ancestors' limbs? Relish them well, you will find that they have the flavor of your own flesh.' A fiction that by no means savors of barbarity. On the pictures which represent these prisoners being executed or at the point of death, they are seen spitting in the face of their slayers or making mouths at them. Indeed they never cease to challenge and defy them by word and look until the breath is out of their body. Verily here we see men who are indeed savages if we compare them with ourselves: for either they must be so in good sooth, or we; there is a wonderful distance between their character and ours.

The men there have several wives, and the higher their reputation for valor the greater is the number of their wives. It is a remarkably beautiful feature in their marriages, that the same jealousy that our wives have to keep us from the love and favors of other women, they have to an equal degree to procure it. Being more solicitous for their husbands' honor than for anything else, they use their best endeavors to have as many companions as they can, seeing that that is a proof of their husband's worth . . . .

And, that it may not be supposed that all this is done through a simple and slavish obligation to follow usage, and under the weight of authority of their ancient customs, without reasoning or judgment, and because their minds are too dull to imagine any other, I must give a few proofs of their intellectual capacity. Besides the warlike song I have just cited I have another, of an amorous nature, which begins thus: 'Adder, stay; stay, adder, that thy colors may serve as a pattern for my sister to work a rich girdle to give to my love: thus shall thy beauty and the dispositions of thy spots be preferred for all time to all other serpents.' This first verse is the burden of the song. Now, I have enough knowledge of poetry to judge this much: that not only is there nothing barbarous in this idea, but that it is altogether Anacreontic. Their language, by the way, is a soft language, with an agreeable tone, and their terminations resemble the Greek.

Three men of this nation, not knowing how dear, in tranquillity and happiness, it will one day cost them to know the corruptions of this side of the world, and that this intercourse will be the cause of their ruin, which indeed I imagine is already advanced (poor wretches, to be allured by the desire to see new things and to leave their own

serene sky to come and see ours!), were at Rouen at a time
when the late King Charles the Ninth was there. The
King had a long talk with them. They were shown our
ways, our pomp, the form of a fine city. After that some-
body asked their opinion, desiring to know what they most
wondered at. They mentioned three things, the third of
which I am sorry to have forgotten, but I still remember
two. They said that in the first place they thought it very
strange that so many big men with beards, strong and
armed, who were about the King (they were probably
thinking of the Swiss who formed his guard) should submit to obey a child, and that they did not rather choose
one of their own number to command them. Secondly
(they have a way of speaking of men as if they were halves
of one another), that they had observed that there were
men amongst us, full and gorged with all kinds of good
things, and that their halves were begging at their doors,
emaciated with hunger and poverty; and they thought it
strange how these necessitous halves could suffer such injustice, and that they did not seize the others by the throat,
or set fire to their houses.

I had a long talk with one of them; but I had an inter-
preter who followed my meaning so badly, and was at such
a loss, in his stupidity, to take in my ideas, that I could get
little satisfaction out of him. When I asked the native,
'What he gained from his superior position among his people?' (for he was a captain, and our sailors called him a
king), he said it was 'to march foremost in war'. How
many men did he lead? He pointed to a piece of ground,
to signify as many as that space could hold: it might be
four or five thousand men. Did all his authority lapse
with the war? He said 'that this remained, that when he
visited the villages that were dependent on him, they made
paths through their thickets, by which he might pass at
his ease.' All this does not sound too ill; but hold! they
don't wear trousers.

THE TEMPEST

Gonzalo: Had I plantation of this isle, my lord,—
Antonio: He'd sow't with nettle-seed.
Sebastian: or docks, or mallows
Gonzalo: And were the king on't, what would I do?

Sebastian: Scape being drunk, for want of wine.
Gonzalo: I' the commonwealth I would by contraries
Execute all things; for no kind of traffic
Would I admit; no name of magistrate;
Letters should not be known; riches, poverty,
And use of service, none; contract, succession,
Bourn, bound of land, tilth, vineyard, none;
No use of metal, corn, or wine, or oil;
No occupation; all men idle, all;
And women too, but innocent and pure;
No sovereignty;—
Sebastian: Yet he would be king on't.
Antonio: The latter end of his commonwealth forgets the
    beginning.
Gonzalo: All things in common nature should produce
Without sweat or endeavour; treason, felony,
Sword, pike, knife, gun, or need of any engine,
Would I not have; but nature should bring forth,
Of its own kind, all foison, all abundance,
To feed my innocent people.
Sebastian: No marrying 'mong his subjects?
Antonio: None, man; all idle; whores and knaves.

151

Gonzalo: I would with such perfection govern, sir,
To excel the golden age.

Sebastian: Save his majesty!

Antonio: Long live Gonzalo!

F. THOMÆ CAMPANELLÆ
Appendix Politica

CIVITAS
SOLIS

IDEA
REIPVBLICÆ PHILO-
SOPHICÆ.

FRANCOFVRTI

Typis Egenolphi Emmelii, Impensis vero Godofredi
Tambachii, Anno Salutis

M. DC. XXIII.

ADDITIONAL BIBLIOGRAPHY

Block, G., *Thomas Campanella: politisches Interesse und philosophische Spekulation,* Tubingen, 1979

Corsano, A., *Tommaso Campanella,* Bari, 1961

Firpo, L., *Ricerche campanelliane,* Florence, 1947

and in English:

Berneri, Marie L., *Journey Through Utopia,* New York, 1971

Negley, Glenn Robert, and J. Max Patrick, eds., *The Quest for Utopia,* New York, 1952

Wilkins, Ernest H., *A History of Italian Literature,* Cambridge, Mass., 1954

Overleaf: Title page of first edition of Campanella's "Civitas Solis", Frankfurt, 1623

TOMMASO CAMPANELLA

Giovanni Domenico Campanella (1568-1639), an Italian contemporary of Bacon and Galileo, was born at Stilo in Calabria. By thirteen he had read most of the Latin authors in the original; at fifteen he entered the Dominican order, under the name Fra Tommaso, and pursued his education in science and philosophy at Telesio's school in Morgentia, and in theology at Cosenza. He quickly became distin-guished for his rationalistic interest in science, for his liberal opposition to authoritarianism, and for his distrust of the Spanish rule in southern Italy. "I was born," he said, "to combat three great evils, tyranny, sophistry, and hypocrisy." Characteristically, he selected for his motto the words *numquam tacebo,* and this unwillingness to keep silence, to-gether with his non-conformist ideas, soon led him into difficulty with the Spanish regime. He was imprisoned in 1598, spending the next twenty-eight years of his life in con-finement and, occasionally, under torture. During these years he composed many of his writings, thus joining that select rank of imprisoned authors which includes Boethius, Raleigh, Cervantes, Bunyan, and his compatriot, Pellico. Ultimately released from prison at the age of fifty-eight, he fled in disguise to Paris, where his last years, spent in editing his many works, were somewhat eased by the patronage of Richelieu and a pension from the king. There he died in 1639, not the least conspicuous of that long line of Renais-sance thinkers which numbers among it Nicholas of Cusa, Tycho Brahe, Bruno, Galileo, and his master, Bernardino Telesio.

Few of Campenella's eighty-eight works are now read, but some of the titles suggest his interests and preoccupa-tions. Thus, the *De Monarchio Hispanica* (1602) attacks

political tyranny; his *De sensu rerum* (1620) defends the
new physiological science of his day; and the *Apologia pro
Galileo* (1622) reveals his devotion to the great Italian scientist. His best known work, the *Civitas Solis, idea reipublicae
Platonicae,* was published at Frankfort in 1623. Although
greatly indebted to Plato and to the medieval monastic ideal,
it also reveals quite clearly the growing admiration for science. Like Bacon, Campanella rejected Aristotelian, or
medieval, philosophy as mere logomachy, and sought to base
metaphysical concepts upon the data of the natural sciences.
His temple of learning, for instance, is a huge natural history
museum, filled with pictures of all things in heaven and
earth arranged according to scientific classifications. From
these specimens the children in his utopia quickly learn the
rudiments of astronomy, geography, biology, anatomy, etc.
Language study, the very center of Renaissance education,
Campanella dismisses as mere memorization; the humane letters which Petrarch, Erasmus, and More had so ardently
defended, Campanella practically ignores; but natural science, in all its aspects, he eulogizes as the source and authority for all philosophy. Thus Hoh, his Platonic guardian,
must be versed in all the several sciences. This essentially
modern attitude toward education, with its stress upon the
use of visual aids, antedated the *Orbis Pictus* of Comenius
by a quarter century. Campanella's ideas may profitably be
compared with those of his great co-eval, Bacon, who may
possibly have seen his book.

Although there are few studies of Campanella in English, the student may consult E. G. Gardner, *Tommaso Cam-
panello and His Poetry* (1923), as well as the pertinent
chapters in Symond's *History of the Renaissance in Italy*
(1876), who also translated much of the poetry in *The Son-
nets of Michel Angelo Buonarotti and Tommaso Campanella*
(1878). The *De Monarchio Hispanica* was twice translated in the seventeenth century, by Edmund Chilmead
(1654), and again by William Prynne (1660), and the illum-

inating *Defense of Galileo* has recently been made available by Grant McColley (1937). For those who read French, L. Blanchet, *Campenella* (1920) is a useful work; and any of the standard histories of science supplies a good introduction to Campanella's importance in this field. Unfortunately, no annotated edition of the *Civitas Solis* exists, and the sole translation, here reproduced, is the somewhat abbreviatd version of T. W. Halliday.

THE CITY OF THE SUN

A Poetical Dialogue between a Grandmaster of the Knights Hospitallers and a Genoese Sea-captain, his guest.

Grandmaster. Prithee, now, tell me what happened to you during that voyage?

Captain. I have already told you how I wandered over the whole earth. In the course of my journeying I came to Taprobane, and was compelled to go ashore at a place, where through fear of the inhabitants I remained in a wood. When I stepped out of this I found myself on a large plain immediately under the equator.

Grand. And what befell you here?

Capt. I came upon a large crowd of men and armed women, many of whom did not understand our language, and they conducted me forthwith to the City of the Sun.

Grand. Tell me after what plan this city is built and how it is governed?

Capt. The greater part of the city is built upon a high hill, which rises from an extensive plain, but several of its circles extend for some distance beyond the base of the hill, which is of such size that the diameter of the city is upwards of two miles, so that its circumference becomes about seven. On account of the humped shape of the mountain, however, the diameter of the city is really more than if it were built on a plain.

It is divided into seven rings or huge circles named from the seven planets, and the way from one to the other of these is by four streets and through four gates, that look towards the four points of the compass. Furthermore, it is so built that if the first circle were stormed, it would of necessity entail a double amount of energy to storm the second; still more to storm the third; and in each succeeding case the strength and energy would have to be doubled; so that he who wishes to capture that city must, as it were, storm it seven times. For my own part, however, I think that not even the first wall could be occupied, so thick are the earthworks and so well fortified is it with breastworks, towers, guns and ditches.

When I had been taken through the northern gate (which is shut with an iron door so wrought that it can be raised and let down, and locked in easily and strongly, its projections running into the grooves of the thick posts by a marvellous device), I saw a level space seventy paces wide between the first and second walls. From hence can be seen large palaces all joined to the wall of the second circuit, in such a manner as to appear all one palace. Arches run on a level with the middle height of the palaces, and are continued around the whole ring. There are galleries for promenading upon these arches, which are supported from beneath by thick and well-shaped columns, enclosing arcades like peristyles, or cloisters of an abbey.

But the palaces have no entrances from below, except on the inner or concave partition, from which one enters directly to the lower parts of the building. The higher parts, however, are reached by flights of marble steps, which lead to galleries for promenading on the inside similar to those on the outside. From these one enters the higher rooms, which are very beautiful, and have windows on the concave and convex partitions. These rooms are divided from one another by richly decorated walls. The convex or outer wall of the ring is about eight spans thick; the concave, three; the intermediate walls are one, or perhaps one and a half. Leaving this circle one gets to the second plain, which is nearly three paces narrower than the first. Then the first wall of the second ring is seen adorned above and below with similar galleries for walking, and

there is on the inside of it another interior wall enclosing
palaces. It has also similar peristyles supported by columns
in the lower part, but above are excellent pictures, round
the ways into the upper houses. And so on afterwards
through similar spaces and double walls, enclosing palaces,
and adorned with galleries for walking, extending along
their outer side, and supported by columns, till the last circuit is reached, the way being still over a level plain.

But when the two gates, that is to say, those of the out-
most and the inmost walls, have been passed, one mounts
by means of steps so formed that an ascent is scarcely
discernible, since it proceeds in a slanting direction, and the
steps succeed one another at almost imperceptible heights.
On the top of the hill is a rather spacious plain, and in the
midst of this there rises a temple built with wondrous art.

Grand. Tell on, I pray you! Tell on! I am dying to
hear more.

Capt. The temple is built in the form of a circle; it is not
girt with walls, but stands upon thick columns, beautifully
grouped. A very large dome, built with great care in the
centre or pole, contains another small vault as it were rising
out of it, and in this is a spiracle, which is right over the
altar. There is but one altar in the middle of the temple,
and this is hedged round by columns. The temple itself is
on a space of more than three hundred and fifty paces.
Without it, arches measuring about eight paces extend
from the heads of these columns outwards, whence other
columns rise about three paces from the thick, strong and
erect wall. Between these and the former columns there
are galleries for walking, with beautiful pavements, and
in the recess of the wall, which is adorned with numerous
large doors, there are immovable seats, placed as it were
between the inside columns, supporting the temple. Port-
able chairs are not wanting, many and well adorned. Nothing is seen over the altar but a large globe, upon which
the heavenly bodies are painted, and another globe upon

which there is a representation of the earth. Furthermore, in the vault of the dome there can be discerned representations of all the stars of heaven from the first to the sixth magnitude, with their proper names and power to influence terrestrial things marked in three little verses for each. There are the poles and greater and lesser circles according to the right latitude of the place, but these are not perfect because there is no wall below. They seem, too, to be made in their relation to the globes on the altar. The pavement of the temple is bright with precious stones. Its seven golden lamps hang always burning, and these bear the names of the seven planets.

At the top of the building several small and beautiful cells surround the small dome, and behind the level space above the bands or arches of the exterior and interior columns there are many cells, both small and large, where the priests and religious officers dwell to the number of forty-nine.

A revolving flag projects from the smaller dome, and this shows in what quarter the wind is. The flag is marked with figures up to thirty-six, and the priests know what sort of year the different kinds of winds bring and what will be the changes of weather on land and sea. Furthermore, under the flag a book is always kept written with letters of gold.

Grand. I pray you, worthy hero, explain to me their whole system of government; for I am anxious to hear it.

Capt. The great rule among them is a priest whom they call by the name HOH, though we should call him Metaphysic. He is head over all, in temporal and spiritual matters, and all business and lawsuits are settled by him, as the supreme authority. Three princes of equal power— viz., Pon, Sin and Mor—assist him, and these in our tongue we should call POWER, WISDOM and LOVE. To POWER belongs the care of all matters relating to war and peace. He attends to the military arts, and, next to HOH, he is ruler in every affair of a warlike nature. He governs

the military magistrates and the soldiers, and has the man-
agement of the munitions, the fortifications, the storming
of places, the implements of war, the armories, the smiths
and workmen connected with matters of this sort.

But WISDOM is the ruler of the liberal arts, of mechanics, of all sciences with their magistrates and doctors, and
of the discipline of the schools. As many doctors as there
are, are under his control. There is one doctor who is
called Astrologus; a second, Cosmographus; a third, Arith-
meticus; a fourth, Geometra; a fifth, Historiographus; a
sixth, Poeta; a seventh, Logicus; an eighth, Rhetor; a ninth,
Grammaticus; a tenth, Medicus; an eleventh, Physiologus;
a twelfth, Politicus a thirteenth, Moralis. They have but
one book, which they call Wisdom, and in it all the sciences are written with conciseness and marvellous fluency
of expression. This they read to the people after the custom of the Pythagoreans. It is Wisdom who causes the
exterior and interior, the higher and lower walls of the
city to be adorned with the finest pictures, and to have all
the sciences painted upon them in an admirable manner.
On the walls of the temple and on the dome, which is
let down when the priest gives an address, lest the sounds
of his voice, being scattered, should fly away from his
audience, there are pictures of stars in their different magnitudes, with the powers and motions of each, expressed
separately in three little verses.

On the interior wall of the first circuit all the mathemat-
ical figures are conspicuously painted—figures more in number than Archimedes or Euclid discovered, marked sym-
metrically, and with the explanation of them neatly written
and contained each in a little verse. There are definitions
and propositions, etc. On the exterior convex wall is first
an immense drawing of the whole earth, given at one view.
Following upon this, there are tablets setting forth for
every separate country the customs both public and private, the laws, the origins and the power of the inhabit-

ants; and the alphabets the different people use can be seen above that of the City of the Sun.

On the inside of the second circuit, that is to say of the second ring of buildings, paintings of all kinds of precious and common stones, of minerals and metals, are seen; and a little piece of the metal itself is also there with an apposite explanation in two small verses for each metal or stone. On the outside are marked all the seas, rivers, lakes and streams which are on the face of the earth; as are also the wines and the oils and the different liquids, with the sources from which the last are extracted, their qualities and strength. There are also vessels built into the wall above the arches, and these are full of liquids from one to three hundred years old, which cure all diseases. Hail and snow, storms and thunder, and whatever else takes place in the air, are represented with suitable figures and little verses. The inhabitants even have the art of representing in stone all the phenomena of the air, such as the wind, rain, thunder, the rainbow, etc.

On the interior of the third circuit all the different families of trees and herbs are depicted, and there is a live specimen of each plant in earthenware vessels placed under the outer partition of the arches. With the specimens there are explanations as to where they were first found, what are their powers and natures, and resemblances to celestial things and to metals: to parts of the human body and to things in the sea, and also as to their uses in medicine, etc. On the exterior wall are all the races of fish, found in rivers, lakes and seas, and their habits and values, and ways of breeding, training and living, the purposes for which they exist in the world, and their uses to man. Further, their resemblances to celestial and terrestrial things, produced both by nature and art, are so given that I was astonished when I saw a fish which was like a bishop, one like a chain, another like a garment, a fourth like a nail, a fifth like a star, and others like images of those things existing among us, the relation in each case being completely manifest. There are sea-urchins to be seen, and the purple shell-fish and mussels; and whatever the watery world possesses worthy of being known is there fully shown in marvellous characters of painting and drawing.

On the fourth interior wall all the different kinds of birds are painted, with their natures, sizes, customs, colors, manner of living, etc.; and the only real phoenix is possessed by the inhabitants of this city. On the exterior are shown all the races of creeping animals, serpents, dragons and worms; the insects, the flies, gnats, beetles, etc., in their different states, strength, venoms and uses and a great deal more than you or I can think of.

On the fifth interior they have all the larger animals of the earth, as many in number as would astonish you. We indeed know not the thousandth part of them, for on the exterior wall also a great many of immense size are also portrayed. To be sure, of horses alone, how great a number of breeds there is and how beautiful are the forms there cleverly displayed!

On the sixth interior are painted all the mechanical arts, with the several instruments for each and their manner of use among different nations. Alongside the dignity of such is placed, and their several inventors are named. But on the exterior all the inventors in science, in warfare, and in law are represented. There I saw Moses, Osiris, Jupiter, Mercury, Lycurgus, Pompilius, Pythagoras, Zamolxis, Solon, Charondas, Phoroneus, with very many others. They even have Mahomet whom nevertheless they hate as a false and sordid legislator. In the most dignified position I saw a representation of Jesus Christ and of the twelve Apostles, whom they consider very worthy and hold to be great. Of the representations of men, I perceived Caesar, Alexander, Pyrrhus and Hannibal in the highest place; and other very renowned heroes in peace and war, especially Roman heroes, were painted in lower positions, under the galleries. And when I asked with astonishment whence they had obtained our history, they told me that among them there was a knowledge of all languages, and that by perseverance they continually send explorers and ambassadors over the whole earth, who learn thoroughly the customs, forces, rule and histories of the nations, bad and good alike. These they apply all to their own republic, and with this they are well pleased. I learnt that cannon and typography were invented by the Chinese before we knew of them. There are magistrates, who announce the meaning of the pictures, and boys are accustomed to learn all the sciences, without toil and as if for pleasure; but in the way of history only until they are ten years old.

LOVE is foremost in attending to the charge of the race. He sees that men and women are so joined together, that they bring forth the best offspring. Indeed, they laugh at us who exhibit a studious care for our breed of horses and dogs, but neglect the breeding of human beings. Thus the education of the children is under his rule. So also is the medicine that is sold, the sowing and collecting of fruits of the earth and of trees, agriculture, pasturage, the preparations for the months, the cooking arrangements, and whatever has any reference to food, clothing, and the intercourse of the sexes. Love himself is ruler, but there are many male and female magistrates dedicated to these arts.

Metaphysic then with these three rulers manage all the above-named matters, and even by himself alone nothing is done; all business is discharged by the four together, but in whatever Metaphysic inclines to the rest are sure to agree.

Grand. Tell me, please, of the magistrates, their services and duties, of the education and mode of living, whether the government is a monarchy, a republic, or an aristocracy.

Capt. This race of men came there from India, flying

from the sword of the Magi, a race of plunderers and ty-
rants who laid waste their country, and they determined
to lead a philosophic life in fellowship with one another.
Although the community of wives is not instituted among
the other inhabitants of their province, among them it is
in use after this manner. All things are common with
them, and their dispensation is by the authority of the
magistrates. Arts and honors and pleasures are common,
and are held in such a manner that no one can appropriate
anything to himself.

They say that all private property is acquired and improved for the reason that each one of us by himself has
his own home and wife and children. From this self-love
springs. For when we raise a son to riches and dignities,
and leave an heir to much wealth, we become either ready
to grasp at the property of the state, if in any case fear
should be removed for the power which belongs to riches
and rank; or avaricious, crafty, and hypocritical, if any
one is of slender purse, little strength, and mean ancestry.
but when we have taken away self-love, there remains
only love for the state.

Grand. Under such circumstances no one will be willing
to labor, while he expects others to work, on the fruit of
whose labors he can live, as Aristotle argues against Plato.

Capt. I do not know how to deal with that argument,
but I declare to you that they burn with so great a love for
their fatherland, as I could scarcely have believed possible;
and indeed with much more than the histories tell us belonged to the Romans, who fell willingly for their country,
inasmuch as they have to a greater extent surrendered
their private property. I think truly that the friars and
monks and clergy of our country, if they were not weakened by love for their kindred and friends, or by the ambition to rise to higher dignities, would be less fond of
property, and more imbued with a spirit of charity towards

all, as it was in the time of the Apostles, and is now in a great many cases.

Grand. St. Augustine may say that, but I say that among this race of men, friendship is worth nothing; since they have not the chance of conferring mutual benefits on one another.

Capt. Nay, indeed. For it is worth the trouble to see that no one can receive gifts from another. Whatever is necessary they have, they receive it from the community, and the magistrate takes care that no one receives more than he deserves. Yet nothing necessary is denied to any one. Friendship is recognized among them in war, in infirmity, in the art contests, by which means they aid one another mutually by teaching. Sometimes they improve themselves mutually with praises, with conversation, with actions and out of the things they need. All those of the same age call one another brothers. They call over twenty-two years of age, fathers; those who are less than twenty-two are named sons. Moreover, the magistrates govern well, so that no one in the fraternity can do injury to another.

Grand. And how?

Capt. As many names of virtues as there are amongst us, so many magistrates there are among them. There is a magistrate who is named Magnanimity, another Fortitude, a third Chastity, a fourth Liberality, a fifth Criminal and Civil Justice, a sixth Comfort, a seventh Truth, an eighth Kindness, a tenth Gratitude, an eleventh Cheerfulness, a twelfth Exercise, a thirteenth Sobriety, etc. They are elected to duties of that kind, each one to that duty for excellence in which he is known from boyhood to be most suitable. Wherefore among them neither robbery nor clever murders, nor lewdness, incest, adultery, or other crimes of which we accuse one another, can be found. They accuse themselves of ingratitude and malignity when any one denies a lawful satisfaction to another, of indolence, of sadness, of anger, of scurrility, of slander, and of lying, which curseful thing they thoroughly hate. Accused persons undergoing punishment are deprived of the common table, and other honors, until the judge thinks that they agree with their correction.

Grand. Tell me the manner in which the magistrates are chosen.

Capt. You would not rightly understand this, unless you first learnt their manner of living. That you may know then, men and women wear the same kind of garment, suited for war. The women wear the toga below the knee, but the men above. And both sexes are instructed in all the arts together. When this has been done as a start, and before their third year, the boys learn the language and the alphabet on the walls by walking round them. They have four leaders, and four elders, the first to direct them, the second to teach them, and these are men approved beyond all others. After some time they exercise themselves with gymnastics, running, quoits, and other games, by means of which all their muscles are strengthened alike. Their feet are always bare, and so are their heads as far as the seventh ring. Afterwards they lead them to the offices of the trades, such as shoemaking, cooking, metalworking, carpentry, painting, etc. In order to find out the bent of the genius of each one, after their seventh year, when they have already gone through the mathematics on the walls, they take them to the readings of all the sciences; there are four lectures at each reading, and in the course of four hours the four in their order explain everything.

For some take physical exercise or busy themselves with public services or functions, others apply themselves to reading. Leaving these studies all are devoted to the more abstruse subjects, to mathematics, to medicine, and to other sciences. There is continual debate and studied argument amongst them, and after a time they become magistrates of

those sciences or mechanical arts in which they are the most
proficient; for every one follows the opinion of his leader
and judge, and goes out to the plains to the works of the
field, and for the purpose of becoming acquainted with the
pasturage of dumb animals. And they consider him the
more noble and renowned who has dedicated himself to
the study of the most arts and knows how to practise them
wisely. Wherefore they laugh at us in that we consider
our workmen ignoble, and hold those to be noble who
have mastered no pursuit; but live in ease, and are so
many slaves given over to their own pleasure and lasciviousness; and thus as it were from a school of vices
so many idle and wicked fellows go forth for the ruin
of the state.

The rest of the officials, however, are chosen by the four
chiefs, Hoh, Pon, Sin and Mor, and by the teachers of that
art over which they are fit to preside. And these teachers
know well who is most suited for rule. Certain men are
proposed by the magistrates in council, they themselves
not seeking to become candidates, and he opposes who
knows anything against those brought forward for election,
or if not, speaks in favor of them. But no one attains to the
dignity of Hoh except him who knows the histories of the
nations, and their customs and sacrifices and laws, and their
form of government, whether a republic or a monarchy.
He must also know the names of the lawgivers and the inventors in science, and the laws and the history of the
earth and the heavenly bodies. They think it also necessary that he should understand all the mechanical arts, the
physical sciences, astrology and mathematics. (Nearly
every two days they teach our mechanical art. They are
not allowed to overwork themselves, but frequent practice
and the paintings render learning easy to them. Not
too much care is given to the cultivation of languages, as
they have a goodly number of interpreters who are gram-
marians in the state.) But beyond everything else it is

necessary that Hoh should understand metaphysics and theology; that he should know thoroughly the derivations,
foundations and demonstrations of all the arts and sciences; the likeness and difference of things; necessity, fate,
and the harmonies of the universe; power, wisdom, and
the love of things and of God; the stages of life and its
symbols; everything relating to the heavens, the earth
and the sea; and the ideas of God, as much as mortal
man can know of Him. He must also be well read in the
Prophets and in astrology. And thus they know long beforehand who will be Hoh. He is not chosen to so great a
dignity unless he has attained his thirty-fifth year. And
this office is perpetual, because it is not known who may
be too wise for it or who too skilled in ruling.

Grand. Who indeed can be so wise? If even any one
has a knowledge of the sciences it seems that he must be
unskilled in ruling.

Capt. This very question I asked them and they replied
thus: "We, indeed, are more certain that such a very
learned man has the knowledge of governing, than you
who place ignorant persons in authority, and consider them
suitable merely because they have sprung from rulers or
have been chosen by a powerful faction. But our Hoh, a
man really the most capable to rule, is for all that never
cruel nor wicked, nor a tyrant, inasmuch as he possesses so
much wisdom. This, moreover, is not unknown to you,
that the same argument cannot apply among you, when
you consider that man the most learned who knows most
of grammar, or logic, or of Aristotle or any other author.
For such knowledge as this of yours much servile labor
and memory work is required, so that a man is rendered
unskilful; since he has contemplated nothing but the
words of books and has given his mind with useless result
to the consideration of the dead signs of things. Hence he
knows not in what way God rules the universe, nor the
ways and customs of Nature and the nations. Wherefore

he is not equal to our HOH. For that one cannot know so
many arts and sciences thoroughly, who is not esteemed
for skilled ingenuity, very apt at all things, and therefore at
ruling especially. This also is plain to us that he who
knows only science, does not really know either that or
the others, and he who is suited for only one science and
has gathered his knowledge from books, is unlearned and
unskilled. But this is not the case with intellects prompt
and expert in every branch of knowledge and suitable
for the consideration of natural objects, as it is necessary
that our HOH should be. Besides in our state the sciences
are taught with a facility (as you have seen) by which
more scholars are turned out by us in one year than by
you in ten, or even fifteen. Make trial, I pray you of these
boys." In this manner I was struck with astonishment
at their truthful discourse and at the trial of their boys,
who did not understand my language well. Indeed it
is necessary that three of them should be skilled in our
tongue, three in Arabic, three in Polish, and three in each
of the other languages, and no recreation is allowed them
unless they become more learned. For that they go out
to the plain for the sake of running about and hurling
arrows and lances, and of firing harquebuses, and for the
sake of hunting the wild animals and getting a knowledge
of plants and stones, and agriculture and pasturage; sometimes the band of boys does one thing, sometimes another.

They do not consider it necessary that the three rulers
assisting HOH should know other than the arts having
reference to their rule, and so they have only a historical
knowledge of the arts which are common to all. But their
own they know well, to which certainly one is dedicated
more than another. Thus POWER is the most learned in
the equestrian art, in marshalling the army, in marking out
of camps, in the manufacture of every kind of weapon and
of warlike machines, in planning stratagems, and in every
affair of a military nature. And for these reasons, they

consider it necessary that these chiefs should have been
philosophers, historians, politicians, and physicists. Concerning the other two triumvirs, understand remarks similar to those I have made about POWER.

Grand. I really wish that you would recount all their
public duties, and would distinguish between them, and
also that you would tell clearly how they are all taught in
common.

Capt. They have dwellings in common and dormitories,
and couches and other necessaries. But at the end of every
six months they are separated by the masters. Some shall
sleep in this ring, some in another; some in the first apart-
ment, and some in the second; and these apartments are
marked by means of the alphabet on the lintel. There are
occupations, mechanical and theoretical, common to both
men and women, with this difference, that the occupations
which require more hard work, and walking a long distance, are practised by men, such as plowing, sowing,
gathering the fruits, working at the threshing-floor, and
perchance at the vintage. But it is customery to choose
women for milking the cows, and for making cheese. In
like manner, they go to the gardens near to the outskirts of
the city both for collecting the plants and for cultivating
them. In fact, all sedentary and stationary pursuits are
practised by the women, such as weaving, spinning, sew-
ing, cutting the hair, shaving, dispensing medicines, and
making all kinds of garments. They are, however, excluded from working in wood and the manufacture of
arms. If a woman is fit to paint, she is not prevented from
doing so; nevertheless, music is given over to the women
alone, because they please the more, and of a truth to boys
also. But the women have not the practice of the drum
and the horn.

And they prepare their feasts and arrange the tables in
the following manner. It is the peculiar work of the boys
and girls under twenty to wait at the tables. In every ring

there are the suitable kitchens, barns, and stores of utensils for eating and drinking, and over every department an old man and an old woman preside. These two have at once the command of those who serve, and the power of chastising, or causing to be chastised, those who are negligent or disobedient; and they also examine and mark each one, both male and female, who excels in his or her duties.

All the young people wait upon the older ones who have passed the age of forty, and in the evening when they go to sleep the master and mistress command that those should be sent to work in the morning, upon whom in succession the duty falls, one or two to separate apartments. The young people, however, wait upon one another, and that alas! with some unwillingness. They have first and second tables, and on both sides there are seats. On one side sit the women, on the other the men; and as in the refectories of the monks, there is no noise. While they are eating, a young man reads a book from a platform, intoning distinctly and sonorously, and often the magistrates question them upon the more important parts of the reading. And truly it is pleasant to observe in what manner these young people, so beautiful and clothed in garments so suitable, attend to them, and to see at the same time so many friends, brothers, sons, fathers and mothers in all their turn living together with so much honesty, propriety and love. So each one is given a napkin, a plate, fish, and a dish of food. It is the duty of the medical officers to tell the cooks what repasts shall be prepared on each day, and what food for the old, what for the young, and what for the sick. The magistrates receive the full-grown and fatter portion, and they from their share always distribute something to the boys at the table who have shown themselves more studious in the morning at the lectures and debates concerning wisdom and arms. And this is held to be one of the most distinguished honors. For six days they ordain to sing with music at table. Only a few, however, sing; or there is one voice accompanying the lute and one for each other instrument. And when all alike in service join their hands, nothing is found to be wanting. The old men placed at the head of the cooking business and of the refectories of the servants praise the cleanliness of the streets, the houses, the vessels, the garments, the workshops and the warehouses.

They wear white undergarments to which adheres a covering, which is at once coat and legging, without wrinkles. The borders of the fastenings are furnished with globular buttons, extended round and caught up here and there by chains. The coverings of the legs descend to the shoes and are continued even to the heels. Then they cover their feet with large socks, or as it were half-buskins fastened by buckles, over which they wear a half-boot, and besides, as I have already said, they are clothed with a toga. And so aptly fitting are the garments, that when the toga is destroyed, the different parts of the whole body are straightway discerned, no part being concealed. They change their clothes for different ones four times in the year, that is when the sun enters respectively the constellations Aries, Cancer, Libra and Capricorn, and according to the circumstances and necessity as decided by the officer of health. The keepers of clothes for the different rings are wont to distribute them, and it is marvellous that they have at the same time as many garments as there is need for, some heavy and some slight, according to the weather. They all use white clothing, and this is washed in each month with lye or soap, as are also the workshops of the lower trades, the kitchens, the pantries, the barns, the store-houses, the armories, the refectories and the baths. Moreover, the clothes are washed at the pillars of the peristyles, and the water is brought down by means of canals which are continued as sewers. In every street of the different rings there are suitable fountains, which send forth their water by means of canals, the water being drawn up from nearly the bottom of the mountain by the sole movement of a cleverly contrived handle. There is water in fountains and in cisterns, whither the rain-water collected from the roofs of the houses is brought through pipes full of sand. They wash their bodies often, according as the doctor and master command. All the mechanical arts are practised under the peristyles, but the speculative are carried on above in the walking galleries and ramparts where are the more splendid paintings, but the more sacred ones are taught in the temple. In the halls and wings of the rings there are solar time-pieces and bells, and hands by which the hours and seasons are marked off.

Grand. Tell me about their children.

Capt. When their women have brought forth children, they suckle them and rear them in temples set apart for all. They give milk for two years or more as the physician orders. After that time the weaned child is given into the charge of the mistresses, if it is a female, and to the masters, if it is a male. And then with other young children they are pleasantly instructed in the alphabet, and in the knowledge of the pictures, and in running, walking and wrestling; also in the historical drawings, and in languages; and they are adorned with a suitable garment of different colors. After their sixth year they are taught natural science, and then the mechanical sciences. The men who are weak in intellect are sent to farms, and when they have become more proficient some of them are received into the state. And those of the same age and born under the same constellation are especially like one another in strength and in appearance, and hence arises much lasting concord in the state, these men honoring one another with mutual love and help. Names are given to them by Metaphysicus, and that not by chance but designedly, and according to each one's peculiarity, as was the custom among the ancient Romans. Wherefore one is called Beautiful (Pulcher), another the Big-nosed (Naso), another

Crooked (Torvus), another Lean (Macer), and so on. But when they have become very skilled in their professions and done any great deed in war or in time of peace, a cog-nomen from art is given to them, such as Beautiful, the great painter (Pulcher, Pictor Magnus), the golden one (Aureus), the excellent one (Excellens), or the strong (Strenuus); or from their deeds, such as Naso the Brave (Nason Fortis), or the cunning, or the great, or very great conqueror; or from the enemy any one has overcome, Africanus, Asiaticus, Etruscus; or if any one has overcome Manfred or Tortelius, he is called Macer Manfred or Tor-telius, and so on. All these cognomens are added by the higher magistrates, and very often with a crown suitable to the deed or art, and with the flourish of music. For gold and silver is reckoned of little value among them except as material for their vessels and ornaments, which are common to all.

Grand. Tell me, I pray you, is there no jealousy among them or disappointment to that one who has not been elected to a magistracy, or to any other dignity to which he aspires?

Capt. Certainly not. For no one wants either necessar-ies or luxuries. Moreover, the race is managed for the good of the commonwealth and not of private individuals, and the magistrates must be obeyed. They deny what we hold —viz., that it is natural to man to recognize his offspring and to educate them, and to use his wife and house and children as his own. For they say that children are bred for the preservation of the species and not for individual pleasure, as St. Thomas also asserts. Therefore the breed-ing of children has reference to the commonwealth and not to individuals, except in so far as they are constituents of the commonwealth. And since individuals for the most part bring forth children wrongly and educate them wrongly, they consider that they remove destruction from the state, and therefore, for this reason, with most sacred fear, they commit the education of the children, who as it were are the element of the republic, to the care of the magistrates; for the safety of the community is not that of a few. And thus they distribute male and female breeders of the best natures according to philosophical rules. Plato thinks that this distribution ought to be made by lot, lest some men seeing that they are kept away from the beautiful women, should rise up with anger and hatred against the magistrates; and he thinks further that those who do not deserve cohabitation with the more beautiful women, should be deceived whilst the lots are being led out of the city by the magistrates, so that at all times the women who are suitable should fall to their lot, not those whom they desire. This shrewdness, however, is not necessary among the inhabitants of the City of the Sun. For with them deformity is unknown. When the women are exercised they get a clear complexion, and become strong of limb, tall and agile, and with them beauty consists of tallness and strength. Therefore, if any woman dyes her face, so that it may become beautiful, or uses high-heeled boots so that she may appear tall, or garments with trains to cover her wooden shoes, she is condemned to capital punishment. But if the women should even desire them, they have no facility for doing these things. For who indeed would give them this facility? Further, they assert that among us abuses of this kind arise from the leisure and sloth of women. By these means they lose their color and have pale complexions, and become feeble and small. For this reason they are without proper complexions, use high sandals, and become beautiful not from strength, but from slothful tenderness. And thus they ruin their own tempers and natures, and consequently those of their offspring. Furthermore, if at any time a man is taken captive with ardent love for a certain woman, the two are allowed to converse and joke together, and to give one another garlands of flowers or leaves, and to make

verses. But if the race is endangered, by no means is further union between them permitted. Moreover, the love
born of eager desire is not known among them; only that
born of friendship.

Domestic affairs and partnerships are of little account,
because, excepting the sign of honor, each one receives
what he is in need of. To the heroes and heroines of the
republic, it is customary to give the pleasing gifts of
honor, beautiful wreaths, sweet food or splendid clothes,
while they are feasting. In the daytime all use white
garments within the city, but at night or outside the city
they use red garments either of wool or silk. They hate
black as they do dung, and therefore they dislike the Japa-
nese, who are fond of black. Pride they consider the most
execrable vice, and one who acts proudly is chastised with
the most ruthless correction. Wherefore no one thinks it
lowering to wait at table or to work in the kitchen or fields.
All work they call discipline, and thus they say that it is
honorable to go on foot, to do any act of nature, to see with
the eye, and to speak with the tongue; and when there is
need, they distinguish philosophically between tears and
spittle.

Every man who, when he is told off to work, does his
duty, is considered very honorable. It is not the custom
to keep slaves. For they are enough, and more than
enough, for themselves. But with us, alas! it is not so.
In Naples there exists seventy thousand souls, and out
of these scarcely ten or fifteen thousand do any work,
and they are always lean from overwork and are getting
weaker every day. The rest become a prey to idleness,
avarice, ill-health, lasciviousness, usury and other vices,
and contaminate and corrupt very many families by holding them in servitude for their own use, by keeping them
in poverty and slavishness, and by imparting to them
their own vices. Therefore public slavery ruins them; useful works, in the field, in military service and in arts, ex-

cept those which are debasing, are not cultivated, the few
who do practise them doing so with much aversion. But in
the City of the Sun, while duty and work is distributed
among all, it only falls to each one to work for about four
hours every day. The remaining hours are spent in learning joyously, in debating, in reading, in reciting, in writing, in walking, in exercising the mind and body, and with
play. They allow no game which is played while sitting,
neither the single die nor dice, nor chess, nor others like
these. But they play with the ball, with the sack, with
the hoop, with wrestling, and hurling at the stake. They
say, moreover, that grinding poverty renders men worth-
less, cunning, sulky, thievish, insidious, vagabonds, liars,
false witnesses, etc.; and that wealth makes them insolent,
proud, ignorant, traitors, assumers of what they know not,
deceivers, boasters, wanting in affection, slanderers, etc.
But with them all the rich and poor together make up the
community. They are rich because they want nothing,
poor because they possess nothing; and consequently they
are not slaves to circumstances, but circumctances serve
them. And on this point they strongly recommend the
religion of the Christians, and especially the life of the
Apostles.

Grand This seems excellent and sacred, but the community of women is a thing too difficult to attain. The
holy Roman Clement says that wives ought to be common
in accordance with the apostolic institution, and praises
Plato and Socrates, who thus teach, but the Glossary in-
terprets this community with regard to obedience. And
Tertullian agrees with the Glossary, that the first Christians had everything in common except wives.

Capt. These things I know little of. But this I saw
among the inhabitants of the City of the Sun that they did
not make this exception. And they defend themselves by
the opinion of Socrates, of Cato, of Plato, and of St.
Clement but, as you say, they misunderstand the opinions

of these thinkers. And the inhabitants of the solar city ascribe this to their want of education, since they are by no means learned in philosophy. Nevertheless, they send abroad to discover the customs of nations, and the best of these they always adopt. Practice makes the women suitable for war and other duties. Thus they agree with Plato, in whom I have read these same things. The reasoning of our Cajetan does not convince me, and least of all that of Aristotle. This thing, however, existing among them is excellent and worthy of imitation—viz., that no physical defect renders a man incapable of being serviceable except the decrepitude of old age, since even the deformed are useful for consultation. The lame serve as guards, watching with the eyes which they possess. The blind card wool with their hands, separating the down from the hairs, with which latter they stuff the couches and sofas; those who are without the use of eyes and hands give the use of their ears or their voice for the convenience of the state, and if one has only one sense, he uses it in the farms. And these cripples are well treated, and some become spies, telling the officers of the state what they have heard.

Grand. Tell me now, I pray you, of their military affairs. Then you may explain their arts, ways of life and sciences, and lastly their religion.

Capt. The triumvir, Power, has under him all the magistrates of arms, of artillery, of cavalry, of foot-soldiers, of architects, and of strategists, and the masters and many of the most excellent workmen obey the magistrates, the men of each are paying allegiance to their respective chiefs. Moreover, Power is at the head of all the professors of gymnastics, who teach military exercise, and who are prudent generals, advanced in age. By these the boys are trained after their twelfth year. Before this age, however, they have been accustomed to wrestling, running, throwing the weight and other minor exercises, under inferior masters. But at twelve they are taught how to strike at the enemy, at horses and elephants, to handle the spear, the sword, the arrow and the sling; to manage the horse; to advance and retreat; to remain in order of battle; to help a comrade in arms; to anticipate the enemy by cunning; and to conquer.

The women also are taught these arts under their own magistrates and mistresses, so that they may be able if need be to render assistance to the males in battles near the city. They are taught to watch the fortifications lest at some time a hasty attack should suddenly be made. In this respect they praise the Spartans and Amazons. The women know well also how to let fly fiery balls, and how to make them from lead; how to throw stones from pinnacles and to go in the way of an attack. They are accustomed also to give up wine unmixed altogether, and that one is punished most severely who shows any fear.

The inhabitants of the City of the Sun do not fear death, because they all believe that the soul is immortal, and that when it has left the body it is associated with other spirits, wicked or good, according to the merits of this present life. Although they are partly followers of Bramah and Pythagoras, they do not believe in the transmigration of souls, except in some cases, by a distinct decree of God. They do abstain from injuring an enemy of the republic and of religion, who is unworthy of pity. During the second month the army is reviewed, and every day there is practice of arms, either in the cavalry plain or within the walls. Nor are they ever without lectures of Moses, of Joshua, of David, of Judas Maccabeus, of Caesar, of Alexander, of Scipio, of Hannibal, and other great soldiers should be read. And then each one gives his own opinion as to whether these generals acted well or ill, usefully or honorably, and then the teacher answers and says who are right.

Grand. With whom do they wage war, and for what reasons, since they are so prosperous?

Capt. Wars might never occur, nevertheless they are exercised in military tactics and in hunting, lest perchance they should become effeminate and unprepared for any emergency. Besides there are four kingdoms in the island, which are very envious of their prosperity, for this reason that the people desire to live after the manner of the inhabitants of the City of the Sun, and to be under their rule rather than that of their own kings. Wherefore the state often makes war upon these because, being neighbors, they are usurpers and live impiously, since they have not an object of worship and do not observe the religion of other nations or of the Brahmins. And other nations of India, to which formerly they were subject, rise up as it were in rebellion, as also do the Taprobanese, whom they wanted to join them at first. The warriors of the City of the Sun, however, are always the victors. As soon as they suffered from insult or disgrace or plunder, or when their allies have been harassed, or a people have been oppressed by a tyrant of the state (for they are always the advocates of liberty), they go immediately to the council for deliberation. After they have knelt in the presence of God that He might inspire their consultation, they do proceed to examine the merits of the business, and thus war is decided on. Immediately after a priest, whom they call Forensic, is sent away. He demands from the enemy the restitution of the plunder, asks that the allies should be freed from oppression, or that the tyrant should be deposed. If they deny these things war is declared by invoking the vengeance of God—the God of Sabaoth—for destruction of those who maintain an unjust cause. But if the enemy refuse to reply, the priest gives him the space of one hour for his answer, if he is a king, but three if it is a republic, so that they cannot escape giving a response. And in this manner war is undertaken against the insolent enemies of natural rights and of religion. When war has been declared, the deputy of Power performs everything, but Power, like the Roman dictator, plans and wills everything, so that hurtful tardiness may be avoided. And when anything of great moment arises he consults Hoh and Wisdom and Love.

Before this, however, the occasion of war and the justice of making an expedition is declared by a herald in the great council. All from twenty years and upwards are admitted to this council, and thus the necessaries are agreed upon. All kinds of weapons stand in the armories, and these they use often in sham fights. The exterior walls of each ring are full of guns prepared by their labors, and they have other engines for hurling which are called cannons, and which they take into battle upon mules and asses and carriages. When they have arrived in an open plain they enclose in the middle the provisions, engines of war, chariots, ladders and machines and all fight courageously. Then each one returns to the standards, and the enemy thinking that they are giving and preparing to flee, are deceived and relax their order: then the warriors of the City of the Sun, wheeling into wings and columns on each side, regain their breath and strength, and ordering the artillery to discharge their bullets they resume the fight against a disorganized host. And they observe many ruses of this kind. They overcome all mortals with their stratagems and engines. Their camp is fortified after the manner of the Romans. They pitch their tents and fortify the wall and ditch with wonderful quickness. The masters of works, of engines and hurling machines, stand ready, and the soldiers understand the use of the spade and the axe.

Five, eight, or ten leaders learned in the order of battle and in strategy consult together concerning the business of war, and command their bands after consultation. It is their wont to take out with them a body of boys, armed and on horses, so that they may learn to fight, just as the whelps of lions and wolves are accustomed to blood. And these in time of danger betake themselves to a place of safety, along with many armed women. After the battle the women and boys soothe and relieve the pain of the warriors, and wait upon them and encourage them with embraces and pleasant words. How wonderful a help is this! For the soldiers, in order that they may acquit themselves as sturdy men in the eyes of their wives and offspring, endure hardships, and so love makes them con-querors. He who in the fight first scales the enemy's walls receives after the battle a crown of grass, a token of honor, and at the presentation the women and boys applaud loudly; that one who affords aid to an ally gets a civic crown of oak-leaves; he who kills a tyrant dedicates his arms in the temple and receives from Hoh the cognomen of his deed, and other warriors obtain other kinds of crowns. Every horse-soldier carries a spear and two strongly tempered pistols, narrow at the mouth, hanging from his saddle. And to get the barrels of their pistols narrow they pierce the metal which they intend to convert into arms. Further, every cavalry soldier has a sword and a dagger. But the rest, who form the light-armed troops, carry a metal cudgel. For if the foe cannot pierce their metal for pistols and cannot make swords, they attack him with clubs, shatter and overthrow him. Two chains of six spans length hang from the club, and at the end of these are iron balls, and when these aimed at the enemy they surround his neck and drag him to the ground; and in order that they may be able to use the club more easily, they do not hold the reins with their hands, but use them by means of the feet. If perchance the reins are interchanged above the trappings of the saddle, the ends are fastened to the stirrups with buckles and not to the feet. And the stirrups have an arrangement for swift movement of the bridle, so that they draw in or let out

the rein with marvellous celerity. With the right foot
they turn the rorse to the left and with the left to the
right. This secret, moreover, is not known to the Tartars.
For, although they govern the reins with their feet, they
are ignorant nevertheless of turning them and drawing
them in and letting them out by means of the block of
the stirrups. The light-armed cavalry with them are the
first to engage in battle, then the men forming the phalanx
with their spears, then the archers for whose services a
great price is paid, and who are accustomed to fight in
lines crossing one another as the threads of cloth, some
rushing forward in their turn and others receding. They
have a band of lancers strengthening the line of battle,
but they make trial of the swords only at the end.

After the battle they celebrate the military triumphs
after the manner of the Romans, and even in a more magnificent way. Prayers by the way of thank-offerings are
made to God, and then the general presents himself in
the temple, and the deeds, good and bad, are related by
the poet or historian, who according to custom was with
the expedition. And the greatest chief, Hoh, crowns the
general with laurel and distributes little gifts and honors
to all the valorous soldiers, who are for some days free
from public duties. But this exemption from work is by
no means pleasing to them, since they know not what it
is to be at leisure, and so they help their companions.
On the other hand, they who have been conquered through
their own fault, or have lost the victory, are blamed; and
they who were the first to take flight are in no way worthy
to escape death, unless when the whole army asks their
lives, and each one takes upon himself a part of their
punishment. But this indulgence is rarely granted, except when there are good reasons favoring it. But he
who did not bear help to an ally or friend is beaten with
rods. That one who did not obey orders is given to the
beasts, in an enclosure, to be devoured, and a staff is put

in his hand, and if he should conquer the lions and the bears that are there, which is almost impossible, he is received into favor again. The conquered states or those willingly delivered up to them, forthwith have all things in common, and receive a garrison and magistrates from the City of the Sun, and by degrees they are accustomed to the ways of the city, the mistress of all, to which they even send their sons to be taught without contributing anything for expense.

It woud be too great trouble to tell you about the spies and their master, and about the guards and laws and ceremonies, both within and without the state, which you can of yourself imagine. Since from childhood they are chosen according to their inclination and the star under which they were born, therefore each one working according to his natural propensity does his duty well and pleasantly, because naturally. The same things I may say concerning strategy and the other functions.

There are guards in the city by day and by night, and they are placed at the four gates, and outside the walls of the seventh ring, above the breastworks and towers and inside mounds. These places are guarded in the day by women, in the night by men. And lest the guard should become weary of watching, and in case of a surprise, they change them every three hours, as is the custom with our soldiers. At sunset, when the drum and symphonia sound, the armed guards are distributed. Cavalry and infantry make use of hunting as the symbol of war, and practise games and hold festivities in the plains. Then the music strikes up, and freely they pardon the offences and faults of the enemy, and after the victories they are kind to them, if it has been decreed that they should destroy the walls of the enemy's city and take their lives. All these things are done on the same day as the victory, and afterwards they never cease to load the conquered with favors, for they say that there ought to be no fighting, except when the con-querors give up the conquered, not when they kill them. If there is a dispute among them concerning injury or any other matter (for they themselves scarcely ever contend except in matters of honor), the chief and his magistrates chastise the accused one secretly, if he has done harm in deeds after he has been first angry. If they wait until the time of battle for the verbal decision, they must give vent to their anger against the enemy, and he who in battle shows the most daring deeds is considered to have defended the better and truer cause in the struggle, and the other yields, and they are punished justly. Nevertheless, they are not allowed to come to single combat, since right is maintained by the tribunal, and because the unjust cause is often apparent when the more just succumbs, and he who professes to be the better man shows this in public fight.

Grand. This is worth while, so that factions should not be cherished for the harm of the fatherland, and so that civil wars might not occur, for by means of these a tyrant often arises, as the examples of Rome and Athens show. Now, I pray you, tell me of their works and matter connected therewith.

Capt. I believe that you have already heard about their military affairs and about their agricultural and pastoral life, and in what way these are common to them, and how they honor with the first grade of nobility whoever is considered to have a knowledge of these. They who are skilful in more arts than these they consider still nobler, and they set that one apart for teaching the art in which he is most skilful. The occupations which require the most labor, such as working in metals and building, are the most praiseworthy among them. No one declines to go to these occupations, for the reason that from the beginning their propensities are well known, and among them, on account of the distribution of labor, no one does work harmful to him, but only that which is necessary for him. The occupations entailing less labor belong to the women. All of them are expected to know how to swim, and for this reason ponds are dug outside the walls of the city and within them near to the fountains.

Commerce is of little use to them, but they know the value of money, and they count for the use of their am-bassadors and explorers, so that with it they may have the means of living. They receive merchants into their states from the different countries of the world, and these buy the superfluous goods of the city. The people of the City of the Sun refuse to take money, but in importing they ac-cept in exchange those things of which they are in need, and sometimes they buy with money; and the young people in the City of the Sun are much amused when they see that for a small price they receive so many things in ex-change. The old men, however, do not laugh. They are unwilling that the state should be corrupted by the vicious customs of slaves and foreigners. Therefore they do busi-ness at the gates, and sell those whom they have taken in war or keep them for digging ditches and other hard work without the city, and for this reason they always send four bands of soldiers to take care of the fields, and with them there are the laborers. They go out of the four gates from which roads with walls on both sides of them lead to the sea, so that goods might easily be carried over them and foreigners might not meet with difficulty on their way.

To strangers they are kind and polite; they keep them for three days at the public expense; after they have first washed their feet, they show them their city and its cus-toms, and they honor them with a seat at the council and public table, and there are men whose duty it is to take care of and guard the guests. But if strangers should wish to become citizens of their state, they try them first for a month on a farm, and for another month in the city, then they decide concerning them, and admit them with certain ceremonies and oaths.

Agriculture is much followed among them; there is not a span of earth without cultivation, and they observe the winds and propitious stars. With the exception of a few left in the city all go out armed, and with flags and drums and trumpets sounding, to the fields, for the purposes of plowing, sowing, digging, hoeing, reaping, gathering fruit and grapes; and they set in order everything, and do their work in a very few hours and with much care. They use wagons fitted with sails which are borne along by the wind even when it is contrary, by the marvellous contrivance of wheels within wheels.

And when there is no wind a beast draws along a huge cart, which is a grand sight.

The guardians of the land move about in the meantime, armed and always in their proper turn. They do not use dung and filth for manuring the fields, thinking that the fruit contracts something of their rottenness, and when eaten gives a short and poor subsistence, as women who are beautiful with rouge and from want of exercise bring forth feeble offspring. Wherefore they do not as it were paint the earth, but dig it up well and use secret remedies, so that fruit is borne quickly and multiplies, and is not destroyed. They have a book for this work, which they call the Georgics. As much of the land as is necessary is cultivated, and the rest is used for the pasturage of cattle.

The excellent occupation of breeding and rearing horses, oxen, sheep, dogs and all kinds of domestic and tame animals, is in the highest esteem among them as it was in the time of Abraham. And the animals are led so to pair that they may be able to breed well.

Fine pictures of oxen, horses, sheep, and other animals are placed before them. They do not turn out horses with mares to feed, but at the proper time they bring them together in an enclosure of the stables in their fields. And this is done when they observe that the constellation

Archer is in favorable conjunction with Mars and Jupiter. For the oxen they observe the Bull, for the sheep the Ram, and so on in accordance with art. Under the Pleiades they keep a drove of hens and ducks and geese, which are driven out by the women to feed near the city. The women only do this when it is a pleasure to them. There are also places enclosed, where they make cheese, butter, and milk-food. They also keep capons, fruit and other things, and for all these matters there is a book which they call the Bucolics. They have an abundance of all things, since every one likes to be industrious, their labors being slight and profitable. They are docile, and that one among them who is head of the rest in duties of this kind they call king. For they say that this is the proper name of the leaders, and it does not belong to ignorant persons. It is wonderful to see how men and women march together collectively, and always in obedience to the voice of the king. Nor do they regard him with loathing as we do, for they know that although he is greater than themselves, he is for all that their father and brother. They keep groves and woods for wild animals, and they often hunt.

The science of navigation is considered very dignified by them, and they possess rafts and triremes, which go over the waters without rowers or the force of the wind, but by a marvellous contrivance. And other vessels they have which are moved by the winds. They have a correct knowledge of the stars, and of the ebb and flow of the tide. They navigate for the sake of becoming acquainted with nations and different countries and things. They injure nobody, and they do not put up with injury, and they never go to battle unless when provoked. They assert that the whole earth will in time come to live in accordance with their customs, and consequently they always find out whether there be a nation whose manner of living is better and more approved than the rest. They admire the Christian institutions and look for a realization of the apostolic life in vogue among themselves and in us. There are treaties between them and the Chinese, and many other nations, both insular and continental, such as Siam and Calicut, which they are only just able to explore. Further-more, they have artificial fires, battles on sea and land, and many strategic secrets. Therefore they are nearly always victorious.

Grand. Now it would be very pleasant to learn with what foods and drinks they are nourished, and in what way and for how long they live.

Capt. Their food consists of flesh, butter, honey, cheese, garden herbs, and vegetables of various kinds. They were unwilling at first to slay animals, because it seemed cruel; but thinking afterwards that it was also cruel to destroy herbs which have a share of sensitive feeling, they saw that they would perish from hunger unless they did an un-justifiable action for the sake of justifiable ones, and so now they all eat meat. Nevertheless, they do not kill willingly useful animals such as oxen and horses. They observe the difference between useful and harmful foods, and for this they employ the science of medicine. They always change their food. First they eat flesh, then fish, then afterwards they go back to flesh, and nature is never incommoded or weakened. The old people use the more digestible kind of food, and take three meals a day, eating only a little. But the general community eat twice, and the boys four times, that they might satisfy nature. The length of their lives is generally one hundred years, but often they reach two hundred.

As regards drinking, they are extremely moderate. Wine is never given to young people until they are ten years old, unless the state of their health demands it. After their tenth year they take it diluted with water, and so do the women, but the old men of fifty and upwards use little or no water. They eat the most healthy things, according to the time of the year.

They think nothing harmful which is brought forth by God, except when there has been abuse by taking too much. And therefore in the summer they feed on fruits, because they are moist and juicy and cool, and counteract the heat and dryness. In the winter they feed on dry articles, and in the autumn they eat grapes, since they are given by God to remove melancholy and sadness; and they also make use of scents to a great degree. In the morning, when they have all risen they comb their hair and wash their faces and hands with cold water. Then they chew thyme or rock parsley or fennel, or rub their hands with these plants. The old men make incense, and with their faces to the east repeat the short prayer which Jesus Christ taught us. After this they go to wait upon the old men, some go to the dance, and others to the duties of the state. Later on they meet at the early lectures, then in the temple, then for bodily exercise. Then for a little while they sit down to rest, and at length they go to dinner.

Among them there is never gout in the hands or feet, no catarrh, nor sciatica, nor grievous colics, nor flatulency, nor hard breathing. For these diseases are caused by indigestion and flatulency, and by frugality and exercise they remove every humor and spasm. Wherefore it is unseemly in the extreme to be seen vomiting or spitting, since they say that this is a sign either of little exercise or of ignoble sloth, or of drunkenness or gluttony. They suffer rather from swellings or from the dry spasm, which they relieve with plenty of good and juicy food. They heal fevers with pleasant baths and with milk-food, and with a pleasant habitation in the country and by gradual exercise. Unclean diseases cannot be prevalent with them because they often clean their bodies by bathing in wine, and soothe them with aromatic oil, and by the sweat of exercise they diffuse the poisonous vapor which corrupts the blood and the marrow. They do suffer a little from consumption, because they cannot perspire at the breast, but they never have asthma, for the humid nature of which a heavy man is required. They cure hot fevers with cold potations of water, but slight ones with sweet smells, with cheese-bread or sleep, with music or dancing. Tertiary fevers are cured by bleeding, by rhubarb or by a similar drawing remedy, or by water soaked in the roots of plants, with purgative and sharp-tasting qualities. But it is rarely that they take purgative medicines. Fevers occuring every fourth day are cured easily by suddenly startling the unprepared patients, and by means of herbs producing effects opposite to the humors of this fever. All these secrets they told me in opposition to their own wishes. They take more diligent pains to cure the lasting fevers, which they fear more, and they strive to counteract these by the observation of stars and of plants, and by prayers to God. Fevers recurring every fifth, sixth, eighth or more days, you never find whenever heavy humors are wanting.

They use baths, and moreover they have warm ones according to the Roman custom, and they make use also of olive oil. They have found out, too, a great many secret cures for the preservation of cleanliness and health. And in other ways they labor to cure the epilepsy, with which they are often troubled.

Grand. A sign this disease is of wonderful cleverness, for from it Hercules, Scotus, Socrates, Callimachus, and Mahomet have suffered.

Capt. They cure by means of prayers to heaven, by strengthening the head, by acids, by planned gymnastics, and with fat cheese-bread sprinkled with the flour of wheaten corn. They are very skilled in making dishes, and in them they put spice, honey, butter and many highly strengthening spices, and they temper their richness with acids, so that they never vomit. They do not drink ice-cold drinks nor artificial hot drinks, as the Chinese do; for they are not without aid against the humors of the body, on account of the help they get from the natural heat of the water; but they strengthen it with crushed garlic, with vinegar, with wild thyme, with mint, and with basil, in the summer or in time of special heaviness. They also know a secret for renovating life after about the seventieth year, and for ridding it of affliction, and this they do by a pleasing and indeed wonderful art.

G. M. Thus far you have said nothing concerning their sciences and magistrates.

Capt. Undoubtedly I have. But since you are so curious I will add more. Both when it is new moon and full moon they call a council after a sacrifice. To this all from twenty years upwards are admitted, and each one is asked separately to say what is wanting in the state, and which of the magistrates have discharged their duties rightly and which wrongly. Then after eight days all the magistrates assemble, to wit, Hoh first, and with him Power, Wisdom and Love. Each one of the three last has three magistrates under him, making in all thirteen, and they consider the affairs of the arts pertaining to each one of them; Power, of war; Wisdom, of the sciences; Love, of food, clothing, education and breeding. The masters of all the bands, who are captains of tens, of fifties, of hundreds, also assemble, the women first and then the men. They argue about those things which are of the welfare of the state, and they choose the magistrates from among those who have already been named in the great council. In this manner they assembel daily, Hoh and his three princes, and they correct, confirm and execute the matters passing to them, as decisions in the elections; other necessary questions they provide of themselves. They do not use lots unless when they are altogether doubtful how to decide. The eight magistrates under Hoh, Power, Wisdom and Love are changed according to the wish of the people, but the first four are never changed, unless they, taking counsel with themselves, give up the dignity of one to another, whom among them they know to be wiser, more renowned, and more nearly

perfect. And then they are obedient and honorable, since
they yield willingly to the wiser man and are taught by
him. This, however, rarely happens. The principals of
the sciences, except Metaphysics, who is Hoh himself, and
is as it were, the architect of all science, having rule over
all, are attached to Wisdom. Hoh is ashamed to be ignorant of any possible thing. Under Wisdom therefore is
Grammar, Logic, Physics, Medicine, Astrology, Astronomy,
Geometry, Cosmography, Music, Perspective, Arithmetic,
Poetry, Rhetoric, Painting, Sculpture. Under the triumvir
Love are Breeding Agriculture, Education, Medicine, Clothing, Pasturage, Coining.

G. M. What about their judges?

Capt. This is the point I was just thinking of explain-
ing. Every one is judged by the first master of his trade,
and thus all the head artificers are judges. They punish
with exile, with flogging, with blame, with deprivation of
the common table, with exclusion from the church and
from the company of women. When there is a case in
which great injury has been done, it is punished with death,
and they repay an eye with an eye, a nose for a nose, a
tooth for a tooth, and so on, according to the law of retaliation. If the offence is wilful the council decides. When
there is strife and it takes place undesignedly, the sentence
is mitigated; nevertheless, not by the judge but by the triumvirate, from whom even it may be referred to Hoh, not
on account of justice but of mercy, for Hoh is able to pardon. They have no prisons, except one tower for shutting
up rebellious enemies, and there is no written statement
of a case, which we commonly call a lawsuit. But the accu-
sation and witnesses are produced in the presence of the
judge and Power; the accused person makes his defence,
and he is immediately acquitted or condemned by the judge;
and if he appeals to the triumvirate, on the following day
he is acquitted or condemned. On the third day he is dismissed through the mercy and clemency of Hoh, or receives

the inviolable rigor of his sentence. An accused person is reconciled to his accuser and to his witnesses, as it were, with the medicine of his complaint, that is, with embracing and kissing. No one is killed or stoned unless by the hands of the people, the accuser and the witnesses beginning first. For they have no executioners and lictors, lest the state should sink into ruin. The choice of death is given to the rest of the people, who enclose the lifeless remains in little bags and burn them by the application of fire, while exhorters are present for the purpose of advising concerning a good death. Nevertheless, the whole nation laments and beseechs God that His anger may be appeased, being in grief that it should as it were have to cut off a rotten member of the state. Certain officers talk to and convince the accused man by means of arguments until he himself acquiesces in the sentence of death passed upon him, or else he does not die. But if a crime has been committed against the liberty of the republic, or against God, or against the supreme magistrates, there is immediate censure without pity. These only are punished with death. He who is about to die is compelled to state in the presence of the people and with religious scrupulousness the reasons for which he does not deserve death, and also the sins of the others who ought to die instead of him, and further the mistakes of the magistrates. If, moreover, it should seem right to the person thus asserting, he must say why the accused ones are deserving of less punishment than he. And if by his arguments he gains the victory he is sent into exile, and appeases the state by means of prayers and sacrifices and good life ensuing. They do not torture those named by the accused person, but they warn them. Sins of frailty and ignorance are punished only with blaming, and with compulsory continuation as learners under the law and discipline of those sciences or arts against which they have sinned. And all these things they have mutually among themselves, since they seem to be in very truth members of the same body, and one of another.

This further I would have you know, that if a trans-gressor, without waiting to be accused, goes of his own accord before a magistrate, accusing himself and seeking to make amends, that one is liberated from the punishment of a secret crime, and since he has not been accused of such a crime, his punishment is changed into another. They take special care that no one should invent slander, and if this should happen they meet the offence with the punish-ment of retaliation. Since they always walk about and work in crowds, five witnesses are required for the convic-tion of a transgressor. If the case is otherwise, after having threatened him, he is released after he has sworn an oath as the warant of good conduct. Or if he is accused a sec-ond or third time, his increased punishment rests on the testimony of three or two witnesses. They have but few laws, and these short and plain, and written upon a flat table, and hanging to the doors of the temple, that is be-tween the columns. And on single columns can be seen the essences of things described in the very terse style of Metaphysics—viz., the essences of God, of the angels, of the world, of the stars, of man, of fate, of virtue, all done with great wisdom. The definitions of all the virtues are also delineated here, and here is the tribunal, where the judges of all the virtues have their seat. The definition of a certain virtue is written under that column where the judges for the aforesaid virtue sit, and when a judge gives judgment he sits and speaks thus: O son, thou hast sinned against this sacred definition of beneficence, or of magnani-mity, or of another virtue, as the case may be. And after discussion the judge legally condemns him to the punish-ment for the crime of which he is accused—viz., for injury, for despondency, for pride, for ingratitude, for sloth, &c. But the sentences are certain and true correctives, savoring more of clemency than of actual punishment.

G. M. Now you ought to tell me about their priests, their sacrifices, their religion, and their belief.

Capt. The chief priest is Hoh, and it is the duty of all the superior magistrates to pardon sins. Therefore the whole state by secret confession, which we also use, tell their sins to the magistrates, who at once purge their souls and teach those that are inimical to the people. Then the sacred magistrates themselves confess their own sinfulness to the three supreme chiefs, and together they confess the faults of one another, though no special one is named, and they confess especially the heavier faults and those harmful to the state. At length the triumvirs confess their sinfulness to Hoh himself, who forthwith recognizes the kinds of sins that are harmful to the state, and succors with timely remedies. Then he offers sacrifices and prayers to God. And before this he confesses the sins of the whole people, in the presence of God, and publicly in the temple, above the altar, as often as it had been necessary that the fault should be corrected. Nevertheless, no transgressor is spoken of by his name. In this manner he absolves the people by advising them that they should beware of sins of the aforesaid kind. Afterwards he offers sacrifice to God, that He should pardon the state and absolve it of its sins, and to teach and defend it. Once in every year the chief priests of each separate subordinate state confess their sins in the presence of Hoh. Thus he is not ignorant of the wrongdoings of the provinces, and forthwith he removes them with all human and heavenly remedies.

Sacrifice is conducted after the following manner: Hoh asks the people which one among them wishes to give himself as a sacrifice to God for the sake of his fellows. He is then placed upon the fourth table, with ceremonies and the offering up of prayers: the table is hung up in a wonderful manner by means of four ropes passing through four cords attached to firm pulley-blocks in the small dome of the temple. This done they cry to the God of mercy, that He may accept the offering, not of a beast as among the heathen, but of a human being. Then Hoh orders the ropes to be drawn and the sacrifice is pulled up above to the centre of the small dome, and there it dedicates itself with the most fervent supplications. Food is given to it through a window by the priests, who live around the dome, but it is allowed a very little to eat, until it has atoned for the sins of the state. There with prayer and fasting he cries to the God of heaven that He might accept its willing offering. And after twenty or thirty days, the anger of God being appeased, the sacrifice becomes a priest, or sometimes, though rarely, returns below by means of the outer way for the priests. Ever after this man is treated with great benevolence and much honor, for the reason that he offered himself unto death for the sake of his coun- try. But God does not require death. The priests above twenty-four years of age offer praises from their places in the top of the temple. This they do in the middle of the night, at noon, in the morning and in the evening, to wit, four times a day they sing their chants in the presence of God. It is also their work to observe the stars and to note with the astrolabe their motions and influences upon human things, and to find out their powers. Thus they know in what part of the earth any change has been or will be, and at what time it has taken place, and they send to find whether the matter be as they have it. They make a note of predictions, true and false, so that they may be able from experience to predict more correctly. The priests, more- over, determine the hours for breeding and the days for sowing, reaping, and gathering the vintage, and are as it were the ambassadors and intercessors and connection be- tween God and man. And it is from among them mostly that Hoh is elected. They write very learned treatises and search into the sciences. Below they never descend, unless for their dinner and supper, so that the essence of their heads do not descend to the stomachs and liver. Only very seldom, and that as a cure for the ills of solitude, do they have converse with women. On certain days Hoh goes up to them and deliberates with them concerning the matters which he has lately investigated for the benefit of the state and all the nations of the world.

In the temple beneath one priest always stands near the altar praying for the people, and at the end of every hour another succeeds him, just as we are accustomed in solemn prayer to change every fourth hour. And this method of supplication they call perpetual prayer. After a meal they return thanks to God. Then they sing the deeds of the Christian, Jewish, and Gentile heroes, and of those of all other nations, and this is very delightful to them. Forsooth, no one is envious of another. They sing a hymn to Love, one to Wisdom, and one each to all the other virtues, and this they do under the direction of the ruler of each virtue. Each one takes the woman he loves most, and they dance for exercise with propriety and stateliness under the peristyles. The women wear their long hair all twisted together and collected into one knot on the crown of the head, but in rolling it they leave one curl. The men, however, have one curl only and the rest of their hair around the head is shaven off. Further, they wear a slight covering, and above this a round hat a little larger than the size of their head. In the fields they use caps, but at home each one wears a biretto white, red, or another color according to his trade or ocupation. Moreover, the magistrates use grander and more imposing-looking coverings for the head.

They hold great festivities when the sun enters the four cardinal points of the heaven, that is when he enters Cancer, Libra, Capricorn, and Aries. On these occasions they have very learned, splendid, and as it were comic performances. They celebrate also every full and every new moon with a festival, as also they do the anniversaries of the founding of the city, and of the days when they have won victories or done any other great achievement. The celebrations take place with the music of female voices, with the noise of trumpets and drums, and the firing of saluta-

tions. The poets sing the praises of the most renowned
leaders and the victories. Nevertheless, if any of them
should deceive even by disparaging a foreign hero, he is
punished. No one can exercise the function of a poet who
invents that which is not true, and a license like this they
think to be a pest of our world, for the reason that it puts
a premium upon virtue and often assigns it to unworthy
persons, either from fear or flattery, or ambition or avarice.
For the praise of no one is a statue erected until after his
death; but whilst he is alive, who has found out new arts
and very useful secrets, or who has rendered great service
to the state either at home or on the battle-field, his name
is written in the book of heroes. They do not bury dead
bodies, but burn them, so that a plague may not arise from
them, and so that they may be converted into fire, a very
noble and powerful thing, which has its coming from the
sun and returns to it. And for the above reasons no chance
is given for idolatry. The statues and pictures of the
heroes, however, are there, and the splendid women set
apart to become mothers often look at them. Prayers are
made from the state to the four horizontal corners of the
world. In the morning to the rising sun, then to the setting
sun, then to the south, and lastly to the north; and in the
contrary order in the evening, first to the setting sun, to
the rising sun, to the north, and at length to the south.
They repeat but one prayer, which asks for health of body
and of mind, and happiness for themselves and all people,
and they conclude it with the petition "As it seems best to
God." The public prayer for all is long, and it is poured
forth to heaven. For this reason the altar is round and is
divided crosswise by ways at right angles to one another.
By these ways Hoh enters after he has repeated the four
prayers, and he prays looking up to heaven. And then a
great mystery is seen by them. The priestly vestments are
of a beauty and meaning like to those of Aaron. They
resemble Nature and they surpass Art.

They divide the seasons according to the revolution of
the sun, and not of the stars, and they observe yearly by
how much time the one precedes the other. They hold that
the sun approaches nearer and nearer, and therefore by
ever lessening circles reaches the tropics and the equator
every year a little sooner. They measure months by the
course of the moon, years by that of the sun. They praise
Ptolemy, admire Copernicus, but place Aristarchus and Phi-
lolaus before him. They take great pains in endeavoring
to understand the construction of the world, and whether
or not it will perish, and at what time. They believe that
the true oracle of Jesus Christ is by the signs in the sun,
in the moon, and in the stars, which signs do not thus
appear to many of us foolish ones. Therefore they wait for
the renewing of the age, and perchance for its end. They
say that is very doubtful whether the world was made from
nothing, or from the ruins of other worlds, or from chaos,
but they certainly think that it was made, and did not exist
from eternity. Therefore they disbelieve in Aristotle,
whom they consider a logician and not a philosopher. From
analogies, they can draw many arguments against the eternity of the world. The sun and the stars they, so to speak,
regard as the living representatives and signs of God, as the
temples and holy living altars, and they honor but do not
worship them. Beyond all other things they venerate the
sun, but they consider no created thing worthy the adora-
tion of worship. This they give to God alone, and thus
they serve Him, that they may not come into the power of
a tyrant and fall into misery by undergoing punishment by
creatures of revenge. They contemplate and know God
under the image of the Sun, and they call it the sign of
God, His face and living image, by means of which light,
heat, life, and the making of all things good and bad proceeds. Therefore they have built an altar like to the Sun
in shape, and the priests praise God in the sun and in the
stars, as it were His altars, and in the heavens, His temple

as it were; and they pray to good angels, who are, so to speak, the intercessors living in the stars, their strong abodes. For God long since set signs of their beauty in heaven, and of His glory in the Sun. They say there is but one heaven, and that the planets move and rise of themselves when they approach the sun or are in conjunction with it.

They assert two principles of the physics of things below, namely, that the Sun is the father, and the Earth the mother; the air is an impure part of the heavens; all fire is derived from the sun. The sea is the sweat of earth, or the fluid of earth combusted, and fused within its bowels; but is the bond of union between air and earth, as the blood is of the spirit and flesh of animals. The world is a great animal, and we live within it as worms live within us. Therefore we do not belong to the system of stars, sun, and earth, but to God only; for in respect to them which seek only to amplify themselves, we are born and live by chance; but in respect to God, whose instruments we are, we are formed by prescience and design, and for a high end. Therefore we are bound to no Father but God, and receive all things from Him. They hold as beyond question the immortality of souls, and that these associate with good angels after death, or with bad angels, according as they have likened themselves in this life to either. For all things seek their like. They differ little from us as to places of reward and punishment. They are in doubt whether there are other worlds beyond ours, and account it madness to say there is nothing. Nonentity is incompatible with the infinite entity of God. They lay down two principles of metaphysics, entity which is the highest God, and nothingness which is the defect of entity. Evil and sin come of the propensity of nothingness; the sin having its cause not efficient, but in deficiency. Deficiency is, they say, of power, wisdom or will. Sin they place in the last of these three, because he who knows and has the power to do good is bound also to have the will, for will arises out of them. They worship God in Trinity, saying God is the supreme Power, whence proceeds the highest Wisdom, which is the same with God, and from these comes Love, which is both Power and Wisdom; but they do not distinguish persons by name, as in our Christian law, which has not been revealed to them. This religion, when its abuses have been removed, will be the future mistress of the world, as great theologians teach and hope. Therefore Spain found the New World (though its first discoverer, Columbus, great- est of heroes, was a Genoese), that all nations should be gathered under one law. We know not what we do, but God knows, whose instruments we are. They sought new regions for lust of gold and riches, but God works to a higher end. The sun strives to burn up the earth, not to produce plants and men, but God guides the battle to great issues. His the praise, to Him the glory!

G. M. Oh, if you knew what our astrologers say of the coming age, and of our age, that has in it more history within a hundred years than all the world had in four thousand years before! Of the wonderful invention of printing and guns, and the use of the magnet, and how it all comes of Mercury, Mars, the Moon, and the Scorpion!

Capt. Ah, Well! God gives all in His good time. They astrologize too much.

NEW
ATLANTIS.

A VVorke unfinished.

Written by the Right Honourable, FRANCIS,
*Lord Verulam, Viscount S*t*. Alban.*

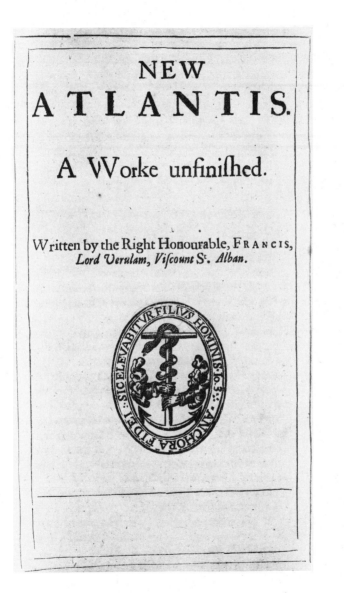

ADDITIONAL BIBLIOGRAPHY

Alley, Ronald, and J. Rotherstein, *Francis Bacon,* London, 1964

Brown, Catherine D., *Francis Bacon,* Boston, 1963

Green, A. Wigfall, *Sir Francis Bacon, His Life and Works,* Denver, 1952

Sturt, M., *Francis Bacon,* London, 1932

Willey, B. *The Seventeenth Century Background,* New York, 1942

Overleaf: Title page of Bacon's "New Atlantis" in the sixth edition of "Sylva Sylvanum", London, 1651.

FRANCIS BACON

In many external respects, the life of Francis Bacon (1561-1626) was similar to that of Sir Thomas More, a century before. Both came from distinguished families, and both received excellent educations. Both studied law and both practised that profession. Both entered public life at a comparatively early age, and both finally arrived, at the end of their political careers, at the Lord Chancellorship. Moreover, each fell into disfavor with his sovereign; each was accused of taking bribes; each was condemned and imprisoned in the Tower. Finally, each was the most distinguished writer and thinker of his time, and each was, in a sense, a martyr to his faith. More died because of his steadfast devotion to his religion. Bacon, so the story goes, met his death through devotion to experimental science. While testing the preservative powers of snow, he contracted a chill and perished. This external similarity does not extend, however, to the characters of the two men. More was a man of the utmost integrity, sweetness, and generosity; Bacon was by no means admirable.

Moreover, aside from the fact that both men wrote utopias, there is little similarity between their writings. More was a classicist and a humanist; his *Utopia* is well-planned, light, satirical, yet eminently profound and sane. Bacon, often mis-called "The father of inductive philosophy," was pre-eminently a modern and a scientist; his *New Atlantis* is incomplete, ill-proportioned, somewhat heavy in style, and dogmatically devoted to the glorification of natural science. So, too, with his other writings. Although he is best known to the general reader for his brief *Essays* (1597, 1625), his great work is the voluminous treatise on scientific method, the *Instauratio Magna*, comprising the *Advancement of Learning* (1605), its Latin enlargement, *De Augmentis Scientiarum* (1623), the *Novum Organum* (1620), which contains an analysis and exposition of the inductive method, and the exemplary natural history, *Sylva Sylvarum* (1627) to which was posthumously appended the *New Atlantis*. This little fragment, written about 1624, embodies in fictional form the ideal of an academy for scientific research. It offers an excellent introduction to Bacon's conception of the dignity and utility of science, together with an early account of the experimental method. Although it was somewhat influenced by More's *Utopia*, which Bacon refers to, and possibly by Campanella's *City of the Sun* which had appeared a year or two earlier, the *New Atlantis* is entirely faithful to the main lines of Bacon's grandiose philosophy. It also embodies, curiously enough, his personal love for grandiose accoutrements and ceremonies.

Bacon's works are easily accessible in many editions. The student should not neglect Macaulay's brilliant essay attacking Bacon's personal character, while defending his philosophic writings. The standard biography is still that of James Spedding, *Life and Letters of Francis Bacon* (7 vols., 1861-1874), but the student will find the briefer lives by R. W. Church (1884), or Charles Williams (1933) somewhat more manageable. For an interesting contemporary account, one should consult the *Life* (1627) by William Rawley, Bacon's chaplain, secretary, and earliest editor. The scientific aspects of Bacon's philosophy, and his influence upon later thinkers, is ably discussed by T. C. Allbutt, *Palissy, Bacon, and the Revival of Natural Science* (1914), by A. E. Taylor, *Francis Bacon* (1926), and, more recently, by F. Steegmuller, *Sir Francis Bacon, the First Modern Mind* (1930). A useful annotated edition of the *New Atlantis* is that by G. C. Moore Smith (1909).

NEW ATLANTIS

W E SAILED from Peru, where we had continued by the space of one whole year, for China and Japan, by the South Sea, taking with us victuals for twelve months; and had good winds from the east, though soft and weak, for five months' space and more. But then the wind came about, and settled in the west for many days, so as we could make little or no way, and were sometimes in purpose to turn back. But then again there arose strong and great winds from the south, with a point east; which carried us up, for all that we could do, towards the north: by which time our victuals failed us, though we had made good spare of them. So that finding ourselves, in the midst of the greatest wilderness of waters in the world, without victual, we gave ourselves for lost men, and prepared for death. Yet we did lift up our hearts and voices to God above, who showeth His wonders in the deep; beseeching Him of his mercy, that as in the beginning He discovered the face of the deep, and brought forth dry land, so He would now discover land to us, that we might not perish.

And it came to pass, that the next day about evening we saw within a kenning before us, toward the north, as it were thick clouds, which did put us in some hope of land: knowing how that part of the South Sea was utterly un-known: and might have islands or continents, that hitherto were not come to light. Wherefore we bent our course thither, where we saw the appearance of land, all that night: and in the dawning of next day, we might plainly discern that it was a land flat to our sight, and full of boscage, which made it show the more dark. And after an hour and a half's sailing, we entered into a good haven, being the port of a fair city. Not great indeed, but well built, and that gave a pleasant view from the sea. And we thinking every minute long till we were on land, came close to the shore and offered to land. But straightways we saw divers of the people, with bastons in their hands, as it were forbidding us to land; yet without any cries or fierceness, but only as warning us off, by signs that they made. Whereupon being not a little discomfited, we were advis' ing with ourselves what we should do.

During which time there made forth to us a small boat, with about eight persons in it, whereof one of them had in his hand a tipstaff of a yellow cane, tipped at both ends with blue, who made aboard our ship, without any show of distrust at all. And when he saw one of our number present himself somewhat afore the rest, he drew forth a little scroll of parchment (somewhat yellower than our parchment, and shining like the leaves of writing tables, but otherwise soft and flexible), and delivered it to our foremost man. In which scroll were written in ancient Hebrew, and in ancient Greek, and in good Latin of the school, and in Spanish these words: "Land ye not, none of you, and provide to be gone from this coast within sixteen days, except you have further time given you; meanwhile, if you want fresh water, or victual, or help for your sick, or that your ship needeth repair, write down your wants, and you shall have that which belongeth to mercy." This scroll was signed with a stamp of cherubim's wings, not spread, but hanging downwards; and by them a cross. This being delivered, the officer returned, and left only a servant with us to receive our answer.

Consulting hereupon amongst ourselves, we were much perplexed. The denial of landing, and hasty warning us away, troubled us much: on the other side, to find that the people had languages, and were so full of humanity, did comfort us not a little. And above all, the sign of the cross to that instrument, was to us a great rejoicing, and as it were a certain presage of good. Our answer was in the Spanish tongue, "That for our ship, it was well; for we had rather met with calms and contrary winds, than any tempests. For our sick, they were many, and in very ill case; so that if they were not permitted to land, they ran in danger of their lives." Our other wants we set down in particular, adding, "That we had some little store of merchandise, which if it pleased them to deal for, it might supply our wants, without being chargeable unto them." We offered some reward in pistolets unto the servant, and a piece of crimson velvet to be presented to the officer; but the servant took them not, nor would scarce look upon them; and so left us, and went back in another little boat which was sent for him.

About three hours after we had despatched our answer there came towards us a person (as it seemed) of a place. He had on him a gown with wide sleeves, of a kind of water chamolet, of an excellent azure color, far more glossy than ours: his under apparel was green, and so was his hat, being in the form of a turban, daintily made, and not so huge as the Turkish turbans; and the locks of his hair came down below the brims of it. A reverend man was he to behold. He came in a boat, gilt in some part of it, with four persons more only in that boat; and was followed by another boat, wherein were some twenty. When he was come within a flight-shot of our ship, signs were made to us that we should send forth some to meet him upon the water, which we presently did in our ship-boat, sending the principal man amongst us save one, and four of our number with him.

When we were come within six yards of their boat, they called to us to stay, and not to approach farther, which we did. And thereupon the man, whom I before described, stood up, and with a loud voice in Spanish, asked, "Are ye Christians?" We answered, "We were;" fearing the less, because of the cross we had seen in the subscription. At

which answer the said person lift up his right hand towards
heaven, and drew it softly to his mouth (which is the gesture they use, when they thank God), and said: "If ye
will swear, all of you, by the merits of the Saviour, that ye
are no pirates; nor have shed blood, lawfully nor unlaw-
fully, within forty days past; you may have license to come
on land." We said, "We are all ready to take that oath."
Whereupon one of those that were with him, being (as it
seemed) a notary, made an entry of this act. Which done,
another of the attendants of the great person, which was
with him in the same boat, after his lord had spoken a little
to him, said aloud: "My lord would have you know, that
it is not of pride, or greatness, that he cometh not aboard
your ship: but for that, in your answer, you declare that
you have many sick amongst you, he was warned by the
conservator of health of the city that he should keep a
distance." We bowed ourselves towards him, and answered: "We were his humble servants; and accounted for
great honor and singular humanity towards us, that which
was already done: but hoped well, that the nature of the
sickness of our men was not infections." So he returned;
and a while after came the notary to us aboard our ship;
holding in his hand a fruit of that country, like an orange,
but of color between orange-tawny and scarlet: which cast
a most excellent odor. He used it (as it seemed) for a preservative against infection. He gave us our oath, "By the
name of Jesus, and His merits:" and after told us, that the
next day by six of the clock in the morning, we should be
sent to, and brought to the strangers' house (so he called
it), where we should be accommodated of things, both for
our whole and for our sick. So he left us; and when we
offered him some pistolets, he smiling, said, "He must not
be twice paid for one labor;" meaning (as I take it) that
he had salary sufficient of the state for his service. For
(as I after learned) they call an officer that taketh rewards,
twice-paid.

The next morning early, there came to us the same officer that came to us at first with his cane, and told us:
"He came to conduct us to the strangers' house: and that he
had prevented the hour, because we might have the whole
day before us for our business. For (said he) if you will
follow my advice, there shall first go with me some few of
you, and see the place, and how it may be made convenient
for you: and then you may send for your sick, and the rest
of your number, which ye will bring on land." We thanked
him, and said, "That his care which he took of desolate
strangers, God would reward." And so six of us went on
land with him; and when we were on land, he went before
us, and turned to us, and said, "He was but our servant,
and our guide." He led us through three fair streets; and
all the way we went there were gathered some people on
both sides, standing in a row; but in so civil a fashion, as if
it had been, not to wonder at us, but to welcome us; and
divers of them, as we passed by them, put their arms a little
abroad, which is their gesture when they bid any welcome.

The strangers' house is a fair and spacious house, built of
brick, of somewhat a bluer color than our brick; and with
handsome windows, some of glass, some of a kind of cam-
bric oiled. He brought us first into a fair parlor above
stairs, and then asked us, "What number of persons we
were? and how many sick?" We answered, "We were in
all (sick and whole) one and fifty persons, whereof our
sick were seventeen." He desired us to have patience a
little, and to stay till he came back to us, which was about
an hour after; and then he led us to see the chambers
which were provided for us, being in number nineteen.
They having cast it (as it seemeth) that four of those
chambers, which were better than the rest, might receive
four of the principal men of our company; and lodge them
alone by themselves; and the other fifteen chambers were
to lodge us, two and two together. The chambers were
handsome and cheerful chambers, and furnished civilly.

Then he led us to a long gallery, like a dorture, where he
showed us all along the one side (for the other side was but
wall and window) seventeen cells, very neat ones, having
partitions of cedar wood. Which gallery and cells, being in
all forty (many more than we needed), were instituted as
an infirmary for sick persons. And he told us withal, that
as any of our sick waxed well, he might be removed from
his cell to a chamber: for which purpose there were set
forth ten spare chambers, besides the number we spake of
before. This done, he brought us back to the parlor, and
lifting his cane a little (as they do when they give any
charge or command), said to us, "Ye are to know that the
custom of the land requireth, that after this day and to-
morrow (which we give you for removing your people
from your ship), you are to keep within doors for three
days. But let it not trouble you, nor do not think yourselves restrained, but rather left to your rest and ease. You
shall want nothing; and there are six of our people appointed to attend you for any business you may have
abroad." We gave him thanks with all affection and respect, and said, "God surely is manifested in this land."
We offered him also twenty pistolets; but he smiled, and
only said: "What? Twice paid!" And so he left us.

Soon after our dinner was served in; which was right
good viands, both for bread and meat: better than any col-
legiate diet that I have known in Europe. We had also
drink of three sorts, all wholesome and good; wine of
the grape; a drink of grain, such as is with us our ale, but
more clear; and a kind of cider made of a fruit of that
country; a wonderful pleasing and refreshing drink. Besides, there were brought in to us great store of those scarlet oranges for our sick; which (they said) were an assured
remedy for sickness taken at sea. There was given us also
a box of small grey or whitish pills, which they wished our
sick should take, one of the pills every night before sleep;
which (they said) would hasten their recovery.

The next day, after that our trouble of carriage and removing of our men and goods out of our ship was somewhat settled and quiet, I thought good to call our company together, and when they were assembled, said unto
them, "My dear friends, let us know ourselves, and how
it standeth with us. We are men cast on a land, as Jonas
was out of the whale's belly, when we were as buried in
the deep; and now we are on land, we are but between
death and life, for we are beyond both the old world and
the new; and whether ever we shall see Europe, God only
knoweth. It is a kind of miracle hath brought us hither,
and it must be little less that shall bring us hence. Therefore in regard of our deliverance past, and our danger present and to come, let us look up to God, and every man re-
form his own ways. Besides we are come here amongst a
Christian people, full of piety and humanity. Let us not
bring that confusion of face upon ourselves, as to show our
vices or unworthiness before them. Yet there is more, for
they have by commandment (though in form of courtesy)
cloistered us within these walls for three days; who knoweth whether it be not to take some taste of our manners
and conditions? And if they find them bad, to banish us
straightways; if good, to give us further time. For these
men that they have given us for attendance, may withal
have an eye upon us. Therefore, for God's love, and as we
love the weal of our souls and bodies, let us so behave ourselves, as we may be at peace with God, and may find grace
in the eyes of this people." Our company with one voice
thanked me for my good admonition, and promised me to
live soberly and civilly, and without giving any the least
occasion of offence. So we spent our three days joyfully,
and without care, in expectation what would be done with
us when they were expired. During which time, we had
every hour joy of the amendment of our sick, who thought
themselves cast into some divine pool of healing, they
mended so kindly and so fast.

The morrow after our three days were past, there came
to us a new man, that we had not seen before, clothed in
blue as the former was, save that his turban was white with
a small red cross on the top. He had also a tippet of fine
linen. At his coming in, he did bend to us a little, and put
his arms abroad. We of our parts saluted him in a very
lowly and submissive manner; as looking that from him
we should receive sentence of life or death. He desired to
speak with some few of us. Whereupon six of us only
stayed, and the rest avoided the room. He said, "I am by
office governor of this house of strangers, and by vocation
I am a Christian priest; and therefore am come to you, to
offer you my service, both as strangers, and chiefly as
Christians. Some things I may tell you, which I think you
will not be unwilling to hear. The state hath given you
license to stay on land for the space of six weeks: and let
it not trouble you, if your occasions ask further time, for
the law in this point is not precise; and I do not doubt, but
myself shall be able to obtain for you such further time as
shall be convenient. Ye shall also understand, that the
strangers' house is at this time rich, and much aforehand;
for it hath laid up revenue these thirty-seven years; for so
long it is since any stranger arrived in this part; and therefore take ye no care; the state will defray you all the time
you stay. Neither shall you stay one day the less for that.
As for any merchandise you have brought, ye shall be well
used, and have your return, either in merchandise or in
gold and silver: for to us it is all one. And if you have
any other request to make, hide it not; for ye shall find we
will not make your countenance to fall by the answer ye
shall receive. Only this I must tell you, that none of you
must go above a karan (that is with them a mile and a half)
from the walls of the city, without special leave."

We answered, after we had looked a while upon one
another, admiring this gracious and parent-like usage, that
we could not tell what to say, for we wanted words to

express our thanks; and his noble free offers left us nothing
to ask. It seemed to us, that we had before us a picture of
our salvation in heaven; for we that were a while since in
the jaws of death, were now brought into a place where
we found nothing but consolations. For the commandment laid upon us, we would not fail to obey it, though
it was impossible but our hearts should be inflamed to tread
further upon this happy and holy ground. We added, that
our tongues should first cleave to the roofs of our mouths,
ere we should forget, either this reverend person, or this
whole nation, in our prayers. We also most humbly be-
sought him to accept of us as his true servants, by as just
a right as ever men on earth were bounden; laying and
presenting both our persons and all we had at his feet. He
said, he was a priest, and looked for a priest's reward;
which was our brotherly love, and the good of our souls
and bodies. So he went from us, not without tears of tenderness in his eyes, and left us also confused with joy and
kindness, saying amongst ourselves, that we were come into
a land of angels which did appear to us daily, and prevent
us with comforts, which we thought not of, much less
expected.

The next day, about ten of the clock, the governor came
to us again, and after salutations, said familiarly, that he
was come to visit us; and called for a chair, and sat him
down; and we being some ten of us (the rest were of the
meaner sort, or else gone abroad), sat down with him; and
when we were set, he began thus: "We of this island of
Bensalem (for so they called it in their language) have this:
that by means of our solitary situation, and of the laws of
secrecy, which we have for our travellers, and our rare
admission of strangers; we know well most part of the
habitable world, and are ourselves unknown. Therefore
because he that knoweth least is fittest to ask questions, it is
more reason, for the entertainment of the time, that ye ask
me questions, than that I ask you."

We answered, that we humbly thanked him, that he would give us leave so to do. And that we conceived by the taste we had already, that there was no worldly thing on earth more worthy to be known than the state of that happy land. But above all (we said) since that we were met from the several ends of the world, and hoped as-suredly that we should meet one day in the kingdom of heaven (for that we were both parts Christians), we de-sired to know (in respect that land was so remote, and so divided by vast and unknown seas from the land where our Saviour walked on earth) who was the apostle of that na-tion, and how it was converted to the faith? It appeared in his face, that he took great contentment in this our ques-tion; he said, "Ye knit my heart to you, by asking this ques-tion in the first place: for it showeth that you first seek the kingdom of heaven: and I shall gladly, and briefly satisfy your demand.

"About twenty years after the ascension of our Saviour it came to pass, that there was seen by the people of Ren-fusa (a city upon the eastern coast of our island, within sight, the night was cloudy and calm), as it might be some mile in the sea, a great pillar of light; not sharp, but in form of a column, or cylinder, rising from the sea, a great way up towards heaven; and on the top of it was seen a large cross of light, more bright and resplendent than the body of the pillar. Upon which so strange a spectacle, the people of the city gathered apace together upon the sands, to wonder; and so after put themselves into a number of small boats to go nearer to this marvellous sight. But when the boats were come within about sixty yards of the pillar, they found themselves all bound, and could go no further, yet so as they might move to go about, but might not approach nearer; so as the boats stood all as in a theatre, beholding this light, as an heavenly sign. It so fell out, that there was in one of the boats one of the wise men of the Society of Salomon's House; which house or college, my good brethren, is the very eye of this kingdom, who having a while attentively and devoutly viewed and con-templated this pillar and cross, fell down upon his face; and then raised himself upon his knees, and lifting up his hands to heaven, made his prayers in this manner:

" ' Lord God of heaven and earth; thou hast vouchsafed of thy grace, to those of our order to know thy works of creation, and true secrets of them; and to discern (as far as appertaineth to the generations of men) between divine miracles, works of Nature, works of art and impostures, and illusions of all sorts. I do here acknowledge and testify before this people, that the thing we now see before our eyes, is thy finger, and a true miracle. And forasmuch as we learn in our books, that thou never workest miracles, but to a divine and excellent end (for the laws of Nature are thine own laws, and thou exceedest them not but upon great cause), we most humbly beseech thee to prosper this great sign, and to give us the interpretation and use of it in mercy; which thou dost in some part secretly promise, by sending it unto us.'

"When he had made his prayer, he presently found the boat he was in movable and unbound; whereas all the rest remained still fast; and taking that for an assurance of leave to approach, he caused the boat to be softly and with silence rowed towards the pillar; but ere he came near it, the pillar and cross of light broke up, and cast itself abroad, as it were into a firmament of many stars, which also vanished soon after, and there was nothing left to be seen but a small ark, or chest of cedar, dry and not wet at all with water, though it swam; and in the fore-end of it, which was towards him, grew a small green branch of palm; and when the wise man had taken it with all rever-ence into his boat, it opened of itself, and there were found in it a book and a letter, both written in fine parch-ment, and wrapped in sindons of linen. The book con-tained all the canonical books of the Old and New Testa-

ment, according as you have them (for we know well what
the churches with you receive), and the Apocalypse itself;
and some other books of the New Testament, which were
not at that time written, were nevertheless in the book
And for the letter, it was in these words:

" 'I Bartholomew, a servant of the Highest, and apostle
of Jesus Christ, was warned by an angel that appeared to
me in a vision of glory, that I should commit this ark to the
floods of the sea.   Therefore I do testify and declare unto
the people where God shall ordain this ark to come to
land, that in the same day is come unto them salvation
and peace, and goodwill from the Father, and from the
Lord Jesus.'

"There was also in both these writings, as well the book
as the letter, wrought a great miracle, conform to that of
the apostles, in the original gift of tongues.   For there
being at that time, in this land, Hebrews, Persians, and
Indians, besides the natives, every one read upon the book
and letter, as if they had been written in his own language.
And thus was this land saved from infidelity (as the remain
of the old world was from water) by an ark, through the
apostolical and miraculous evangelism of St. Bartholomew."   And here he paused, and a messenger came, and
called him forth from us.   So this was all that passed in
that conference.

The next day, the same governor came again to us,
immediately after dinner, and excused himself, saying,
"That the day before he was called from us somewhat
abruptly, but now he would make us amends, and spend
time with us, if we held his company and conference
agreeable."   We answered, that we held it so agreeable and
pleasing to us, as we forgot both dangers past, and fears
to come, for the time we heard him speak; and that we
thought an hour spent with him was worth years of our
former life.   He bowed himself a little to us, and after we

were set again, he said, "Well, the questions are on your part."

One of our number said, after a little pause, that there was a matter we were no less desirous to know than fearful to ask, lest we might presume too far. But encouraged by his rare humanity towards us (that could scarce think ourselves strangers, being his vowed and professed servants), we would take the hardness to propound it; humbly beseeching him, if he thought it not fit to be answered, that he would pardon it, though he rejected it. We said, we well observed those his words, which he formerly spake, that this happy island, where we now stood, was known to few, and yet knew most of the nations of the world, which we found to be true, considering they had the languages of Europe, and knew much of our state and business; and yet we in Europe (notwithstanding all the remote discoveries and navigations of this last age) never heard any of the least inkling or glimpse of this island. This we found wonderful strange; for that all nations have interknowledge one of another, either by voyage into foreign parts, or by strangers that come to them; and though the traveller into a foreign country doth commonly know more by the eye than he that stayeth at home can by relation of the traveller; let both ways suffice to make a mutual knowledge, in some degree, on both parts. But for this island, we never heard tell of any ship of theirs, that had been seen to arrive upon any shore of Europe; no, nor of either the East or West Indies, nor yet of any ship of any other part of the world, that had made return for them. And yet the marvel rested not in this. For the situation of it (as his lordship said) in the secret conclave of such a vast sea might cause it. But then, that they should have knowledge of the languages, books, affairs, of those that lie such a distance from them, it was a thing we could not tell what to make of; for that it seemed to us a condition and propriety of divine powers and beings, to be hidden and unseen to others, and yet to have others open, and as in a light to them.

At this speech the governor gave a gracious smile and said, that we did well to ask pardon for this question we now asked, for that it imported, as if we thought this land a land of magicians, that sent forth spirits of the air into all parts, to bring them news and intelligence of other countries. It was answered by us all, in all possible humbleness, but yet with a countenance taking knowledge, that we knew that he spake it but merrily. That we were apt enough to think, there was somewhat supernatural in this island, but yet rather as angelical than magical. But to let his lordship know truly what it was that made us tender and doubtful to ask this question, it was not any such conceit, but because we remembered he had given a touch in his former speech, that this land had laws of secrecy touching strangers. To this he said, "You remember it aright; and therefore in that I shall say to you, I must reserve some particulars, which it is not lawful for me to reveal, but there will be enough left to give you satisfaction.

"You shall understand (that which perhaps you will scarce think credible) that about three thousand years ago, or somewhat more, the navigation of the world (especially for remote voyages) was greater than at this day. Do not think with yourselves, that I know not how much it is increased with you within these threescore years; I know it well, and yet I say, greater then than now; whether it was, that the example of the ark, that saved the remnant of men from the universal deluge, gave men confidence to adventure upon the waters, or what it was; but such is the truth. The Phoenicians, and especially the Tyrians, had great fleets; so had the Carthaginians their colony, which is yet farther west. Toward the east the shipping of Egypt, and of Palestine, was likewise great. China, also, and the great Atlantis (that you call America), which have now but junks and canoes, abounded then in tall ships. This island

(as appeareth by faithful registers of those times) had then
fifteen hundred strong ships, of great content. Of all this
there is with you sparing memory, or none; but we have
large knowledge thereof.

"At that time, this land was known and frequented by
the ships and vessels of all the nations before named. And
(as it cometh to pass) they had many times men of other
countries, that were no sailors, that came with them; as
Persians, Chaldeans, Arabians, so as almost all nations of
might and fame restored hither; of whom we have some
stirps and little tribes with us at this day. And for our
own ships, they went sundry voyages, as well to your
straits, which you call the Pillars of Hercules, as to other
parts in the Atlantic and Mediterranean Seas; as to Paguin
(which is the same with Cambalaine) and Quinzy, upon
the Oriental Seas, as far as to the borders of the East
Tartary.

"At the same time, and an age after or more, the inhabitants of the great Atlantis did flourish. For though the
narration and description which is made by a great man
with you, that the descendants of Neptune planted there,
and of the magnificent temple, palace, city and hill; and
the manifold streams of goodly navigable rivers, which as
so many chains environed the same site and temple; and
the several degrees of ascent, whereby men did climb up to
the same, as if it had been a Scala Coeli; be all poetical
and fabulous; yet so much is true, that the said country of
Atlantis, as well that of Peru, then called Coya, as that of
Mexico, then named Tyrambel, were mighty and proud
kingdoms, in arms, shipping, and riches; so mighty, as at
one time, or at least within the space of ten years, they
both made two great expeditions; they of Tyrambel
through the Atlantic to the Mediterranean Sea; and they of
Coya, through the South Sea upon this our island; and for
the former of these, which was into Europe, the same author amongst you, as it seemeth, had some relation from

the Egyptian priest, whom he citeth. For assuredly, such a thing there was. But whether it were the ancient Athenians that had the glory of the repulse and resistance of those forces, I can say nothing; but certain it is there never came back either ship or man from that voyage. Neither had the other voyage of those of Coya upon us had better fortune, if they had not met with enemies of greater clemency. For the king of this island, by name Altabin, a wise man and a great warrior, knowing well both his own strength and that of his enemies, handled the matter so, as he cut off their land forces from their ships, and entoiled both their navy and their camp with a greater power than theirs, both by sea and land; and compelled them to render themselves without striking a stroke; and after they were at his mercy, contenting himself only with their oath, that they should no more bear arms against him, dismissed them all in safety.

But the divine revenge overtook not long after those proud enterprises. For within less than the space of one hundred years the Great Atlantis was utterly lost and destroyed; not by a great earthquake, as your man saith, for that whole tract is little subject to earthquakes, but by a particular deluge, or inundation; those countries having at this day far greater rivers, and far higher mountains to pour down waters, than any part of the old world. But it is true that the same inundation was not deep, not past forty foot, in most places, from the ground, so that although it destroyed man and beast generally, yet some few wild inhabitants of the wood escaped. Birds were also saved by flying to the high trees and woods. For as for men, although they had buildings in many places higher than the depth of the water, yet that inundation, though it were shallow, had a long continuance, whereby they of the vale that were not drowned perished for want of food, and other things necessary.

So as marvel you not at the thin population of America, nor at the rudeness and ignorance of the people; for you must account your inhabitants of America as a young people, younger a thousand years at the least than the rest of the world, for that there was so much time between the universal flood and their particular inundation. For the poor remnant of human seed which remained in their mountains, peopled the country again slowly, by little and little, and being simple and a savage people (not like Noah and his sons, which was the chief family of the earth), they were not able to leave letters, arts, and civility to their posterity; and having likewise in their mountainous habitations been used, in respect of the extreme cold of those regions, to clothe themselves with the skins of tigers, bears, and great hairy goats, that they have in those parts; when after they came down into the valley, and found the intolerable heats which are there, and knew no means of lighter apparel, they were forced to begin the custom of going naked, which continueth at this day. Only they take great pride and delight in the feathers of birds, and this also they took from those their ancestors of the mountains, who were invited unto it, by the infinite flight of birds, that came up to the high ground, while the waters stood below. So you see, by this main accident of time, we lost our traffic with the Americans, with whom of all others, in regard they lay nearest to us, we had most commerce.

As for the other parts of the world, it is most manifest that in the ages following (whether it were in respect of wars, or by a natural revolution of time) navigation did everywhere greatly decay, and specially far voyages (the rather by the use of galleys, and such vessels as could hardly brook the ocean) were altogether left and omitted. So then, that part of intercourse which could be from other nations, to sail to us, you see how it hath long since ceased; except it were by some rare accident, as this of yours. But now of the cessation of that other part of intercourse,

which might be by our sailing to other nations, I must yield
you some other cause. For I cannot say, if I shall say
truly, but our shipping, for number, strength, mariners,
pilots, and all things that appertain to navigation, is as
great as ever; and therefore why we should sit at home, I
shall now give you an account by itself; and it will draw
nearer, to give you satisfaction, to your principal question.

"There reigned in this island about 1,900 years ago, a
king, whose memory of all others we most adore; not super-
stitiously, but as a divine instrument, though a mortal man:
his name was Salomona; and we esteem him as the lawgiver of our nation. This king had a large heart, inscrutable
for good; and was wholly bent to make his kingdom and
people happy. He therefore taking into consideration how
sufficient and substantive this land was, to maintain itself
without any aid at all of the foreigner; being 5,000 miles
in circuit, and of rare fertility of soil, in the greatest part
thereof; and finding also the shipping of this country might
be plentifully set on work, both by fishing and by transpor-
tations from port to port, and likewise by sailing unto some
small islands that are not far from us, and are under the
crown and laws of this state; and recalling into his memory
the happy and flourishing estate wherein this land then
was, so as it might be a thousand ways altered to the worse,
but scarce any one way to the better; though nothing
wanted to his noble and heroical intentions, but only (as
far as human foresight might reach) to give perpetuity to
that which was in his time so happily established, therefore
amongst his other fundamental laws of this kingdom he
did ordain the interdicts and prohibitions which we have
touching entrance of strangers; which at that time (though
it was after the calamity of America) was frequent; doubt-
ing novelties and commixture of manners. It is true, the
like laws against the admission of strangers without license
is an ancient law in the kingdom of China, and yet continued in use. But there it is a poor thing; and hath made

them a curious, ignorant, fearful foolish nation. But our lawgiver made his law of another temper. For first, he hath preserved all points of humanity, in taking order and making provision for the relief of strangers distressed; whereof you have tasted."

At this speech (as reason was) we all rose up, and bowed ourselves. He went on:

"That king also still desiring to join humanity and policy together; and thinking it against humanity, to detain strangers here against their wills; and against policy, that they should return, and discover their knowledge of this estate, he took this course; he did ordain, that of the strangers that should be permitted to land, as many at all times might depart as many as would; but as many as would stay, should have very good conditions, and means to live from the state. Wherein he saw so far, that now in so many ages since the prohibition, we have memory not of one ship that ever returned, and but of thirteen persons only, at several times, that chose to return in our bottoms. What those few that returned may have reported abroad, I know not. But you must think, whatsoever they have said, could be taken where they came from but for a dream. Now for our travelling from hence into part abroad, our lawgiver thought fit altogether to restrain it. So is it not in China. For the Chinese sail where the will, or can; which showeth, that their law of keeping out strangers is a law of pusillanimity and fear. But this restraint of ours hath only one exception, which is admirable; preserving the good which cometh by communicating with strangers, and avoiding the hurt: and I will now open it to you. And here I shall seem a little to digress, but you will by-and-by find it pertinent.

Ye shall understand, my dear friends, that amongst the excellent acts of that king, one above all hath the pre-eminence. It was the erection and institution of an order, or society, which we call Salomon's House; the noblest

foundation, as we think, that ever was upon the earth, and
the lantern of this kingdom. It is dedicated to the study
of the works and creatures of God. Some think it beareth
the founder's name a little corrupted, as if it should be
Solomon's House. But the records write it as it is spoken.
So as I take it to be denominate of the king of the Hebrews, which is famous with you, and no strangers to us;
for we have some parts of the works which with you are
lost; namely, that natural history which he wrote of all
plants, from the cedar of Libanus to the moss that groweth
out of the wall; and of all things that have life and motion
This maketh me think that our king finding himself to
symbolize, in many things, with that king of the Hebrews,
which lived many years before him, honored him with the
title of this foundation. And I am rather induced to be
of this opinion, for that I find in ancient records, this order
or society is sometimes called Solomon's House, and sometimes the College of the Six Days' Works; whereby I am
satisfied that our excellent king had learned from the Hebrews that God had created the world, and all that therein
is, within six days: and therefore he instituted that house,
for the finding out of the true nature of all things, whereby
God might have the more glory in the workmanship of
them, and men the more fruit in their use of them, did
give it also that second name.

But now to come to our present purpose. When the
king had forbidden to all his people navigation into any
part that was not under his crown, he made nevertheless
this ordinance; that every twelve years there should be set
forth out of this kingdom, two ships, appointed to several
voyages; that in either of these ships there should be a
mission of three of the fellows or brethren of Salomon's
House, whose errand was only to give us knowledge of
the affairs and state of those countries to which they were
designed; and especially of the sciences, arts, manufactures,
and inventions of all the world; and withal to bring unto

us books, instruments, and patterns in every kind: that the ships, after they had landed the brethren, should return; and that the brethren should stay abroad until the new mission, the ships are not otherwise fraught than with store of victuals, and good quantity of treasure to remain with the brethren, for the buying of such things, and rewarding of such persons, as they should think fit. Now for me to tell you how the vulgar sort of mariners are contained from being discovered at land, and how they that must be put on shore for any time, color themselves under the names of other nations, and to what places these voyages have been designed; and what places of rendezvous are appointed for the new missions, and the like circumstances of the practice, I may not do it, neither is it much to your desire. But thus you see we maintain a trade, not for gold, silver, or jewels, nor for silks, nor for spices, nor any other commodity of matter; but only for God's first creature, which was light; to have light, I say, of the growth of all parts of the world." And when he had said this, he was silent, and so were we all; for indeed we were all astonished to hear so strange things so probably told. And he perceiving that we were willing to say somewhat, but had it not ready, in great courtesy took us off, and descended to ask us questions of our voyage and fortunes, and in the end concluded that we might do well to think with ourselves, what time of stay we would demand of the state, and bade us not to scant ourselves; for he would procure such time as we desired. Whereupon we all rose up and presented ourselves to kiss the skirt of his tippet, but he would not suffer us, and so took his leave. But when it came once amongst our people, that the state used to offer conditions to strangers that would stay, we had work enough to get any of our men to look to our ship, and to keep them from going presently to the governor, to crave conditions; but with much ado we restrained them, till we might agree what course to take.

We took ourselves now for freemen, seeing there was no danger of our utter perdition, and lived most joyfully, go-ing abroad and seeing what was to be seen in the city and places adjacent, within our tedder; and obtaining acquaint-ance with many of the city, not of the meanest qualiry, at whose hands we found such humanity, and such a freedom and desire to take strangers, as it were, into their bosom, as was enough to make us forget all that was dear to us in our own countries; and continually we met with many things, right worthy of observation and relation; as indeed, if there be a mirror in the world, worthy to hold men's eyes, it is that country.

One day there were two of our company bidden to a feast of the family, as they call it; a most natural, pious, and reverend custom it is, showing that nation to be com-pounded of all goodness. This is the manner of it; it is granted to any man that shall live to see thirty persons descended of his body, alive together, and all above three years old, to make this feast, which is done at the cost of the state. The father of the family, whom they call the Tirsan, two days before the feast, taketh to him three of such friends as he liketh to choose, and is assisted also by the governor of the city or place where the feast is cele-brated, and all the persons of the family, of both sexes, are summoned to attend him. These two days the Tirsan sitteth in consultation, concerning the good estate of the family. There, if there be any discord or suits between any of the family, they are compounded and appeased. There, if any of the family be distressed or decayed, order is taken for their relief, and competent means to live. There, if any be subject to vice, or take ill courses, they are reproved and censured. So likewise direction is given touching marriages, and the courses of life which any of them should take, with divers other the like orders and advices. The governor assisteth to the end, to put in execution, by his public authority, the decrees and orders

of the Tirsan, if they should be disobeyed, though that
seldom needeth; such reverence and obedience they give
to the order of Nature. The Tirsan doth also then ever
choose one man from amongst his sons, to live in house
with him; who is called ever after the Son of the Vine.
The reason will hereafter appear.

On the feast day, the father or Tirsan cometh forth after
divine service into a large room where the feast is cele-
brated; which room hath an half-pace at the upper end.
Against the wall, in the middle of the half-pace, is a chair
placed for him, with a table and carpet before it. Over
the chair is a state, made round or oval, and it is of ivy;
an ivy somewhat whiter than ours, like the leaf of a silver
asp, but more shining; for it is green all winter. And the
state is curiously wrought with silver and silk of divers
colors, broiding or binding in the ivy; and is ever of the
work done of some of the daughters of the family; and
veiled over at the top, with a fine net of silk and silver.
But the substance of it is true ivy; whereof after it is taken
down, the friends of the family are desirous to have some
leaf or sprig to keep.

The Tirsan cometh forth with all his generation or lineage, the males before him, and the females following him;
and if there be a mother, from whose body the whole
lineage is descended, there is a traverse placed in a loft
above on the right hand of the chair, with a privy door,
and a carved window of glass, leaded with gold and blue;
where she sitteth, but is not seen. When the Tirsan is
come forth, he sitteth down in the chair; and all the lineage place themselves against the wall, both at his back,
and upon the return of the half-pace, in order of their
years, without difference of sex, and stand upon their feet.
When he is set, the room being always full of company, but
well kept and without disorder, after some pause there cometh in from the lower end of the room a Taratan (which
is as much as an herald), and on either side of him two

young lads: whereof one carrieth a scroll of their shining yellow parchment, and the other a cluster of grapes of gold, with a long foot or stalk. The herald and children are clothed with mantles of sea-water green satin; but the herald's mantle is streamed with gold, and hath a train.

Then the herald with three curtsies, or rather inclinations, cometh up as far as the half-pace, and there first taketh into his hand the scroll. This scroll is the king's charter, containing gift of revenue, and many privileges, exemptions, and points of honor, granted to the father of the family; and it is ever styled and directed, "To such an one, our well-beloved friend and creditor," which is a title proper only to this case. For they say, the king is debtor to no man, but for propagation of his subjects; the seal set to the king's charter is the king's image, embossed or moulded in gold; and though such charters be expedited of course, and as of right, yet they are varied by discretion, according to the number and dignity of the family. This charter the herald readeth aloud; and while it is read, the father or Tirsan standeth up, supported by two of his sons, such as he chooseth. Then the herald mounteth the half-pace, and delivereth the charter into his hand: and with that there is an acclamation, by all that are present, in their language, which is thus much, "Happy are the people of Bensalem."

Then the herald taketh into his hand from the other child the cluster of grapes, which is of gold; both the stalk, and the grapes. But the grapes are daintily enamelled; and if the males of the family be the greater number, the grapes are enamelled purple, with a little sun set on the top; if the females, then they are enamelled into a greenish yellow, with a crescent on the top. The grapes are in number as many as there are descendants of the family. This golden cluster the herald delivereth also to the Tirsan; who presently delivereth it over to that son that he had formerly chosen, to be in house with him: who beareth

it before his father, as an ensign of honor, when he goeth
in public ever after; and is thereupon called the Son of the
Vine.

After this ceremony ended the father or Tirsan retireth;
and after some time cometh forth again to dinner, where
he sitteth alone under the state, as before; and none of
his descendants sit with him, of what degree or dignity
so ever, except he hap to be of Salomon's House. He
is served only by his own children, such as are male; who
perform unto him all service of the table upon the knee,
and the women only stand about him, leaning against the
wall. The room below this half-pace hath tables on the
sides for the guests that are bidden; who are served with
great and comely order; and towards the end of dinner
(which in the greatest feasts with them lasteth never above
an hour and a half) there is an hymn sung, varied according to the invention of him that composeth it (for they
have excellent poesy), but the subject of it is always the
praises of Adam, and Noah, and Abraham; whereof the
former two peopled the world, and the last was the father
of the faithful: concluding ever with a thanksgiving for
the nativity of our Saviour, in whose birth the births of
all are only blessed.

Dinner being done, the Tirsan retireth again; and having withdrawn himself alone into a place, where he maketh
some private prayers, he cometh forth the third time, to
give the blessing; with all his descendants, who stand
about him as at the first. Then he calleth them forth by
one and by one, by name as he pleaseth, though seldom
the order of age be inverted. The person that is called
(the table being before removed) kneeleth down before the
chair, and the father layeth his hand upon his head, or her
head, and giveth the blessing in these words: "Son of
Bensalem (or daughter of Bensalem), thy father saith it;
the man by whom thou hast breath and life speaketh the
word; the blessing of the everlasting Father, the Prince of

Peace, and the Holy Dove be upon thee, and make the days
of thy pilgrimage good and many." This he saith to
every of them; and that done, if there be any of his sons of
eminent merit and virtue, so they be not above two, he
calleth for them again, and saith, laying his arm over their
shoulders, they standing: "Sons, it is well you are born,
give God the praise, and persevere to the end." And
withal delivereth to either of them a jewel, made in the
figure of an ear of wheat, which they ever after wear in the
front of their turban, or hat; this done, they fall to music
and dances, and other recreations, after their manner, for
the rest of the day. This is the full order of that feast.

By that time six or seven days were spent, I was fallen
into straight acquaintance with a merchant of that city,
whose name was Joabin. He was a Jew and circumcised;
for they have some few stirps of Jews yet remaining among
them, whom they leave to their own religion. Which they
may the better do, because they are of a far differing disposition from the Jews in other parts. For whereas they
hate the name of Christ, and have a secret inbred rancour
against the people amongst whom they live; these, contrariwise, give unto our Saviour many high attributes, and
love the nation of Bensalem extremely. Surely this man
of whom I speak would ever acknowledge that Christ was
born of a Virgin; and that He was more than a man; and
he would tell how God made Him ruler of the seraphims,
which guard His throne; and they call Him also the Milken
Way, and the Eliah of the Messiah, and many other high
names, which though they be inferior to His divine
majesty, yet they are far from the language of other Jews.

And for the country of Bensalem, this man would make
no end of commending it, being desirous by tradition
among the Jews there to have believed that the people
thereof were of the generations of Abraham, by another
son, whom they call Nachoran; and that Moses by a secret
cabala ordained the laws of Bensalem which they now use;

and that when the Messias should come, and sit in His throne at Hierusalem, the King of Bensalem should sit at His feet, whereas other kings should keep a great distance. But yet setting aside these Jewish dreams, the man was a wise man and learned, and of great policy, and excellently seen in the laws and customs of that nation.

Amongst other discourses one day I told him, I was much affected with the relation I had from some of the company of their custom in holding the feast of the family, for that, methought, I had never heard of a solemnity wherein Nature did so much preside. And because propa- gation of families proceedeth from the nuptial copulation, I desired to know of him what laws and customs they had concerning marriage, and whether they kept marriage well, and whether they were tied to one wife? For that where the population is so much affected, and such as with them it seemed to be, there is commonly permission of plurality of wives. To this he said: "You have reason for to com- mend that excellent institution of the feast of the family; and indeed we have experience, that those families that are partakers of the blessings of that feast, do flourish and prosper ever after, in an extraordinary manner. But hear me now, and I will tell you what I know. You shall un- derstand that there is not under the heavens so chaste a nation as this of Bensalem, nor so free from all polution or foulness. It is the virgin of the world; I remember, I have read in one of your European books, of an holy hermit amongst you, that desired to see the spirit of fornication, and there appeared to him a little foul ugly Ethiope; but if he had desired to see the spirit of chastity of Bensalem, it would have appeared to him in the likeness of a fair beautiful cherubim. For there is nothing, amongst mortal men, more fair and admirable than the chaste minds of this people. Know, therefore, that with them there are no stews, no dissolute houses, no courtezans, nor anything of that kind. Nay, they wonder, with detestation, at you in

Europe, which permit such things. They say ye have put marriage out of office; for marriage is ordained a remedy for unlawful concupiscence; and natural concupiscence seemeth as a spur to marriage. But when men have at hand a remedy, more agreeable to their corrupt will, marriage is almost expulsed. And therefore there are with you seen infinite men that marry not, but choose rather a libertine and impure single life, than to be yoked in marriage; and many that do marry, marry late, when the prime and strength of their years is past. And when they do marry, what is marriage to them but a very bargain; wherein is sought alliance, or portion, or reputation, with some desire (almost indifferent) of issue; and not the faithful nuptial union of man and wife, that was first instituted. Neither is it possible that those that have cast away so basely so much of their strength, should greatly esteem children (being of the same matter) as chaste men do. So likewise during marriage is the case much amended, as it ought to be if those things were tolerated only for necessity; no, but they remain still as a very affront to marriage. The haunting of those dissolute places, or resort to courtesans, are no more punished in married men than in bachelors. And the depraved custom of change, and the delight in meretricious embracements (where sin is turned into art), maketh marriage a dull thing, and a kind of imposition or tax. They hear you defend these things, as done to avoid greater evils; as advoutries, deflowering of virgins, unnatural lust, and the like. But they say, this is a preposterous wisdom; and they call it Lot's offer, who to save his guests from abusing, offered his daughters; nay, they say further, that there is little gained in this; for that the same vices and appetites do still remain and abound, unlawful lust being like a furnace, that if you stop the flames altogether it will quench, but if you give it any vent it will rage; as for masculine love, they have no touch of it; and yet there are not so faithful and inviolate friendships in the world again as are there, and to speak generally (as I said before) I have not read of any such chastity in any people as theirs. And their usual saying is that whosoever is unchaste cannot reverence himself; and they say that the reverence of a man's self, is, next religion, the chiefest bridle of all vices."

And when he had said this the good Jew paused a little; whereupon I, far more willing to hear him speak on than to speak myself; yet thinking it decent that upon his pause of speech I should not be altogether silent, said only this; that I would say to him, as the widow of Sarepta said to Elias: "that he was come to bring to memory our sins;" and that I confess the righteousness of Bensalem was greater than the righteousness of Europe. At which speech he bowed his head, and went on this manner:

"They have also many wise and excellent laws, touching marriage. They allow no polygamy. They have ordained that none do intermarry, or contract, until a month be past from their first interview. Marriage without consent of parents they do not make void, but they mulct it in the inheritors; for the children of such marriages are not admitted to inherit above a third part of their parents' inheritance. I have read in a book of one of your men, of a feigned commonwealth, where the married couple are permitted, before they contract, to see one another naked. This they dislike; for they think it a scorn to give a refusal after so familiar knowledge; but because of many hidden defects in men and women's bodies, they have a more civil way; for they have near every town a couple of pools (which they call Adam and Eve pools), where it is permitted to one of the friends of the man, and another of the friends of the woman, to see them severally bathe naked."

And as we were thus in conference, there came one that seemed to be a messenger, in a rich huke, that spake with the Jew; whereupon he turned to me, and said, "You will pardon me, for I am commanded away in haste." The next

morning he came to me again, joyfully as it seemed, and
said, "There is word come to the governor of the city, that
one of the fathers of Salomon's House will be here this day
seven-night; we have seen none of them this dozen years.
His coming is in state; but the cause of his coming is secret.
I will provide you and your fellows of a good standing to
see his entry." I thanked him, and told him I was most
glad of the news.

The day being come he made his entry. He was a man
of middle stature and age, comely of person, and had an
aspect as if he pitied men. He was clothed in a robe of fine
black cloth with wide sleeves, and a cape: his under garment was of excellent white linen down to the foot, girt
with a girdle of the same; and a sindon or tippet of the
same about his neck. He had gloves that were curious, and
set with stone; and shoes of peach-colored velvet. His
neck was bare to the shoulders. His hat was like a helmet,
or Spanish montero; and his locks curled below it decently;
they were of color brown. His beard was cut round and
of the same color with his hair, somewhat lighter. He
was carried in a rich chariot, without wheels, litter-wise,
with two horses at either end, richly trapped in blue velvet
embroidered; and two footmen on each side in the like attire. The chariot was of all cedar, gilt and adorned with
crystal; save that the fore-end had panels of sapphires, set
in borders of gold, and the hinder-end the like of emeralds
of the Peru color. There was also a sun of gold, radiant
upon the top, in the midst; and on the top before a small
cherub of gold, with wings displayed. The chariot was
covered with cloth of gold tissued upon blue. He had
before him fifty attendants, young men all, in white satin
loose coats up to the mid-leg, and stockings of white silk;
and shoes of blue velvet; and hats of blue velvet, with fine
plumes of divers colors, set round like hat-bands. Next
before the chariot went two men, bare-headed, in linen
garments down to the foot, girt, and shoes of blue velvet,

who carried the one a crosier, the other a pastoral staff like
a sheep-hook; neither of them of metal, but the crosier of
balm-wood, the pastoral staff of cedar. Horsemen he had
none, neither before nor behind his chariot; as it seemeth,
to avoid all tumult and trouble. Behind his chariot went
all the officers and principals of the companies of the city.
He sat alone, upon cushions, of a kind of excellent plush,
blue; and under his foot curious carpets of silk of divers
colors, like the Persian, but far finer. He held up his bare
hand, as he went, as blessing the people, but in silence.
The street was wonderfully well kept; so that there was
never any army had their men stand in better battle-array
than the people stood. The windows likewise were not
crowded, but every one stood in them, as if they had been
placed.

When the show was passed, the Jew said to me, "I shall
not be able to attend you as I would, in regard of some
charge the city hath laid upon me for the entertaining of
this great person." Three days after the Jew came to me
again, and said, "Ye are happy men; for the father of
Salomon's House taketh knowledge of your being here,
and commanded me to tell you, that he will admit all your
company to his presence, and have private conference with
one of you, that ye shall choose; and for this hath appointed the next day after to-morrow. And because he
meaneth to give you his blessing, he hath appointed it in
the forenoon."

We came at our day and hour, and I was chosen by
my fellows for the private access. We found him in a
fair chamber, richly hanged, and carpeted under foot,
without any degrees to the state; he was set upon a low
throne, richly adorned, and a rich cloth of state over his
head of blue satin embroidered. He was alone, save that
he had two pages of honor, on either hand one, finely
attired in white. His under garments were the like that we
saw him wear in the chariot; but instead of his gown, he

had on him a mantle with a cape, of the same fine black, fastened about him. When we came in, as we were taught, we bowed low at our first entrance; and when we were come near his chair, he stood up, holding forth his hand ungloved, and in posture of blessing; and we every one of us stooped down, and kissed the end of his tippet. That done, the rest departed, and I remained. Then he warned the pages forth of the room, and caused me to sit down beside him, and spake to me thus in the Spanish tongue:

"God bless thee, my son; I will give thee the greatest jewel I have. For I will impart unto thee, for the love of God and men, a relation of the true state of Salomon's House. Son, to make you know the true state of Salomon's House, I will keep this order. First, I will set forth unto you the end of our foundation. Secondly, the preparations and instruments we have for our works. Thirdly, the several employments and functions whereto our fellows are assigned. And fourthly, the ordinances and rites which we observe.

"The end of our foundation is the knowledge of causes, and secret motions of things; and the enlarging of the bounds of human empire, to the effecting of all things possible.

"The preparations and instruments are these. We have large and deep caves of several depths; the deepest are sunk 600 fathoms; and some of them are digged and made under great hills and mountains; so that if you reckon together the depth of the hill, and the depth of the cave, they are, some of them, above three miles deep. For we find that the depth of an hill, and the depth of a cave from the flat, is the same thing; both remote alike from the sun and heaven's beams, and from the open air. These caves we call the lower region. And we use them for all coagula-tions, indurations, refrigerations, and conservations of bodies. We use them likewise for the imitation of natural mines and the producing also of new artificial metals, by compositions and materials which we use and lay there for many years. We use them also sometimes (which may seem strange) for curing of some diseases, and for pro-longation of life, in some hermits that choose to live there, well accommodated of all things necessary, and indeed live very long; by whom also we learn many things.

"We have burials in several earths, where we put divers cements, as the Chinese do their porcelain. But we have them in greater variety, and some of them more fine. We also have great variety of composts and soils, for the mak-ing of the earth fruitful.

"We have high towers, the highest about half a mile in height, and some of them likewise set upon high mount-ains, so that the vantage of the hill with the tower, is in the highest of them three miles at least. And these places we call the upper region, account the air between the high places and the low, as a middle region. We use these towers, according to their several heights and situations, for insulation, refrigeration, conservation, and for the view of divers meteors—as winds, rain, snow, hail; and some of the fiery meteors also. And upon them, in some places, are dwellings of hermits, whom we visit sometimes, and in-struct what to observe.

"We have great lakes, both salt and fresh, whereof we have use for the fish and fowl. We use them also for bur-ials of some natural bodies, for we find a difference in things buried in earth, or in air below the earth, and things buried in water. We have also pools, of which some do strain fresh water out of salt, and others by art do turn fresh water into salt. We have also some rocks in the midst of the sea, and some bays upon the shore for some works, wherein is required the air and vapor of the sea. we have likewise violent streams and cataracts, which serve us for many motions; and likewise engines for multiplying and enforcing of winds to set also on divers motions.

"We have also a number of artificial wells and fountains,

made in imitation of the natural sources and baths, as tincted upon vitriol, sulphur, steel, brass, lead, nitre, and other minerals; and again we have little wells for infusions of many things where the waters take the virtue quicker and better than in vessels or basins. And amongst them we have a water, which we call water of Paradise, being by that we do it made very sovereign for health and prolongation of life.

"We have also great and spacious houses, where we imitate and demonstrate meteors — as snow, hail, rain, some artificial rains of bodies, and not of water, thunders, lightnings; also generations of bodies in air — as frogs, flies, and divers others.

"We have also certain chambers, which we call chambers of health, where we qualify the air as we think good and proper for the cure of divers diseases, and preservation of health.

"We have also fair and large baths, of several mixtures, for the cure of diseases, and the restoring of man's body from arefaction; and others for the confirming of it in strength of sinews, vital parts, and the very juice and substance of the body.

"We have also large and various orchards and gardens, wherein we do not so much respect beauty as variety of ground and soil, proper for divers trees and herbs, and some very spacious, where trees and berries are set, whereof we make divers kinds of drinks, besides the vineyards. In these we practice likewise all conclusions of grafting, and inoculating, as well of wild-trees as fruit trees, which produceth many effects. And we make by art, in the same orchards and gardens, trees and flowers, to come earlier or later than their seasons, and to come up and bear more speedily than by their natural course they do. We make them also by art greater much than their nature; and their fruit greater and sweeter, and of differing taste, smell, color, and figure, from their nature. And many of them we so order, as that they become of medicinal nature.

"We have also means to make divers plants rise by mixtures of earths without seeds, and likewise to make divers new plants, differing from the vulgar, and to make one tree or plant turn into another.

"We have also parks, and enclosures of all sorts, of beasts and birds; which we use not only for view or rareness, but likewise for dissections and trials, that thereby may take light what may be wrought upon the body of man. Wherein we find many strange effects: as continuing life in them, though divers parts, which you account vital, be perished and taken forth; resuscitating of some that seem dead in appearance, and the like. We try also all poisons, and other medicines upon them, as well of chirurgery as physic. By art likewise we make them greater or smaller than their kind is, and contrariwise dwarf them and stay their growth; we make them more fruitful and bearing than their kind is, and contrariwise barren and not generative. Also we make them differ in color, shape, activity, many ways. We find means to make commixtures and copulations of divers kinds, which have produced many new kinds, and them not barren, as the general opinion is. We make a number of kinds of serpents, worms, flies, fishes of putrefaction, whereof some are advanced (in effect) to be perfect creatures, like beasts or birds, and have sexes, and do propagate. Neither do we this by chance, but we know beforehand of what matter and commixture, what kind of those creatures will arise.

"We have also particular pools where we make trials upon fishes, as we have said before of beasts and birds.

"We have also places for breed and generation of those kinds of worms and flies which are of special use; such as are with you your silkworms and bees.

"I will not hold you long with recounting of our brewhouses, bake-houses, and kitchens, where are made divers drinks, breads, and meats, rare and of special effects. Wines we have of grapes, and drinks of other juice, of fruits, of grains, and of roots, and of mixtures with honey, sugar, manna, and fruits dried and decocted; also of the tears or wounding of trees, and of the pulp of canes. And these drinks are of several ages, some to the age or last of forty years. We have drinks also brewed with several herbs, and roots, and spices; yea, with several fleshes, and whitemeats; whereof some of the drinks are such as they are in effect meat and drink both, so that divers, especially in age, do desire to live with them with little or no meat or bread. And above all we strive to have drinks of extreme thin parts to insinuate into the body, and yet without all biting, sharpness, or fretting; insomuch as some of them put upon the back of your hand, will with a little stay pass through to the palm, and yet taste mild to the mouth. We have also waters, which we ripen in that fashion, as they become nourishing, so that they are indeed excellent drinks, and many will use no other. Bread we have of several grains, roots, and kernels; yea, and some of flesh, and fish, dried; with divers kinds of leavings and season- ings; so that some do extremely move appetites, some do nourish so, as divers do live of them, without any other meat, who live very long. So for meats, we have some of them so beaten, and made tender, and mortified, yet without all corrupting, as a weak heat of the stomach will turn them into good chilus, as well as a strong heat would meat otherwise prepared. We have some meats also and bread, and drinks, which taken by men, enable them to fast long after; and some other, that used make the very flesh of men's bodies sensibly more hard and tough, and their strength far greater than otherwise it would be.

"We have dispensatories or shops of medicines; wherein you may easily think, if we have such variety of plants, and living creatures, more than you have in Europe (for we know what you have), the simples, drugs, and ingredi-

ents of medicines, must likewise be in so much the greater
variety. We have them likewise of divers ages, and long
fermentations. And for their preparations, we have not
only all manner of exquisite distillations, and separations,
and especially by gentle heats, and percolations through
divers strainers, yea, and substances; but also exact forms
of composition, whereby they incorporate almost as they
were natural simples.

"We have also divers mechanical arts, which you have
not; and stuffs made by them, as papers, linen, silks, tissues,
dainty works of feathers of wonderful lustre, excellent
dyes, and many others, and shops likewise as well for such
as are not brought into vulgar use amongst us, as for those
that are. For you must know, that of the things before
recited, many of them are grown into use throughout the
kingdom, but yet, if they did flow from our invention, we
have of them also for patterns and principals.

"We have also furnaces of great diversities, and that
keep great diversity of heats; fierce and quick, strong and
constant, soft and mild, blown, quiet, dry, moist, and the
like. But above all we have heats, in imitation of the sun's
and heavenly bodies' heats, that pass divers inequalities,
and as it were orbs, progresses, and returns whereby we
produce admirable effects. Besides, we have heats of
dungs, and of bellies and maws of living creatures and of
their bloods and bodies, and of hays and herbs laid up
moist, of lime unquenched, and such like. Instruments also
which generate heat only by motion. And farther, places
for strong insulations; and again, places under the earth,
which by nature or art yield heat. These divers heats we
use, as the nature of the operation which we intend requireth.

"We have also perspective-houses, where we make demonstrations of all lights and radiations, and of all colors;
and out of things uncolored and transparent, we can represent unto you all several colors, not in rainbows, as it

is in gems and prisms, but of themselves single. We represent also all multiplications of light, which we carry to great distance, and make so sharp, as to discern small points and lines. Also all colorations of light: all delusions and deceits of the sight, in figures, magnitudes, motions, colors; all demonstrations of shadows. We find also divers means, yet unknown to you, of producing of light, originally from divers bodies. We procure means of seeing objects afar off, as in the heaven and remote places; and represent things near as afar off, and things afar off as near; making feigned distances. We have also helps for the sight far above spectacles and glasses in use; we have also glasses and means to see small and minute bodies, perfectly and distinctly; as the shapes and colors of small flies and worms, grains, and flaws in gems which cannot otherwise be seen, observations in urine and blood not otherwise to be seen. We make artificial rainbows, halos, and circles about light. We represent also all manner of reflections, refractions, and multiplications of visual beams of objects.

"We have also precious stones, of all kinds, many of them of great beauty and to you unknown; crystals likewise, and glasses of divers kind; and amongst them some of metals vitrificated, and other materials, besides those of which you make glass. Also a number of fossils, and imperfect minerals, which you have not. Likewise loadstones of prodigious virtue: and other rare stones, both natural and artificial.

"We have also sound-houses, where we practice and demonstrate all sounds and their generation. We have harmony which you have not, of quarter-sounds and lesser slides of sounds. Divers instruments of music likewise to you unknown, some sweeter than any you have; with bells and rings that are dainty and sweet. We represent small sounds as great and deep, likewise great sounds, extenuate and sharp; we make divers tremblings and warblings of sounds, which in their original are entire. We represent and imitate all articulate sounds and letters, and the voices and notes of beasts and birds. We have certain helps; which set to the ear do further the hearing greatly; we have also divers strange and artificial echoes, reflecting the voice many times, and as it were tossing it; and some that give back the voice louder than it came, some shriller and some deeper; yea, some rendering the voice, differing in the letters or articulate sound from that they receive. We have all means to convey sounds in trunks and pipes, in strange lines and distances.

"We have also perfume-houses, wherewith we join also practices of taste. We multiply smells which may seem strange; we imitate smells, making all smells to breathe out of other mixtures than those that give them. We make divers imitations of taste likewise, so that they will deceive any man's taste. And in this house we contain also a confiture-house, where we make all sweetmeats, dry and moist, and divers pleasant wines, milks, broths, and salads, far in greater variety than you have.

"We have also engine-houses, where are prepared engines and instruments for all sorts of motions. There we imitate and practise to make swifter motions than any you have, either out of your muskets or any engine that you have; and to make them and multiply them more easily and with small force, by wheels and other means, and to make them stronger and more violent than yours are, exceeding your greatest cannons and basilisks. We represent also ordnance and instruments of war and engines of all kinds; and likewise new mixtures and compositions of gunpowder, wild-fires burning in water and unquenchable, also fireworks of all variety, both for pleasure and use. We imitate also flights of birds; we have some degrees of flying in the air. We have ships and boats for going under water and brooking of seas, also swimming-girdles and supporters. We have divers curious clocks and other like motions of return, and some perpetual motions. We imitate also motions of living creatures by images of men, beasts, birds, fishes and serpents; we have also a great number of other various motions, strange for equality, fineness and subtilty.

"We have also a mathematical-house, where are represented all instruments, as well of geometry as astronomy, exquisitely made.

"We have also houses of deceits of the senses, where we represent all manner of feats of juggling, false apparitions, impostures and illusions, and their fallacies. And surely you will easily believe that we, that have so many things truly natural which induce admiration, could in a world of particulars deceive the senses if we would disguise those things, and labor to make them more miraculous. But we do hate all impostures and lies, insomuch as we have severely forbidden it to all our fellows, under pain of ignominy and fines, that they do not show any natural work or thing adorned or swelling, but only pure as it is, and without all affectation of strangeness.

"These are, my son, the riches of Salomon's House.

"For the several employments and offices of our fellows, we have twelve that sail into foreign countries under the names of other nations (for our own we conceal), who bring us the books and abstracts, and patterns of experiments of all other parts. These we call merchants of light.

"We have three that collect the experiments which are in all books. These we call depredators.

"We have three that collect the experiments of all mechanical arts, and also of liberal sciences, and also of practices which are not brought into arts. These we call mystery-men.

"We have three that try new experiments. Such as themselves think good. These we call pioneers or miners.

"We have three that draw the experiments of the former four into titles and tables, to give the better light for the drawing of observations and axioms out of them. These we call compilers. We have three that bend themselves, looking into the experiments of their fellows, and cast about how to draw out of them things of use and practice for man's life and knowledge, as well for works as for plain demonstration of causes, means of natural divinations, and the easy and clear discovery of the virtues and parts of bodies. These we call dowry-men or benefactors.

"Then after divers meetings and consults of our whole number, to consider of the former labors and collections, we have three that take care of them to direct new experiments, of a higher light, more penetrating into Nature than the former. These we call lamps.

"We have three others that do execute the experiment so directed, and report them. These we call inoculators.

"Lastly, we have three that raise the former discoveries by experiments into greater observations, axioms, and aphorisms. These we call interpreters of Nature.

"We have also, as you must think, novices and apprentices, that the succession of the former employed men do not fail; besides a great number of servants and attendants, men and women. And this we do also: we have consultations, which of the inventions and experiences which we have discovered shall be published, and which not: and take all an oath of secrecy for the concealing of those which we think fit to keep secret: though some of those we do reveal sometime to the state, and some not.

"For our ordinances and rites, we have two very long and fair galleries: in one of these we place patterns and samples of all manner of the more rare and excellent inventions: in the other we place the statues of all principal inventors. There we have the statue of your Columbus, that discovered the West Indies: also the inventor of ships: your Monk that was the inventor of ordnance and of gunpowder: the inventor of music: the inventor of letters: the inventor of printing: the inventor of observations of astronomy: the inventor of works in metal: the inventor of

glass: the inventor of silk of the worm: the inventor of
wine: the inventor of corn and bread: the inventor of
sugars; and all these by more certain tradition than you
have.   Then we have divers inventors of our own, of
excellent works; which since you have not seen, it were
too long to make descriptions of them; and besides, in the
right understanding of those descriptions you might easily
err.   For upon every invention of value we erect a statue
to the inventor, and give him a liberal and honorable
award.   These statues are some of brass, some of marble
and touchstone, some of cedar and other special woods gilt
and adorned; some of iron, some of silver, some of gold.

"We have certain hymns and services, which we say
daily, of laud and thanks to God for His marvellous works.
And forms of prayers, imploring His aid and blessing for
the illumination of our labors; and turning them into good
and holy uses.

"Lastly, we have circuits or visits, of divers principal
cities of the kingdom; where as it cometh to pass we do
publish such new profitable inventions as we think good.
and we do also declare natural divinations of diseases,
plagues, swarms of hurtful creatures, scarcity, tempest,
earthquakes, great inundations, comets, temperature of the
year, and divers other things; and we give counsel thereupon, what the people shall do for the prevention and remedy of them."

And when he had said this, he stood up; and I, as I had
been taught, knelt down; and he laid his right hand upon
my head, and said, "God bless thee, my son, and God bless
this relation which I have made.   I give thee leave to
publish it, for the good of other nations; for we here are
in God's bosom, a land unknown."   And so he left me;
having assigned a value of about two thousand ducats for
a bounty to me and my fellows.   For they give great
largesses, where they come, upon all occasions.

THE REST WAS NOT PERFECTED